Hometown Appetites

Hometown Appetites

·

The Story of
Clementine Paddleford,
the Forgotten Food Writer
Who Chronicled How
America Ate

·

KELLY ALEXANDER

and

CYNTHIA HARRIS

GOTHAM BOOKS

GOTHAM BOOKS
Published by Penguin Group (USA) Inc.
375 Hudson Street, New York, New York 10014, U.S.A.
Penguin Group (Canada), 90 Eglinton Avenue East, Suite 700, Toronto, Ontario M4P 2Y3,
Canada (a division of Pearson Penguin Canada Inc.); Penguin Books Ltd, 80 Strand,
London WC2R 0RL, England; Penguin Ireland, 25 St Stephen's Green, Dublin 2, Ireland
(a division of Penguin Books Ltd); Penguin Group (Australia), 250 Camberwell Road,
Camberwell, Victoria 3124, Australia (a division of Pearson Australia Group Pty Ltd);
Penguin Books India Pvt Ltd, 11 Community Centre, Panchsheel Park, New Delhi - 110 017,
India; Penguin Group (NZ), 67 Apollo Drive, Rosedale, North Shore 0632, New Zealand
(a division of Pearson New Zealand Ltd); Penguin Books (South Africa) (Pty) Ltd,
24 Sturdee Avenue, Rosebank, Johannesburg 2196, South Africa

Penguin Books Ltd, Registered Offices: 80 Strand, London WC2R 0RL, England

Published by Gotham Books, a member of Penguin Group (USA) Inc.

First printing, September 2008
1   3   5   7   9   10   8   6   4   2

Gotham Books and the skyscraper logo are trademarks of Penguin Group (USA) Inc.

LIBRARY OF CONGRESS CATALOGING-IN-PUBLICATION DATA
Alexander, Kelly.
Hometown appetites : the story of Clementine Paddleford, the forgotten food writer
who chronicled how America ate / by Kelly Alexander and Cynthia Harris.
p.   cm.
Includes index.
ISBN 978-1-592-40389-9 (hardcover)   1. Paddleford, Clementine, 1898–1967.
2. Women food writers—United States—Biography.   I. Harris, Cynthia.   Title.
TX649.P33A44 2008
641.5092—dc22
[B]   2008015264

Printed in the United States of America
Set in Bulmer MT with Murray Hill Display • Designed by Elke Sigal

*This book is dedicated to the memory of
Clementine Paddleford.*

•

*It was also written in remembrance of
one of her great champions, the late R. W. Apple Jr.*

· · · C O N T E N T S · · ·

Why Clem Matters

When Kelly Alexander, then a senior editor at *Saveur*—the magazine I'd co-founded in 1994 and was currently running as editor in chief—came into my office one November day back in 2001 and asked if I'd let her write a piece about Clementine Paddleford, I said yes right away. The truth is that I didn't know much about Paddleford; I'd heard the name, of course, and remembered that she'd been associated with the old *New York Herald Tribune*, but that was about it. I did, however, know a fair amount about Kelly.

In the early years of the twenty-first century, we had a situation at *Saveur* that I believe was unique among American food magazines: Every one of our top-level editors was also a writer, and a good one, and every one of them regularly penned stories for the magazine—often long features involving substantial research and extensive travel, which they somehow managed while still doing a damn good job at their office duties. Their stories were consistently among the strongest pieces we published (they won a number of James Beard Awards and other prizes), and because these writer-editors (now, alas, long scattered) pretty much lived and breathed the magazine, the things they wrote also tended to be particularly definitive of the values we stood for. They spoke the language, in other words, in more ways than one. Thus if one of them—Kelly in this case—came to me and said "This is a good *Saveur* story," that was good enough for me.

Once I'd sent Kelly off to begin her research at the repository of all things Paddlefordian—Manhattan, Kansas (a town to which I have familial connections, coincidentally; the local graveyard is full of distant cousins of my father's)—it did occur to me that I ought to do a little homework, and I got ahold of a copy of Paddleford's masterwork, *How America Eats,* originally published in 1960, though based on earlier columns from the *Herald Tribune* and *This Week* magazine. As I started reading this obviously feisty, indefatigable Kansan's reports (and recipes) from half a century earlier, I was seduced by their unpretentious tone and evocative detail, but I was also quite astonished. Though her writing was new to me, Clementine Paddleford had apparently invented *Saveur* when I was still in my highchair— not really invented it, of course, but concerned herself with exactly the same culinary issues and approached her subject matter from exactly the same point of view we did.

This connection seemed particularly vivid to me because I had recently been revising *Saveur*'s "mission statement" at the request of the magazine's proprietor—one of those curious souls who seems incapable of understanding or communicating anything that can't be expressed in PowerPoint—and in it, our subject matter was defined as (pardon the bullet points):

Why Clem Matters

- The history and traditions of food
- The rituals of preparation and of dining
- The passionate personalities who create the things we eat and drink
- The ingredients and products we know and love, and those we want to discover
- The origins of those ingredients and products and of the world's great dishes, both elegant and everyday
- Our family and cultural roots
- The very environment we live in and draw nourishment from in every sense

If you'd tweaked those points slightly to limit their scope to these United States, you could have used them as the back-cover blurb on *How America Eats*.

Paddleford wasn't exactly the first person to travel the country talking to cooks and collecting recipes: In 1935, the WPA Federal Writers' Project had sent scriveners to all forty-eight states to collect regional recipes and report on what were not yet then called foodways for a massive volume to be called (presciently?) *America Eats*. For various reasons, however, the project was never completed, and the book remained unpublished—though a section on the Midwest cowritten by Nelson Algren, later famous as the author of books like *The Man with the Golden Arm* and *A Walk on the Wild Side* (and as Simone de Beauvoir's lover), came out under the series title in 1992, and earlier this year a volume based on the original materials, by cookery writer Pat Willard, appeared under the title *American Eats! On the Road with the WPA—The Fish Fries, Box Supper Socials, and Chitlin Feasts That Define Real American Food*.

Meanwhile, without exclamation points or juicy subtitles, dogeared copies of *How America Eats* sit on library shelves and in used bookstores all over the country, probably checked out or picked up much less often than they should be.

True, Paddleford's prose can be a little bouncy ("Deep in the heart of Texas, I made 'San Antone' my headquarters for junketing jaunts, rustling up ranch recipes"), and, sure, the croutons in her Caesar salad recipe are cubes of "sandwich bread," her cassoulet includes very un-cassouletish boneless veal, and her "carne con chili" is garnished strangely with black olives. But decades before terms like "authentic" and "local" had become culinary buzzwords, this hungry and instinctually curious woman was knocking on front doors, peering into kitchen windows, tramping through fields and orange groves, sitting down at picnic tables and in fancy restaurants and everywhere in between, and getting to know foods both familiar and untried and the people who cooked them.

In search of the recipes for the varied Christmas cookies sent annually to a friend of hers, she goes to Abilene—the one in her home state, Kansas—"a place where the best recipes are hand-downs from mothers to daughters, from neighbor to neighbor along with those country counting-out rhymes which children teach to children." She calls on Arece Lambert Anderson, daughter of Louis Ferdinard Lambert, "Dean of the [Pennsylvania] mushroom industry," and learns that her family's favorite mushroom dish is chipped creamed beef with mushrooms—served over crisp golden waffles made right at the table. On a visit to writer Isabel Currier in Marblehead, Massachusetts (which yields, among other things, instructions for constructing a meaty, cinnamon-spiced lumberjack pie), her host's remark that it's "a labor of love, to clean greens by the peck" sets Paddleford off on a reverie about her own late grandfather, "a shut-mouth man" whose favorite culinary subject was "a mess-o'-greens dinner, topped off with cornmeal dumplings." Wherever she is and whatever she's eating, she connects the food with the people who make it and the places it comes from, and makes it all the most accessible—and ultimately delicious— by presenting it in context.

On the evidence of *How America Eats* alone—never mind the hundreds of thousands of words she wrote in her other books and in magazine and newspaper articles never collected between hard covers—Clementine Paddleford patently cared about our nation's culinary heritage and realized that if it wasn't documented and publically appreciated, it might well disappear. This is an almost trendy sentiment today, but it was a rare thing in mid-twentieth-century America. She probably would have laughed to hear herself described as a sociologist or anthropologist, but those are in part what she was. More to the point, she was also an engaging writer who knew good food when she had it, and dedicated her career to helping us know it too.

—*Colman Andrews*
Riverside, Connecticut

· · · **P R O L O G U E** · · ·

The Getting-Aroundest Person

As the propellers on the DC-6 slowed for a landing in Hilo, Hawaii, the passengers found the vista a curiosity. It was 1962 and Hawaii's Big Island was not the well-touristed spot it is to-day: No boutique hotels, no swim-up bars, no strip malls. The natural scenery was practically the only attraction. But what an attraction: Royal Palm trees, their shaggy green-brown leaves flapping skyward, beckoned the travelers from Honolulu to pause awhile on the flat stretches of land and sand in the glitter-ing ocean. Peering below, the passengers began their usual rus-tlings, gathering bags, opening and closing compacts, folding newspapers. One woman, in her early sixties with a thick mane of bobbed gray-white hair secured by a headband, wearing a shawl and a swirling skirt, kept her big cornflower blue eyes fo-cused on the view. She liked nothing better than an exotic site. A fan of guidebooks, this voyager knew the name of nearly every tree that glided past as the plane began to touch down—monkey pod, litchi, macadamia, and avocado. The plane settled into

Lyman Field's airspace and then landed. Wide-brimmed sun hat on her head and white gloves on her hands, this passenger debarking was the champion food writer Clementine Paddleford. She was searching out Hawaii's cuisine and helping to put it on the map.

In any short list from the pantheon of American food writers, you will not generally find Clementine Paddleford alongside James Beard and Julia Child. Yet her name belongs right up there with the great names in food history—she was a star deserving still of top billing, the first person to truly define "regional American food," a missing link between how we got from the hard-core study of home economics, which is what food writing was like before Paddleford came along, to the modern American preoccupation with food.

While Paddleford had all the talent in the world, fate and circumstance combined to cruelly bury her legacy. Thus, Paddleford has been robbed of the lasting reputation she built at great effort. There is an upside, though. Her work can now be seen with clarity, as if it were being read for the first time. She was a pioneer in uncovering this country's regional food specialties and recording it for the generations. Most likely the first person to properly codify the concept of "regional American food," Paddleford set about explaining to her nation of readers that people ate what was fresh and local, and combined these ingredients with the recipes that they and their families had brought with them from their respective homelands. She interpreted the concept of America as a melting pot culinary culture long before the term became cliché. She captured the kitchen legacies of Americans from all over before those treasures of the hearth were subsumed into brand names and fast foods.

The Getting-Aroundest Person

Paddleford's humble beginnings equipped her almost from birth for her task. She grew up on a prairie farm in northeastern Kansas where her father was a farmer and a grocer. After graduating from Kansas State Agricultural College in 1921 with a degree in industrial journalism, she worked from 1924 to 1929 as women's editor of a farm magazine. Then, harnessing her wits to her outsized ambition, she reached the top: She became food editor of the *New York Herald Tribune* during the years of its greatest influence—from 1936 until its demise in 1966. The *New Yorker* writer Mark Singer was succinct: "In a town teeming with dailies, the *Trib* was the best written and best edited and, except on lousy days, the most fun." But she was known nationally from 1940 to her death in 1967 as a columnist for *This Week* magazine, a Sunday supplement that appeared in the *Trib* and forty-two other major U.S. newspapers. It meant that what Paddleford wrote, thirteen million households read.

In these two posts Paddleford flexed her talent and established her primacy. Although she took a commercial flight in Hawaii, she herself had a certificate to pilot a Piper Cub, to speed her zigzag trips from kitchen to kitchen. In a mess hall for lumberjacks in the Northwest, in chili parlors in Texas, a hobo camp in Kansas, or the elegant precincts of the Four Seasons in New York City, as well as in private homes in every state she visited, she ate, questioned, and reported smartly and with unflagging enthusiasm. And always, she provided recipes. She was named *Time* magazine's "Best-Known Food Editor" in 1953, and was the subject of a Peter Arno cartoon in *The New Yorker* in 1964.

How is it that Paddleford, so well-known then, is acknowledged by few historians today? The short answer: Timing and circumstances contrived to eclipse her reputation. The death of the *Herald Tribune* in 1966, combined with a disability from an illness, meant she could not climb aboard the rocket that was waiting for foodies—television.

But as she arrived at Hilo in 1962, the world was her pineapple. The airport was alongside a bay on Kamehamha Avenue, Hilo's main street. Paddleford hailed a cab and sat back. Having grown up rural amid all manner of crops, she was an inveterate appreciator of flora and fauna and couldn't keep from leaning out to look at the gorgeous surroundings. She had already explored the food scene in Honolulu, and had fallen in love with what was being grown and eaten in America's newest state, at the time only three years on the flag.

This was late summer. The "Duke of Earl" was heard from every radio. Jackie Kennedy took eager television viewers on a virtual tour of the White House, John Steinbeck won the Nobel Prize for Literature, and Marilyn Monroe was found dead in her apartment. These were dramatic times, but cuisine, high or low, was decidedly not a part of the action. The field of food reporting was confined to print: Julia Child's first program, *The French Chef*, did not debut until the next year, Emeril Lagasse was three years old, and the Food Network did not exist. The number of culinary educational institutions could be counted on one hand. Even the idea of "ethnic food" was limited to things like Italian ices and bagels. It was a time when, as R. W. Apple Jr., the late *New York Times* correspondent and food writer, put it, "Few people in Philadelphia knew what enchiladas were and few in Chicago knew what cioppino was."

As Paddleford well understood when she barged into homes and restaurants across the country, food writing in America was still being invented. Before 1824, almost nothing beyond re- prints of English recipe manuals was published. Then Mary Randolph, a pre-eminent home economist, produced *The Virginia House-wife*. Her recipes document traditional Southern specialties including cornmeal bread, grilled calf's head, and okra soup. "Let every thing be done at the proper time, keep every thing in its proper place, and put every thing to its proper use," was her timeless advice to her sisterhood.

The first food-related book to seize the public imagination came in 1896: Fannie Merritt Farmer's *Boston Cooking–School Cookbook*. Edward Weiss, former owner of Paprikas Weiss in New York, an early force in the gourmet food movement and a frequent source for Paddleford, said that Fannie Farmer marked "the beginnings of the breakdown of the oral tradition," when mothers stood facing the stove and taught daughters to cook a family's favorite foods, and became a marker for an era when the country's young women moved many miles from home to work or start families and could no longer learn at the maternal elbow. Farmer's book was perhaps most noteworthy for its inclusion of accurate ingredient measurements that any woman could fol- low—teaspoons and cups, rather than handfuls and dashes. Af- ter Farmer's innovation, things changed even more: the packaged "convenience food" industry was born, *The Joy of Cooking*, an- other and bigger book than *Fannie Farmer*, was published in the mid-1930s, and newspapers began running recipes that home economists devised.

Still, that was about it. Restaurants were not considered ex- citing, definitely not places to send reporters to. In 1962 the ma- jority of chefs in this country were just guys—nearly all professional cooks were male in those days—most of the time nameless in their white jackets. They weren't well compensated for their efforts, and they weren't known as sex symbols.

In American homes, what prevailed had nothing to do with design or ambience. What was on most people's minds was how to get dinner on the table. The science of home economics dominated. Instead of articles about $100 foie gras–stuffed hamburgers or sources for "authentic imported" wasabi, newspaper food sections were stocked with columns of recipes aimed solely at beleaguered housewives. Instead of real articles, most newspaper food sections were poorly concealed promotion pieces. Meatpacking companies like Chicago's Swift, which had pioneered the first refrigerated railroad car and went on to make millions, bought advertisements that provided homemakers with everything they needed to prepare dinner, including the ham (well, a coupon for one, anyway). If there was any article with recipes it was devoid of interesting stories from the people who dreamed them up. Even the food magazines were not particularly inspiring: Their pictures of perfectly decorated tables and expertly garnished casseroles gave readers something to aspire to, but offered no proof that America had any kind of bona fide food tradition.

In the midst of this was Clementine Paddleford. In terms of authority and excitement, she was the only source. She was perhaps the first American writer to understand that "food writing" was not different from other sorts of reporting. To produce good, engaging articles, a writer must have subject knowledge, a reporter's keen instincts, and verbal facility. Paddleford did not make the mistake, as so many of her colleagues and many male editors did, of thinking that there was something less demanding about writing on food. As Apple put it, Paddleford's stories were "intensively researched," a quality that separated them even further from the pap that was out there.

For instance, an article in *This Week* in early 1949 details the charms of the diner aboard the historic Katy railroad—the MKT, serving Missouri, Kansas, and Texas—and it involved much more than a list of foods consumed. "The search was on. We were ferreting around the Southwest, good cooks the objective. We asked newspaper people, housewives, ministers, butchers, grocers, truck drivers, where to go for a really fine meal. We had luck. The consensus was that about the best dinner one could eat in those parts was a diner dinner on the Katy Railroad."

She described the train ("streamlined, its red and silver engine sleek and powerful") and gave a history of its dining car ("Previously the Katy Railroad had dining stations in various towns where the train stopped and travelers dashed out to eat, hurrying through the courses—while outside the great engine chuff, chuff, chuffed, chaff, chaff, chaffed, as if resentful of all the time wasting"). Then came a concise tour of the dining car itself: "The end walls showed scenes of Dallas skyscrapers. Fresh flowers on each table, the linen immaculate, silver and glassware shining." Several dishes made the meal remarkable, not least of which were the "kornette rolls" that had been a staple of the dining room since before 1912. This is a typical tour de force: "Hello, it was the Katy's kornette boy. He wore a huge stainless steel warmer like a breastplate held by a strap fastened 'round the neck. He lifted the front cover, 'A kornette?' So tiny—one, two, three are not too many of these dainty corn morsels. 'Kornette boy! This way, please!' Here's something that should be eaten in sets of a dozen."

In addition to a keen ability to make mouths water through

Kornettes

1 quart whole milk

1 pound finely ground white cornmeal, about 3 cups

½ cup butter, plus 2 tablespoons for greasing pans

1 tablespoon sugar

1 teaspoon salt

Preheat oven to 375 degrees. Place cornmeal in a medium bowl. In a small saucepan, scald milk and immediately pour over cornmeal, a little at a time, stirring well with a whisk to make a thick batter. While still very hot, stir in butter, sugar, and salt. Let stand 5 minutes.

Fill a pastry bag and drop dough onto a greased baking sheet in cakes about the size of a silver dollar. Chill 5 hours.

Bake about 20 minutes until golden.

Yield: about 80 kornettes

words alone, Paddleford's story on the Katy illustrates her habit of integrating vivid historical detail. "She obviously took the time to learn something about railroads, which is why the stuff stands up," Apple asserted.

Paddleford's writing was a sharp departure from the kind of material that the home economists, who then were exclusive "writers" of recipes in American newspapers, were putting out there. Before Paddleford, almost no text accompanied a recipe in any major newspaper in this country. The idea was "here it is, now cook it." Paddleford saw a lot of room for improvement, and she dived right in to the fray. For one thing, her focus was not on science—perfecting a formula for a dish was not her plan. Instead, her work focused on history and tradition and sought to undermine ideas that most people had about American cooking—that it had no authenticity, that it consisted of meals made entirely from packaged foods, that it was unexciting and uninviting—by bringing to life the people and the joy behind good home-cooked food. This was no small feat, but Paddleford was an old-fashioned journalist and knew how to get good information. She relied on two things: her instincts and her sources. Of top concern to her was making contacts, and she became an ace at that; she knew how to cultivate friendships, and how to keep in touch long after she had met people she would need, as her straight-line attack on the Hills' house in Hilo shows. She sent out form letters to her contacts with her travel schedule, and she made it a point to respond to every letter she received. She was also not afraid to maneuver to meet influential people who could help her research. Opportunistic, oh yes, but she had a worthy goal: she was genuinely concerned with helping home cooks, and for this she had relied on an ever-growing network.

Her beat was unique, too. She sought to find ways people used local ingredients and family recipes to prepare delicious food—in other words, she wanted to invent a modern way to re-invigorate the old oral tradition of recipe-sharing. Thus, her sources were no refined coterie of French culinary school graduates. They were in large part an army of readers. Recognizing her voice as the voice of a friend, they bombarded her with thousands of hand-written letters a year—suggesting favorite cooks, recipes, and restaurants. She also had a network of regional food editors and cooking instructors.

Most important to Paddleford, though, was being "in the field"—traveling the country and dropping into the homes and hearths of real cooks to learn their secrets, frustrations, hopes, and dreams. Dubbed "Hopalong Paddleford" by her employers and "the Nellie Bly of culinary journalism, a go-anywhere, taste-anything, ask-everything kind of reporter" by Apple, she traveled an estimated fifty thousand miles a year from county to county, town to town, state to state, and country to country, seeking the best.

Of course, anyone as well-known as she who traveled as much as she did would be bound to meet magnetic people. In Hawaii, Paddleford had a mission: She knew that few of her readers would get to a state not accessible by auto, just as comparatively few would ever sit at a shiny place setting in the rolling Katy dining car, and so she planned to offer them a taste of it to replicate at home.

In Honolulu, she had visited with Yoshie Isoshima, a cooking teacher whose classes at the local YWCA were packed with women eager to "perpetuate foods familiar to the average Japanese family." Paddleford praised Isoshima's friendliness and her ability to translate her ingredients into measurements that an American cook could use. At the Hills' house, though, the mission was lavished with glamour. She had met Mr. and Mrs. Hill at a cocktail party in New York City. "Do let us know when you come our way," Mrs. Hill said, by way of invitation.

Typical of Paddleford, what might have been an offhand remark was the igniting element for a journey. Hawaii's natural charms struck the Kansan as marvelously foreign, and she reveled in them. This was her second trip in two years.

After her flight, she hailed a taxi that turned right onto Kalanianaolea Street and sped past a wharf in an industrial oil storage area, then on to a neighborhood of original Hawaiian homes arranged in a little row as if on a reservation. Then to a dead-end street, Keokeo Loop Road. Here six houses stood before a backdrop of the Kohala Mountains. Even from the taxi, one house stood out: the home of the Hills, Hilo's upper crust. A giant granite block that rose up with its back to the mountains, it was easily the largest house on the street. It had hard modern edges, to be sure, but these were mellowed by the landscape. Framing the doorway were white-tipped plumeria flowers with their sun-yellow centers, shocking-pink frangipani trees, and orbs of white gardenias. As the taxi stopped, Paddleford, capes and skirts gathered, emerged and inhaled the jasmine air.

Arriving at the Hills' spread, Paddleford was ready to go to work. Her face, while not beautiful, was awfully friendly, and it held a knowing smile. Around her neck was a black ribbon that careful inspection would show held a tracheal tube in place—an ever-present reminder to those she greeted of her bout with throat cancer as a young woman. Her need to press a finger to the little metal device each time she spoke did nothing to keep her from turning on the charm to get recipes and quotes. People were drawn to her natural curiosity and enthusiasm and poured out cooking secrets to someone they believed really cared.

And so it was with the Hills. "Doc" Hill, a transplanted Idahoan, was president of the state Senate and the local power company and chief executive of the island's top realty concern. He was a self-made leader, beloved in the community from the years before he made it big, when he drove around with a homemade optometrist's kit to help outfit island people with eyeglasses. Paddleford's interest, however, lay exclusively with the magnate's wife, Ouida Hill, a five-foot redhead from Roanoke, Virginia, with a warm voice and social hobbies: riding, swimming, gardening, and, most significant, entertaining. Paddleford took in the décor, which was grand and outré for its era. A large black lacquer Chinese screen decorated with gold cranes divided one enormous room that included a cocktail area with gilt details and Italian friezes. In an interview in this room, Paddleford's hostess said she threw parties up to three or four times a week.

Mrs. Hill was just the kind of powerhouse, a "right-hand helper" to her husband, as Paddleford would eventually write, that readers, even those from the most meager backgrounds, would embrace. To Paddleford, Mrs. Hill's party-giving secrets were matters as significant as Castro's weapons plans were to diplomatic reporters. That is because her style of food writing took home cooks along and let them experience the vicarious fun of snooping to see how men and women in every corner of the globe fed their families and guests. Paddleford realized her responsibilities. If someone in Indianapolis had a problem with a recipe from Hawaii, it would be Paddleford who would have to straighten things out. Accuracy was of supreme concern, and despite her natural charisma, she brought to her duties a solemn seriousness.

The Hills were Paddleford's favorite sort of subject. A simple formula: They were Americans and knew how to cook. Paddleford's definition of "authenticity" involved reality. To her, whatever people cooked, wherever they learned it, was the genuine article. It did not matter to her that neither host was from Hawaii, that their ballyhooed parties were on a scale of grandeur few could compete with, or that the food the Hills served was more likely to include imported squab than native poi. What mattered to Paddleford was giving her readers the chance to feel they had brushed shoulders with the Hills themselves, and to enable them to recreate the foods that Paddleford described.

Mrs. Hill reported to Paddleford that at the 53rd Annual Governors Conference, most of the wives were surprised at how similar the dishes she served were to what they were accustomed to on the mainland, the chief exceptions being such exotic touches as local snow peas and taro root. Paddleford noted that and went on to sample the food Mrs. Hill arranged for this interview: parfait glasses sparkling with pink guava ice cream, trays pushing up golden yellow chess tarts with tops as broad and brown-yellow as sunflowers, and old-fashioned sherbet glasses filled with delicate-looking frozen bananas, sugar coated and spiked with cream.

With their cool, custard-like texture, almost like ice cream but not quite, the bananas sent her yellow pencil flying. "You can't believe your tongue!" Paddleford scribbled in her notebook. She knew these beauties would do for any sort of party,

Ouida Hill's Frozen Bananas

5 ripe bananas

1 ¼ cups heavy cream

¼ cup sugar, or more to taste

Peel bananas. Wrap each in waxed paper, twirling both ends to create a tight seal. Place in freezer until very firm, overnight or at least 3 to 4 hours.

Chill 6 wide-mouthed dessert glasses or shallow bowls in the freezer for 5 minutes. Remove glasses from freezer and pour 1 tablespoon of the cream into each. Unwrapping the bananas one by one, slice half of them ¼ inch thick, distributing the slices evenly among the glasses. Sprinkle 1 teaspoon of the sugar over the bananas in each glass. Then drizzle 1 tablespoon of the cream atop the sugared bananas. Slice and divide remaining bananas among the glasses and repeat the process, sprinkling each serving with 1 teaspoon of the sugar and then topping with an additional 1 tablespoon of the cream. Serve immediately.

Yield: 6 servings

anywhere. Mrs. Hill was taken aback: The dessert was an off-hand concoction, a dish she had made so often and with such lack of forethought that she was shocked the great food writer was interested. It was just a dessert of her own invention, she explained to Paddleford, something she thought of long ago and far away from the island paradise. Paddleford persisted and learned another secret.

Whether it was dreamt up under the Mauno Loa Volcano or near the Blue Ridge Mountains was of no consequence to Paddleford. "Good food is good food wherever you find it," she wrote, and the Hills' house was no exception. "Cool Idea from Hawaii—Frozen Bananas" was the title of the article about the Hills and their island hospitality in *This Week* magazine, September 2, 1962. By the time it was in print, Paddleford was thousands of miles away, on another assignment.

Hometown Appetites

CHAPTER 1

Just Watch My Footprints

*N*ow here was a scandal. The year was 1913, the time was about six o'clock in the morning, and the place was the train depot in the prairie town of Manhattan, Kansas, in the Flint Hills 125 miles west of Kansas City. The usual eastward movement of businessmen and farmers was in full flow, but if one looked closely she could easily spot the intrigue: An area merchant, male, was at the very moment boarding a train with a female not his wife. The local newspaper reporter who staked out the station each morning joyfully scribbled in her notebook. "Could this scoop land on the front page?" the journalist likely prayed. She was all of fifteen years old.

Clementine Paddleford, a gangly teen with a close-cropped bob that accentuated her eyes, had been awake since 4 A.M., having already adapted to her writing routine. First, she practiced piano, then completed her household chores, and finally left her home on Poyntz Avenue and headed straight for the railroad platform. She was still in high school, but Paddleford had a professional newspaper career on the front burner.

Hardly a metropolis, Manhattan, then a town of seven thousand people, happened to be a place where a young girl could learn a thing or two about journalism if so inclined. For one thing, Kansas State Agricultural College, opened in 1863 as the first college created as a land-grant institution, had its main campus in the town. The school had recently begun offering a four-year course in industrial journalism, so local people were becoming familiar with the subject. For another, Paddleford's family, who had relocated from a farm to the nearby town of Stockdale before finally settling in Manhattan just a couple of years before, took in boarders, some of whom might have taken journalism classes. Ultimately, though, some people just seem to have been born with a nose for news, and the fifteen-year-old at the depot was one.

To earn extra money, she had taken a reporting job with a local newspaper. Her task was to write short newsy columns—reports of comings and goings—for the *Daily Chronicle*. The depot was always Paddleford's first destination: What better place?

Sadly, before the intrepid reporter's big scoop could make it back to the newsroom, reality intervened in the form of her father who quickly learned his daughter's plans for her column and even more quickly put his foot down.

Usually, no one in town was safe from this reporter's prying ways. There was apparently nothing she wouldn't do in pursuit of story. Busybody Paddleford even made house calls, dropping in on her neighbors and asking her standard question: "What has happened in your house since yesterday?" That these conversations yielded actual published articles says something about the nature of small towns, to be sure, but it says far more about Paddleford's tenacity—her early journalistic intuition, while a bit on the pesky side, certainly had perfect pitch.

Paddleford's journalistic activities, ambitious and amateurish, were a perfect antidote to boredom for a teenager who lived before radios were commonplace in homes. Journalism was a moderately exotic form of entertainment, but Paddleford was by no means an average girl.

Clementine Haskin Paddleford, born on September 27, 1898, on Mill Creek near Stockdale, to Solon Marion and Jennie Stroup Romick Paddleford, did not arrive with a silver spoon in her mouth, but there might have been an iron bit in there: She was determined to prevail and fearless in pursuit of success. No one could be timid who starts out at fifteen covering train depots and grows up to travel 800,000 miles in twelve years to cover the world of food. The wanderlust that ruled her life probably derived from the men in her family, chiefly a grandfather, Stephen Decatur Paddleford, and her father, Solon.

Stephen, known as Cate, was born in the summer of 1830 to a family of farmers in Broome County, New York, in the Southern Tier near the border with Pennsylvania. Like many of his young and poor contemporaries, he caught gold rush fever and at eighteen, joined the forty-niners in their trek west. After wildcatting, he settled down, but only for eleven years. He then packed up his wife and three kids and headed east to Kansas, where the government had opened free land to homesteaders willing to live and farm there. A pioneer of the Bluestem Prairie,

Cate was among the earliest settlers to farm on Mill Creek in Riley County, five miles west of Stockdale.

Pioneer prairie life was tough; it required taming wild land and extra grit just to feed a family. The circumstances inspired a work ethic immortalized in novels of the frontier such as Willa Cather's "My Ántonia," in which an immigrant Bohemian family attempts to conquer the great Nebraska prairie, published in 1918, and Ole Edvart Rolvaag's "Giants in the Earth," in which some hearty Norwegians undertake a similar farm-or-die quest in the Dakotas, published in 1927. The women in these novels were strong in ways that seem almost unimaginable today. They struggled to keep house and raise families as storms of locusts destroyed their crops, they had limited access to medical help, and they had almost no resources beyond what the land yielded. Like many such prairie families, the Paddlefords experienced grim years, and the women were what held them together.

One of these was Cate's wife, Caroline. Caroline took solace in her home and, no matter what, safeguarded the few precious things she had. Her granddaughter Clementine derived inspiration from her, remembering Caroline as "the most immaculate housekeeper in Riley County," writing that one "could eat off grandma's cellar floor." Paddleford also reported that Caroline's "washings were the whitest that flapped on a Kansas breeze," and that her grandmother would hang "the best linens on the clothesline strung across the front yard just to show neighbors as they went driving by." Caroline was also a good farm cook whose recipes for stick-to-your-ribs, satisfying foods were remembered fondly by her granddaughter; Paddleford eventually published one of Caroline's cake recipes in a column on Kansas cooking:

Grandma Paddleford's Marble Layer Cake

4 cups sifted cake flour

5 teaspoons baking powder

½ teaspoon salt

1 cup butter, softened

2 cups sugar

2 teaspoons vanilla extract

4 eggs, separated

1½ cups whole milk

2 ounces unsweetened chocolate, melted

Preheat oven to 350 degrees. Grease and flour 2 9-inch cake pans.

Sift flour, baking powder, and salt into a large bowl.

In a separate bowl, cream butter and sugar thoroughly. Add vanilla. Beat in well-beaten yolks. Add flour alternately with milk, beating until smooth after each addition. Fold in the stiffly beaten egg whites.

Divide batter in half. To one half, add chocolate and stir in. Put into layer pans, alternating spoonfuls of light and dark batters. Gently drop the pans a few inches onto the counter to settle the batter. Gently smooth tops of layers with

continued on next page

spatula. Bake 18 to 25 minutes or until a toothpick inserted into the center of the layer comes up dry. Put layers together with fudge frosting and frost outside of cake.

Yield: 9-inch layer cake

Fudge Frosting

4½ cups confectioners' sugar

¾ cup cocoa powder

12 tablespoons unsalted butter, melted

¾ cup hot, freshly brewed coffee

1 tablespoon vanilla extract

Sift confectioners' sugar and cocoa together into a medium bowl. Stir in butter, then coffee, then vanilla, mixing well with a wooden spoon after each addition until frosting is smooth.

Caroline set a formidable example, but the most important figure in the young woman's life was her mother, Jennie, whose family were also considered pioneers of the Bluestem Prairie. Jennie's work ethic was ingrained, but she also had an extra helping of gumption. Jennie came from farming stock, but she had attended college, unusual for a woman in her day. In 1883, Jennie took one of the earliest home economics courses Kansas State offered. After two years she left to teach school, a path not uncommon for women in the prairies. Three years later she married Solon, another Kansas State student whose brother had been a college classmate. After a brief adventure trying to secure land in the Oklahoma Territories—Solon had inherited his father's wanderlust—Jennie and her husband settled on a farm at Mill Creek not far from Solon's parents. On September 29, 1890, Glenn Decatur Paddleford was born. The second child, Margaret, born nearly five years later, died in infancy. Three years later, in 1898, came Clementine, who became the apple of her mother's eye.

The little girl's early years, spent on farms, were unusually influential in her later work. She was a participant and a close-in witness to the labors and joys of living and eating by the seasons, as well as to the particular hardships of farm life for women, and she developed a deep empathy for the plight of these farm women trying to feed their families with as much sophistication and dignity as their circumstances would permit.

This perspective was an enduring gift; many years later, the editor at *This Week* magazine, William I. Nichols, wrote of Paddleford's ability to draw from a well of "unusually happy memories of her growing-up years." If the daughter inherited wanderlust from the male members of her family, her charisma, spunk, and pluck came from Jennie. Any question about Paddleford's adult character may be answered by looking at the ways Jennie's own iron will served as a model.

Her family's first spread was near Stockdale, which at its height had a population of one hundred. But the mother-daughter bond was made sturdy after February 15, 1906, when Solon and Jennie purchased 260 acres east of the Big Blue River south of town. On a knoll close to a low hill, they built a two-story farmhouse with a big wraparound front porch—the kind for lying about and daydreaming, for sitting on a swing and watching fireflies on hot summer evenings. Paddleford deeply relished her surroundings, which she described as an idyllic farm shaded by elm trees and made beautiful by her mother's prized lilac hedge.

The hedge itself bespoke Jennie's character and determination. "It stood for some sturdy fiber of her will which was the ramrod of her soul," Paddleford wrote. It was not planted on a whim. After a winter of planning her flower beds and mail-ordering seeds, Jennie was eagerly awaiting the first thaw so that she could grab her spade and begin working. Then her husband announced that a new pig run would be built along the west side of the house leading from the hog barn in back to the alfalfa fields below—in prime view of anyone enjoying the front porch. "It is the only place for it," he declared to his family, "you can see that with half an eye." This statement, logical as it might have been, did not sit well with Jennie, who had long dreamed of sitting on her porch and enjoying flowers, including deep purple and lavender lilacs blooming from a twenty-foot-tall hedge.

"I won't have those old sows spoil our view from the porch," Jennie said as she stomped from the room, slamming the door behind her. Despite this protest, Solon did indeed install his pig run. After a week of putting up with its unsightly—and smelly—presence, Jennie disappeared one morning and did not return until after dark. When she came back, it was with a buggy full of lilac cuttings. The next morning, Jennie planted a hedge, right in front of the pig run, "tirelessly, turning the sod twenty, thirty, forty, broad holes," Paddleford wrote. "These will shut out the sight of those old sows," Jennie declared. "Nothing finer than lilacs for a door-yard lane." Once finished, Jennie eyed her work with pride, then turned and gave her daughter a piece of earthy philosophy: "Never grow a wishbone, daughter, where your backbone ought to be."

This lesson in perseverance made an indelible impression. Not only did lilacs become a symbol of motherhood to her—as an adult, Paddleford wore a spray of lilacs in honor of Jennie every Mother's Day—but it also shaped the nature that Paddleford would become famous for: There would be no wishbones here.

In the Blue Valley farmhouse the little girl passed a mere six years of her childhood, yet she gathered a lifetime of memories and lessons. One had to do with Jennie's strict insistence that her daughter be a part of her community—she staunchly held that even though the Paddlefords were considered fairly prosperous in their social circle, her children were not to judge themselves above the others. Jennie worked hard to teach good citizenship in her daughter. "My mother should have been a Communist," Paddleford once confided to Nichols. "Everything had to be shared." At the insistence of Jennie, Paddleford had to tolerate other children on her piano seat and in her playhouse, and she even had to offer her treats around. On receiving her first-ever store-bought chocolates, young Clementine was ecstatic. But she was not permitted to hoard them. Once a week she was made to pass her candy around to the rest of the family. Jennie explained that nothing should be squirreled, but her daughter was not utterly converted. In anticipation of a future drought, she put eight pieces of the chocolate into a sack and hid it in the hay barn. When her candy box was finally empty, she headed for her stash. As she retrieved the sack the bottom fell out and melted chocolate drizzled through. A small brown river flowed into the alfalfa. Jennie had been right: There was no reward for keeping one's riches to oneself. "Nothing must be hoarded, to share a present gives a pleasure twice," Paddleford wrote of this episode. As a paradigm for a career spent distributing prize recipes by newsprint, it's hard to beat.

By far the most valuable lesson the mother gave her daughter involved an attitude toward the kitchen and the preparation of food. Unlike some other farm women who viewed cooking as a chore, Jennie felt that putting dinner on the table for family was a great source of joy. She believed that eating together meant sharing a life and a history, and that if she could keep her family happy around the dining table they could get through just about anything. Jennie respected tradition and mealtimes were especially sacred to her. "Togetherness was a word uncoined in my mother's generation," Paddleford wrote. "But she knew the secret of its meaning. At our supper table there was a family togetherness plus.... Supper was a time for laughter. Arguments were forbidden."

Christmas at the Paddlefords' was several days in preparation and included a multi-course meal that Jennie spent weeks planning. As it neared, the house began to smell richly of balsam and gingerbread. The floor-to-ceiling Christmas tree, a conifer cut fresh from the pasture, was covered with hand-decorated cookies. The promise of mincemeat pies and plum pudding inspired the daughter of the house to exert extra effort in the kitchen. To her fell the job of cracking black walnuts, which were prominent in a number of goodies including plum pudding, fudge, divinity, taffy, and vanilla opera caramels. She used a hammer borrowed from the tool shed to smash each nut on the bottom of a sadiron she held firmly between her knees. She then dug out the meats with a hairpin. This was laborious, time-consuming, and achingly boring, but the kind of work that causes one to savor each bite of each candy—it was worth the effort.

Jennie went all out, and she had a knack for turning ordinary ingredients—like plain old soda crackers—into something special, like inventive cocktail hors d'oeuvre that the kids at the table put away by the handful. (Years later, when she was a professional food editor at the *Christian Herald*, Paddleford would publish these "souffléd crackers," which she'd gussied up with a sprinkle of cayenne pepper, and suggest to her readers that this "new . . . and good" recipe was great for serving alongside oyster stew.) Jennie splurged on exotic ingredients such as celery, cranberries, and oranges, which were ordered in advance from John Sweet's general store. Grandfather Cate always ordered sharp cheddar cheese from New York State; it was his taste of home. Most anticipated of all, though, were the oysters. Every November, Sweet ordered them from Kansas City and they arrived overland in big wooden barrels; these Jennie used to make her silken oyster stew: "How tantalizing that milky, creamy sea smell," Paddleford would remember.

Jennie Paddleford's Oyster Stew

28 oysters, well chilled

6 tablespoons butter

2 teaspoons Worcestershire sauce

1 teaspoon sweet paprika

½ teaspoon celery salt

1 cup whole milk

1 cup half-and-half

Salt, to taste

Shuck oysters over a medium bowl to catch oyster liquor, putting shucked oysters into another bowl. Discard shells.

Melt 4 tablespoons of the butter in a medium saucepan over medium-high heat. Stir in Worcestershire sauce, paprika, and celery salt, then add oysters and bring to a simmer. Add 1 cup of the reserved oyster liquor to pan, discarding any remaining liquor, and bring to a boil. Add milk and half-and-half to pan and heat, stirring once or twice, until just about to boil (do not allow to boil, or stew will curdle), 3 to 5 minutes. Season with salt.

Divide remaining 2 tablespoons butter among 4 warm soup bowls just before ladling in stew.

Yield: 4 servings

Jennie Paddleford's Souffléd Crackers

20 unsalted soda crackers

1 egg white

5 teaspoons grated Parmigiano-Reggiano cheese

Pinch caraway seed for each cracker

Preheat oven to 450 degrees.

Soak soda crackers in a medium bowl of ice water, a few at a time, until slightly swollen and soft, about 20 seconds. (Don't soak too long or they will disintegrate.) Arrange softened crackers in a single layer on a parchment paper–lined baking sheet.

Whisk egg white in a small bowl until very soft peaks form. Brush each cracker with some of the egg white, then sprinkle each with ¼ teaspoon of the cheese and a pinch of caraway seed.

Bake until slightly puffed and golden, 7 to 10 minutes.

Makes 4 to 6 cocktail appetizers

Variation: For Red Pepper Souffléd Crackers, omit egg white, cheese, and caraway. Brush each cracker with ⅛ teaspoon melted butter and sprinkle with cayenne. Proceed with recipe.

Jennie spent her days cooking, but Solon was involved, too. He planted and harvested the corn every year, so it was only fitting that he popped it when the time came. "Popcorn and Christmas were one and the same to his way of thinking," Paddleford wrote of her father. "Popcorn was his hobby, Christmas his delight." Solon popped batches and batches of corn, their distinctive nutty-buttery fragrance clinging to every sofa cushion, carpet, and curtain in the house.

These holiday festivities were the highlight of the year, especially since farm life could be monotonous and bleak during the harsh Kansas winters, and it was not a lot easier in the summer. Many times the rain failed and the crops died as the land became parched. On rare occasions, the climate struck back and the fields were flooded to ruin.

To endure Mother Nature's temper, Jennie punctuated the days by seizing every excuse to make merry. In keeping with farm life's celebration of the seasons, summer brought the Fourth of July picnic in John Sweet's grove. This provided a welcome opportunity for neighbors to socialize and take a break from their labors, especially wheat threshing. Farm families and town folks gathered under the whispering cottonwoods to have a good time and to hear rah-rah speeches given from a platform decorated with bunting. Crowding the table were cakes and pies. Paddleford's own favorite summer indulgence was her mother's strawberry shortcake, made from the first of the season. "When the berries were full and red ripe . . . my job was to pick half a milk-pail full for the first shortcake. It was as exciting as a treasure hunt, one's hand searching out the heart-shaped fruit deep under the leaves," she wrote later.

Solon Paddleford's Popcorn Balls

3 tablespoons butter

1 gallon hot freshly popped corn (1 cup unpopped)

2 cups light corn syrup

2 cups sugar

1 teaspoon white vinegar

2 teaspoons salt

½ teaspoon baking soda

1 teaspoon vanilla extract

1 tablespoon water

Measure all ingredients in advance of preparation, as they will be combined quickly. Keep a bowl of cold water nearby for dipping hands into while forming popcorn balls.

Butter a large bowl and a spatula with 1 tablespoon of the butter. Pour hot popcorn into the bowl.

Make caramel: Mix corn syrup, sugar, the rest of the butter, vinegar, and salt in a saucepan. Heat slowly and stir until the sugar is dissolved and the mixture blended. Boil until a drop forms a soft, cracking ball, about 275 degrees when measured with a candy thermometer, then remove from the heat.

continued on next page

Dissolve the baking soda and vanilla in water. Stir in the dissolved baking soda and the diluted vanilla, then pour the mixture slowly over hot popped corn. Stir with the spatula. Each kernel should have a thick coat. With your hands, shape the corn into balls, being as light-fingered as possible. Dip hands into cold water to keep the mixture from becoming too sticky. If token gifts are to be centered in the balls, wrap them first in waxed paper.

Yield: 25 large balls

Memories of the following dessert loomed large for Paddleford—it became iconic for her, and indeed for the rest of her life she relished writing about strawberry season and did so with particular poetic gusto. Of strawberry shortcake she once wrote: "The juice ran in rivulets, making a crimson lake on the plate." This eloquence, florid as it may have been, did not go unnoticed; for one thing, it was unlike any other food writing of the time, and for another, it is mighty hunger-inducing: Such reading made mouths water. The film critic Judith Crist, who got her start at the *Herald Tribune* in the middle 1940s, was a great admirer of Paddleford, particularly of her yearly strawberry columns. "She was the first food writer I ever encountered who made me feel her enthusiasm for what she was talking about, yes, but also made me taste it," Crist says. "I remember a column she wrote about the first strawberries for the season and I wanted to rush out and buy a quart and I could just taste them on my palate."

Strawberries may have been the premier of Paddleford's farm-born tastes, but there were other special food-related

Jennie Paddleford's Strawberry Shortcake

3 cups all-purpose flour

5 teaspoons baking powder

⅛ teaspoon ground nutmeg

1 teaspoon salt

1 cup sugar, plus more to taste

½ cup plus 2 tablespoons cold butter, cut into small pieces

1 egg, beaten

½ cup whole milk

3 quarts strawberries

1 pint thick cream for passing (optional)

Preheat oven to 400 degrees.

Sift together flour, baking powder, nutmeg, salt, and ½ cup of the sugar into a large bowl. Combine with the ½ cup butter in the bowl of a food processor and pulse until the mixture resembles coarse meal with lumps the size of small peas. Transfer dough to a bowl. Make a well and add to it the egg and milk. Work dough very gently with fingertips or pastry spatula; knead until it just holds together, about 10 seconds. Dots of butter should be visible; do not overwork dough. Generously flour work surface, then roll

continued on next page

dough out to form two circles that are ½ inch thick and 8 to 10 inches in diameter. Wrap the disks tightly and chill.

Set aside 16 of the best looking berries. Hull the rest, then halve and place in a bowl with the remaining ½ cup sugar or more, depending on the ripeness of the fruit. Let strawberries macerate for at least 15 but no more than 45 minutes.

Remove dough disks from refrigerator. On 2 ungreased sheet pans, bake dough rounds 12 to 15 minutes, until golden on the outside and just cooked through in the center. Remove from oven and cool 10 to 15 minutes.

Slather the remaining 2 tablespoons of butter evenly on each disk. Transfer larger disk to a plate that will accommodate it and the juicy berries running off it. Pile macerated berries on top and then cover with the other biscuit. Garnish with reserved whole berries and serve with a pitcher of cold cream, if you like.

Yield: 8 servings

events that held sway, too, especially birthdays. "There was always time at Blue Valley Farm to celebrate a birthday," Paddleford said.

Her own birthday parties lived large in her memory, and none more than her tenth. More than a dozen children were invited for an afternoon of games and supper. Jennie's sure hand at creating fanciful table displays had never been put to better use:

The table was covered with pink crepe paper and an acetylene lamp gave everything a golden glow. There was an enormous platter of fried chicken and mounds of buttery mashed potatoes. When Jennie called her child into the dining room to discuss seating arrangements, the little girl got so excited by the display she put her hand on a nearby sofa and kicked her feet up in pure joy. One foot hit the table, knocking the lamp's china globe into a pitcher of lemonade. Fine glass shattered everywhere. "The day of my life!" Jennie exclaimed. But when the mother saw her daughter's distress, she said: "You are not to cry. You are ten years old. I will get supper again."

And so she did. Two neighbor ladies came over to assist as the birthday girl's brother, Glenn, was dispatched to kill more chickens. Eureka Bolt, Jennie's kitchen helper, made more mashed potatoes while Jennie redecorated the table. By eight o'clock the tired, hungry children pulled chairs up to a setting that was entirely different from the original but equally breathtaking to the celebrant: The pink crepe paper had been replaced by a hand-embroidered tablecloth and the lamp with three ordinary oil lamps, each crowned with a wreath of flowers. The fried chicken, mashed potatoes and gravy, peas, iced tea, and birthday cake and ice cream were a huge success—Paddleford's guests went home sated and happy, exhausted from an afternoon extended to a late-night feast. Jennie decreed the event "the longest birthday party anyone ever had." The mother's exertion in easing her child's disappointment and shame combined with her triumphant outcome makes it hard not to imagine this was the moment when an appreciation for the art—not just the science—of home economics was born in young Paddleford.

Kansas Fried Chicken

2½- to 3-pound broiler chicken, cut into 8 pieces,
backbone removed, at room temperature

Kosher salt and freshly ground black pepper, to taste

⅔ cup all-purpose flour

2 tablespoons butter

4 tablespoons lard

2 cups hot whole milk

Wash chicken pieces and pat dry with paper towels. Season generously with kosher salt. Season flour by stirring in a little salt and pepper. Roll chicken pieces in the flour and pat on evenly with fingertips. Reserve any leftover flour for gravy.

Melt butter and lard in large, heavy skillet over moderate heat. When hot but not smoking, add chicken, largest pieces first; allow room for turning. If skillet won't hold 8 pieces in one layer, fry in installments, grouping white and dark meat in separate batches, so white meat stays juicy. Keep skillet partly covered with a lid so fat doesn't splatter but the chicken doesn't steam. As chicken pieces brown, turn them. White meat will be finished when the meat close to bone is still light pink; remove white meat while dark meat

continued on next page

continues to cook. Dark meat will be finished when thoroughly cooked and fork-tender.

When the chicken is ready, drain on a rack set in a baking pan, putting the pan into a warm oven while making gravy. Pour off all but 2 to 3 tablespoons of fat in the skillet and whisk into the remaining pan fat 2 tablespoons of the remaining seasoned flour. Cook over medium-low heat for a minute until the mixture begins to bubble. Then slowly add milk, whisking constantly until thickened. Continue to cook about 5 minutes. For thicker gravy, continue cooking for a few extra minutes; for thinner gravy, add more milk. Season gravy with salt and pepper to taste.

Yield: 4 servings

With a mother so creative and determined, it is clear where Paddleford acquired her own active imagination and her intense desire to make good on her dreams. Understanding the trials and tribulations—and the joys, too—of farmers was inextricably linked to what it was to be a food writer in Paddleford's era, and, willy-nilly, she had learned the subject from the inside out.

But the days on the farm were numbered. Perhaps seeking a more controllable home life and a more consistent income, Solon and Jennie sold Blue Valley Farm on September 7, 1911, and moved into Stockdale. Solon had arranged to manage the grocery store and post office near the railroad tracks, and his family moved into a house next to the bank.

The stop in Stockdale proved brief. Within two years, Solon

was again bitten by the spirit of adventure. He moved when the opportunity came in the fall of 1913 to purchase the Star Grocery Store, a larger operation in a larger town nearby, Manhattan.

Compared to Stockdale, and certainly the Blue Valley Farm, Manhattan was an actual city, known best as the home of Kansas State. It was here that the teenage Paddleford began her career. What drove her to journalism? Hearing fellow students talk about it played a role, as did curiosity about her surroundings, and a spirit of supreme industriousness. But probably more important, Paddleford was an inveterate writer of letters to grandparents or notes in her own carefully maintained scrapbooks; she kept track of things. Journalism was a natural for her once she learned what it was.

Even in those days, Paddleford paid special attention to the food that accompanied various activities. She took care to note in her scrapbooks the menus for many of her teenage outings. For instance, one winter afternoon, her classmate Emery Taylor rounded up as many of the high school's 1917 senior class as possible and took them to a lake where they ice skated until full dark. Back in town, the group ended up at another student's house where they dined on "scrambled brains, frog legs, and steak." Like strawberries, steak became a symbol of good home cooking to Paddleford—long after she became rich and famous and employed her own cook, a simple steak was what she made on her maid's night off.

Although Manhattan was a farm town, it was not isolated from world affairs. On April 6, 1917, in the spring semester of Clementine's senior year, the United States entered the World

Planked Steak with Duchess Potatoes

Steak

1 Porterhouse, rib-eye, or strip steak 1¾ inches thick,
about 2 pounds

Salt and freshly ground black pepper, to taste

Prepared plank (see note below)

2 to 3 teaspoons vegetable oil

Allow steak to come to room temperature about 45 minutes before searing. Wipe steak dry. Cut off superfluous fat. Season steak heavily with salt and pepper on both sides at least 10 minutes and up to 30 minutes before cooking, meanwhile preheating the broiler. Heat vegetable oil in a frying pan and then sear the steak evenly on each side, seven minutes total, turning steak over once or twice.

In a heavy cast-iron skillet large enough to hold the steak comfortably, broil steak for 7 minutes. Set aside.

Duchess Potatoes

2 russet potatoes, peeled and cut into about 6 pieces each

2½ teaspoons salt

3 egg yolks, lightly beaten

continued on next page

6 tablespoons whole milk or cream

3 tablespoons melted butter

⅛ teaspoon black pepper

3 egg whites, beaten to stiff peaks

Place potatoes in cold water with 1 teaspoon of the salt in a medium pot over high heat. Boil until potato chunks are fork-tender, about 12 to 15 minutes. Drain and mash with a potato masher or put through a food mill for a finer texture. Set aside.

In a medium bowl, beat egg yolks with milk, butter, remaining salt, and pepper, then add to the warm potatoes. Allow the mixture to sit for 10 minutes or until cool. Adjust seasoning. Fold in egg whites.

To serve: Using a pastry bag, pipe a border of duchess potatoes about 1 inch thick close to edge of the prepared plank. Place steak in center of plank. Place plank in hot oven and bake until potatoes are browned on top, about 1½ minutes. Rotate plank once during broiling for even browning. Rest meat for about 10 minutes before serving, keeping potatoes loosely tented with foil. Sprinkle with salt and pepper, and serve on plank, if you like.

Preparing the plank: Soak an untreated 12-inch-square hardwood board—avoiding cedar—which may be purchased at a lumberyard, in hot water for at least 30 minutes. Dry and oil with vegetable oil.

War and her brother, Glenn, registered for military service. Though he was not called to duty, his sister had many friends who were and she was naturally unsettled. In her scrapbook there is a newspaper clipping of a poem likely written by Paddleford herself, who was known among her classmates as a poet. It reads:

As the Rookie Thinks

When you saunter through the gate,
They say, "You'll like it,"
When they take your cigarettes, they say, "You'll like it."
When they hand you out your clothes,
And rub cold cream on your nose,
And disturb your sweet repose, they say "You'll like it."
But
When you're settled down in peace,
You'll say, You like it.
When the pains of three shots cease
You'll say, You like it.
You'll be right there on the job,
To salute the newest gob,
And to say without a sob,
"You'll like it."

On June 1, 1917, Paddleford graduated from Manhattan High School. Like her parents before her she would be a student at Kansas State, joining the student body of 2,406. Just as there was no question about where she would matriculate, there was also no question on her course of study: industrial journalism. The most popular major for women of the day was home economics but Paddleford had already fulfilled the required courses in this area during her high school vacations, so she was unleashed into her chosen field.

The campus she entered had no especially steep hills to scale on the way to class, and the buildings were spread openly along the fields of grass. The architecture, carried out in white Kansas limestone, retains a fairly sturdy institutional look. In those days, it resembled more of a converted farm than an academy: Herds of sheep grazed the campus. A picturesque entrance, which today opens to what is Kansas State University, was always known as Lover's Lane. It is a tree-lined walkway that blooms gloriously in spring and is strewn with colorful leaves in autumn.

The first dormitories for the Aggies were not built until 1926 (and when they finally came into existence, they had no reliable water supply, were heated only by steam, and the electricity was fairly primitive), so students lived in private homes; some male students even lived in dairy barns. Paddleford emulated her mother's boarders and lived at home. Although she was under the eye of her parents, she got free rein to enjoy a full social life in addition to her ambitious class schedule. Ever the recordkeeper, Paddleford pasted into her scrapbook invitations and souvenirs from dances, sorority and fraternity parties, plays, swimming and hiking outings, and Kansas Authors Club events she attended. Paddleford loved swimming and seized every opportunity. She and a group of friends often drove east to the small town of Wamego for a day of splashing around in "Ye Old Swimming Hole." Such outings proved poignant memories. After Paddleford recovered from cancer and learned that the aperture in her throat meant she could never swim again lest she put her life in jeopardy, she recalled those times with special fondness.

Hiking dates and men who made passes are noted in the scrapbooks, but one pursuer stands out: Lloyd David Zimmerman, an engineering student from Lockney, Texas, fell head over heels in love with Paddleford. A smart-looking man with his hair brushed fashionably back from his face to reveal inviting, wide-set eyes, a vast forehead, a square jaw and a knowing smile, Zimmerman was a good catch. Paddleford and Zimmerman probably met at a school dance, and by May 11, 1918, had become more than casually acquainted. Paddleford herself, despite her urge to record every moment, blacked out a note in her guest book that Zimmerman wrote that day. Zimmerman's name next appears in the book three months later, when he wrote, "This is a starter—Just watch my Footprints thru this book hereafter!" Paddleford's initial attempt to conceal a budding romance failed; whatever Zimmerman said to Paddleford was enough for her to continue to accept the company of the man she called "Zimm." "Why do good looking men always like funny looking girls?" she asked her mother, only somewhat joking.

And he did like Paddleford. Thereafter many notes and invitations from Zimm to his young lady followed; based on volume alone, it is a wonder the young man had any time left over for his engineering studies. Quantity was matched with ardor: His notes practically beg for an audience, a dance, a meeting. Paddleford kept all of her invitations and dance cards, and even took lessons so that she could add to the usual repertoire of steps—shuffle, toddle, and cheek-to-cheek. The lessons instead involved what the college authorities called "freak dancing," or steps that involved close body-to-body "wiggling." Paddleford surely enjoyed wiggling away with her buddies—she was no prude, and Lloyd Zimmerman was a happy partner. One of Zimmerman's cards to Paddleford depicts a couple sitting in a chair, the woman on the man's lap and the two locked in a kiss. "Bugs—just look at this and say you are in her place and I under'neath—and love me lots in your mind, till I see you Fri. evening, when spiritual love will be overthrown. Your-Zimm." Considering Paddleford's formidable reputation and authority in later life, it is charming to think of "Bugs" as a term of endearment for her.

Zimmerman was not one to play it cool, and he was especially outspoken in his writing. He inscribed on Paddleford's 1921 Gamma Chi Kappa Sigma dance book: "I love you dear, I'll tell you here, At our last KE Party in School I'll love you forever And ever, and ever, and ever, In a little home all our own." On the other side of the little booklet he wrote: "Bare Knees, Bare backs-and rolled hose. Such sights, Are what drive me wild-you know. Zimm." Not hard to fall in love with an Arrow Collar Man who could dash off such overheated messages.

Her liaison with Zimmerman may have been on a rolling boil, but Paddleford was not easily sidetracked. Food played a huge part at dances and parties and when she went to the local restaurants and cafés she never failed to walk away with a menu and paste it in to the scrapbook. The menus she collected were from restaurants on the Kansas State student strip, including the Student's Inn, Rex Roy Café, Harrison's, and Colson's College Inn Café. Handwritten notes disclose that Rex Roy's Café was open all night and that Paddleford dubbed the Student's Inn "The Pie Store." On the Harrison's menu, Paddleford wrote, "Johnie has cheated me out of ten gallons of ice cream since last fall" and "The hang out for the gang." On the Colson College Inn menu, she wrote, "The place for microbes and good looking men." Menu collecting was a habit Paddleford never lost. When she died she left more than seven hundred.

Other good meals and openings to a wider world came in academic guise. As a member of the Kansas Authors Club, Paddleford traveled to conferences. Carl Sandburg, then just bursting onto the Chicago arts scene, and a young Karl Menninger from Topeka, were among the people she met on the conference circuit. At these meetings, the banquets were grand, and Paddleford reveled in the opportunities.

Like many college students, Paddleford had to make money. Although the Paddlefords had been relatively well off compared with other families in the countryside, life in the city was more expensive, even with boarders to help pay the mortgage. If Paddleford wanted spending money, she had to earn it. So she turned to what she knew she could do, and began to write articles on a freelance basis for farm magazines and state and local newspapers. In those days the idea of buying articles from a college student was, if unusual, not out of the question, and Paddleford took hold. Her opportunities expanded in her junior year when she became associate editor of the college newspaper *The Collegian*; editor of the three-thousand-circulation *Morning Chronicle*, the local paper for which she snooped as a high-schooler, and a stringer for *The Kansas Post*, *The Kansas City Star* and *Topeka Daily Capitol*.

Roast Pork

(Adapted from *Practical Cookery*, 6th ed. Manhattan, KS:
Department of Food Economics and Nutrition, Kansas State
Agricultural College, 1924)

**5-pound pork shoulder, cleaned of sinew, pieces of bone,
skin, and excess fat, rolled and tied**

2 teaspoons salt, plus more to season pork

1 teaspoon black pepper, plus more to season pork

1 tablespoon vegetable oil

5 cups cold water

Wipe pork with damp cloth or paper towel and season generously with salt and pepper on all surfaces. In a large, heavy Dutch oven, heat oil over medium-high heat. Sear meat on all sides until it is an even, deep golden brown. Blot most of the rendered fat out of the pan with a paper towel.

Add the cold water to Dutch oven, along with 2 teaspoons salt and 1 teaspoon pepper. Bring to a low simmer. Cover and simmer over low heat until the roast is fork-tender, about 2½ to 3 hours, turning the roast several times during cooking to ensure that the meat remains moist. Water will slowly reduce throughout the process; if it starts to seem too low, a little fresh water should be added so that meat doesn't dry out. If necessary, during the last 20 to 30 minutes of cooking,

continued on next page

remove the lid to evaporate excess liquid so that only about 1½ cups remain. Reserve remaining liquid. To serve, let roast rest 20 minutes and slice, using leftover liquid to baste.

Yield: 8 to 10 generous servings

Parker House Rolls

2 tablespoons sugar

2 tablespoons butter

1 teaspoon salt

1 cup whole milk, scalded

1 teaspoon active dry yeast

2 tablespoons lukewarm water

3 cups all-purpose flour, sifted

4 tablespoons melted butter

Measure sugar, 2 tablespoons of butter and salt into a large bowl. Add scalded milk and cool to lukewarm, stirring occasionally. Soften yeast in the lukewarm water and add to the milk mixture. Add flour gradually, kneading it into dough with floured hands. Cover tightly and let rise until doubled in size.

Turn onto a lightly floured board, knead slightly, and roll out ½ to ¾ inch thick. Cut with a round or oval 2½-inch

continued on next page

floured biscuit cutter. Crease each roll in the middle with a floured knife handle and fold over. Dip roll into melted butter on both sides.

Place 1 inch apart on greased baking sheet, cover with a dishtowel, and let rise until doubled in size.

Preheat oven to 400 degrees. Brush tops of rolls again with melted butter before baking. Bake 15 to 20 minutes.

Yield: 10 rolls

In these endeavors, Paddleford got strong support from her journalism professor Charles Rogers. Rogers would remain one of Paddleford's friends long after her college years ended and her own fame far exceeded his. They exchanged many letters over the years. She remained ever grateful for his mentoring. Years later, when her ward, Claire Jorgensen, was looking for work in journalism Paddleford had her spend time with Rogers, who went on to write a beautiful letter of recommendation.

In her senior year, Paddleford became editor of *The Collegian*. Immediately and with great gusto she began to assess the newspaper and make changes, and to crack down on what she perceived as laziness on the part of the staff, who happened to be her classmates. They were not pleased. In the so-called "Dooms-day Edition," the yearly issue in which students traditionally aired their grievances over various administrative policies (a tradition that exists at K-State to this day, since renamed "The Game Day Edition" and now devoted exclusively to sports) the staff squawked. "The *Collegian* staff are all threatening to resign because of the extensive and entirely inhumane editorial scope of *the Collegian*," the complaint read. "They say it is a practical impossibility for the staff to live up to all the reforms that Clementine preaches and they aren't even going to try."

The new editor wasn't just blowing smoke, though—she had really earned her chops. In those days a reporter was measured by the number of column inches of work printed in the paper. By her sophomore year Paddleford was far and away the leader in *The Collegian* with 234 inches of type; her nearest competition, Laura Moore, had 112. For the faculty newspaper *The Industrialist*, Paddleford placed first with ninety inches, followed by Greta Lund with twenty-one. With such prodigious output, it is easy to see how the other students felt they could not compete.

In light of her record as a student journalist, Paddleford seemed quite the all-consumed "professional student," but she squeezed in other extracurricular activities, too. She played on the championship women's basketball team all through school. The players, all from their home state, were known as "The Invincible Seven." Their winning streak started in the spring of 1918 and continued for four years. Paddleford declared her group "one of the fastest girls' basketball teams that has ever played on the Aggie court."

In college she began to take on a whole range of subjects to cover in the paper, things that stretched beyond campus life: agriculture, humor, social events, and workers' issues. For instance, a profile of one Louise Smith explained that women were beginning to enter the world of retail internships. Smith, who took a clothing salesmanship course that required her to clerk in a local shop, "believed there would be less dissatisfaction among shop girls if they knew something of the scientific side of the work." Reporting such stories gave Paddleford's voice depth and exposed her to larger issues in society, but more than anything it honed her skills; she seems instinctively to have known that the only way to be a good writer was to practice as much as possible. Soon enough she would be put to the test outside the environment of family and college.

On Thursday, June 2, 1921, Paddleford graduated from college, as neither of her parents had. Once again there was no question in her mind where her future was. She knew that New York City was the hub of all the newspapers in the world, and her heart was set on it. Still, it could not have been easy to leave everything and everyone she had ever known to go to the intimidating city. If her mind was reeling with possibilities, her heart was heavy. Not for the last time in her life, Paddleford decided to put work first—not for her was the giddiness of her newly engaged friends who were already planning families and church suppers.

Paddleford was scared to leave Kansas, as she reported in her journal, but she decided not to show it. The morning of her leave-taking was matter-of-fact as ever. On returning from a brief graduation trip with friends, she walked into the room where her mother was sitting and breezily said, "Good-bye, Mom, I'm off for New York." Although the exchange could not have been entirely glib, Paddleford was not one to agonize; her mother after all had told her not to grow a wishbone instead of a backbone.

For her part, Jennie could not have anticipated anything less from her headstrong daughter. Still, it must not have been easy for Jennie to have bid farewell. "Take along some shelled corn to drop so you can find your way back," she said. "I'll send you the egg money until you get a job."

Paddleford knew what a rare gift she had from her mother, in a day when women did not routinely leave their families and travel alone to faraway dangerous cities. "Even when she knew I was making mistakes," Paddleford wrote, "she let me make them without a backfire of 'I told you so's.' Not for anything would she have let the long shadow of mamma fall across her children's paths."

One thing Paddleford was not leaving behind was her relationship with Lloyd Zimmerman. He had a plan to go to graduate school in New York, and would be heading there with his own set of friends. He was ambitious, too, and given the era, all who knew them must have expected marriage was in the wind. So Paddleford would not be entirely alone in the Manhattan on the Hudson. Her love for Jennie would have been the only hesitation, but she did not let it stop her from boarding the train east.

· · · CHAPTER 2 · · ·

My Own Boss Absolutely

In the late summer of 1921, Warren G. Harding was in the White House, Allied forces occupied the Rhineland, the U.S. Congress had just passed a quota on immigration, and Adolf Hitler became head of the Nazi Party. On the heels of World War I, isolationism was in and multiculturalism wasn't even on the horizon. For Clementine Paddleford, newly arrived in New York City and the proud renter of a room in a boarding house at 520 West 122nd Street, on Morningside Heights north of Columbia University, this meant facing one of Manhattan's challenges and figuring out how to conquer it: the subway.

There she was, in homemade outfits Jennie had lovingly stitched from patterns Paddleford had picked, summer-weight wool suits, blouses with big bows at the neck, a tote bag at her side loaded with pencils and pads, the picture of a career gal of the day, and a greenhorn at that. As her first act of independence in the city, Paddleford enrolled in graduate-level journalism courses at New York University, despite her proximity to

Columbia. These met three evenings a week and required a long subway trip.

Manhattan, Kansas, was not completely homogenous, but it was segregated: The African American section of town consisted of housing along Yuma and Colorado Streets; water fountains and toilets were labeled "Colored." Minstrel skits of the typical sort were performed while Paddleford was in college. Up to now, she had been exposed to very little but white farm people. For the twenty-two-year-old girl, the culture shock of the subway was immediate. "It's funny and yet it's awful," she wrote to Jennie of her subway riding, "especially when you're glued in between a Jew, an Italian, Chinaman or Negro."

New York City held other surprises: "Grimy streets, messy garbage cans and noisy kids," she wrote.

Paddleford wasn't going to give up, although at the beginning things were pretty tough. Paddleford had no job, and knew no one besides her roommate, Pauline Richards, a fellow Kansas State alumna, and Zimm. Her early experience was mostly being "cooped in one room all day long without seeing anyone." Things with Zimm weren't quite so easy, either: The young engineer ended up taking an internship in sales, probably for Westinghouse, in the greater Philadelphia area, which left Paddleford alone except for weekends. Her long wistful letters to Jennie and Zimm, written in her longhand, were filled with excruciating detail about her life, for example, how much time she spent ironing or how much she spent on grocery items. Here she was in this big exciting city, but so far her life was a disapointment.

Zimm's life and times seemed little better. His letters revolved on office details and achingly boring office politics. His every note spoke of longing for her and the times when they could meet again: "You know dear," he wrote, "that whatever I say, or whatever way it can be twisted to make a different meaning, that the one and only meaning that I could and have ever intended it to have is: that I love you and you only, and that there is no other woman in this world for me." One letter contained a wedding ring advertisement cut from a magazine. "Look 'em over dear—for as sure as there is a God and Heaven, you are going to have one some day. I will—on that day—be the happiest person in the world," he wrote.

Boredom and solitude were alleviated when Zimmerman visited. One fall day, they packed a picnic, boarded a ferry across the Hudson River, and then took a streetcar to the Palisades. The next day they visited the "Success," an Australian ship that transported convicts from England to Australia in 1790, and then toured the Van Cortlandt House, preserved as a museum in the park named after the family. After the mansion, they headed for the Botanical Gardens in Bronx Park. By the time they arrived the gardens were closed, so they hiked through the park instead. "The woods are wonderful here. I have never seen Kansas foliage quite as brilliantly colored," she wrote. "The leaves fall so soon in Kansas but here they hang on for weeks becoming more beautiful as the season advances."

Such weekends were blissful, but also reminders of her usually lonesome days. "Sometimes I fairly hate New York," she wrote Jennie. "How I do wish you could come and live with me after Christmas, we could be so happy I know. If I only had work or classes that took me out among people I would be perfectly content, but all day long I sit here alone in the room."

A regular job would have given her a place to go, people to befriend, and a dependable paycheck. Both her parents and

Zimmerman sent her money, and she was undoubtedly eager to take care of herself. Paddleford applied for a job with *The New York Sun*, but instead was given a chance to write, on a freelance basis, a series called "The Woman Who Sees." The assignment was to relate shocking or inspiring incidents. She was paid $8 for each piece published. Most of her work was in the man-bites-dog mode, including, "Girl Saves Her Hat in Subway Crush," "Phone Booth Used as a Windbreak," and "Girl Uses a Fake Limp to Get Seat." Years after, Paddleford confessed that she may have made up tales because of "time constraints," although she sheepishly added that she "might have seen them."

Paddleford also wrote book reviews for *Administration*, a business magazine, and for *The Sun* and *The New York Telegram*. She also kept up her Kansas contacts and occasionally filed a piece for *The Topeka Daily Capitol* and *The Wichita Eagle*. In addition, a professor at N.Y.U., in whom she periodically confided her career worries, referred her to the office of a Fifth Avenue interior designer, one Mrs. Adler, for whom Paddleford wrote press releases. She also took a job waiting on tables at the Union Theological Seminary—near her apartment—and worked as a babysitter for two wealthy Upper West Side families. At Christmas season, she also took a job as a clerk in the umbrella department at Gimbel's. That position ended when Paddleford lost her temper at a customer who banged on the counter and shouted "Miss!" at her. "Don't you 'miss' me!" Paddleford replied, opening a large umbrella in the customer's face. She hated the job and didn't think much of her co-workers, although she was determined not to let them steal her customers. "I got perfectly sick of swallowing people's sass and answering questions," she wrote her mother. "It would kill me . . . if I ever had to do something of the kind for a living." Despite all, she nearly went broke paying for N.Y.U. classes and the rent and groceries. She worried constantly. "Do you know I doubt if I can ever make enough to live," she wrote Jennie.

But Paddleford was also discovering the duality that E. B. White later described as New York's "queer prizes"—the gift of loneliness came with the gift of privacy. "In New York you know so few people," Paddleford wrote her mother, "one can do almost what they please and no one is the wiser." She also began to fall in love with some places, especially the Bowery. One warm spring afternoon, she and a friend hit the shops of antiques and jumble. She bought a brass kettle, a cream pitcher, a sugar bowl, and a serving tray. She said she was attracted to brass because it was "considered aristocratic to have sitting around."

The Lower East Side, Little Italy, and Chinatown also captivated her. "There is something about the tall buildings, the hurrying cold indifferent crowds, the hurdy gurdy music, the sticky smells that come up from dark uncertain looking basements, that appeals to me," she wrote. "Sometimes I hate it, everything, down to the last banana skin and stray cat, but when I think of leaving it, all of the racket, the dirt, the beauty and ugliness all mixed in so comfortably together, I almost revolt at the thought."

Some time before the summer of 1922, Zimmerman had finished his internship in Philadelphia and his company placed him in a job in the area of South Bend, Indiana, and Chicago. At the same time, Paddleford's roommate, Pauline Richards, was planning a move back to Kansas. Paddleford was despondent: "For two days I have done nothing except sit down, stand up, and walk the floor, thinking, thinking," she wrote.

Although she was offered a job at a small local newspaper in upstate New York, Paddleford's pride kept her from taking it. She knew she could land a bigger and better position. She constantly chased leads, bombarding editors with letters, sometimes lying in wait for them at their offices. "I will never come back to Kansas without a job," she swore.

But in the spring of 1922, she was invited to the wedding of a college friend in Chicago. Paddleford jumped at the chance for a change of scenery and the opportunity to see her boyfriend, and took the train west.

She arranged to meet some editors to discuss freelance assignments while in Chicago. With apparent ease, she landed a spot as a feature writer for the *Agricultural News Service* and as an editor of the *Milk Market Reporter*. Within two weeks, she was out of 122nd Street and had moved her belongings to Chicago by train. Her first room was another boarding house, this at 53 East Superior Street.

Paddleford found her new city more fulfilling, both professionally and personally. Then came an ironic turn. Although Zimmerman had been living in the area, he had just accepted a job with Westinghouse in Houston, back in Texas. "No one likes to be known as a quitter," he wrote to Paddleford, "but god knows it is hard to stay here—especially when you are used to a god's bounty like the West." Zimmerman was clear about Paddleford's dreams for herself. "I know that you are going to be a well known writer some day—and I am not saying this in a joking tone either dear," he wrote. "You should at least know I don't kid you on your profession any more?" So despite his departure, he encouraged his love to take the Chicago chance.

Landing in Chicago meant Paddleford got a welcome opportunity to meet young women in journalism. New York may have had its own network of established women reporters and editors, but Paddleford didn't get to meet them because she didn't have a job. In Chicago, it was easier to find good contacts. One was Margery Currey, and when Paddleford met her, opportunities opened up. Currey was a society editor for *The Chicago Tribune* and part of the so-called Chicago Renaissance, which supported and guided writers, particularly women. Currey knew other influential literary figures, including Margaret Anderson, a feminist, the founder of the literary magazine *The Little Review*, which published early works by Ezra Pound, T. S. Eliot, Ernest Hemingway, and James Joyce. She was also friends with Edith Wyatt, a noted Progressive, social activist, and co-founder of *Poetry* magazine, and the playwright Susan Glaspell, co-founder of the Provincetown Players.

Currey took Paddleford under her wing. Her parties, which constituted a salon, enfolded Ben Hecht, Sherwood Anderson, Carl Sandburg, and Maxwell Bodenheim. Currey realized that women in journalism needed a sanctuary, and she also opened her home to members of the Theta Sigma Phi, which was styled the national fraternity for women in journalism. Paddleford had joined this organization in college. Theta Sigma Phi's members in Chicago had a residence at 1215 Astor Street. In a renovated Chinese laundry on Stony Island Avenue near the University of Chicago, Currey lived and was host to literary readings by these young female writers. The gatherings included Paddleford as well as her roommates Tracy Samuels, a lively advertising copywriter, and Marcelle Laval, a writer of children's books. With the support of her Theta Sigma Phi sisters, Paddleford felt part of a community whose members were intent on helping each other. These bonds proved not only useful but enduring; the friendships Paddleford forged during these days would be the most important of her life.

And they weren't only with women. She resumed building a retinue of male escorts. These men squired her around, took her to dinner, dancing, and to the theater. Some of them were fellow Kansans, others new professional contacts. Some helped her find stories, provided introductions, and coached her for interviews. Paddleford's heart may have been with Zimm, but practicality meant she needed to meet other men.

Soon after arriving, Paddleford found better employment. While continuing as editor for the *Milk Market Reporter*, she took a job with the Hayes-Loeb Company, a publicity organization, for $35 a week. After her bosses grasped how fast Paddleford could crank out copy, the in-box on her desk overflowed with account files. She wrote promotional material for the Sears, Roebuck Agricultural Foundation; Sears, Roebuck's radio station WLS, the Real Silk Hosiery Mills, Blue Valley Creamery, Marshall Field, Montgomery Ward, and Phoenix Laboratories. She did ghostwriting for Samuel R. Guard, director of the Sears Foundation. She took assignments to write agricultural and economic articles for *The Country Gentleman*, *The Field Illustrated*, and *The Farm Journal*.

In early 1923, Guard sent Paddleford to cover hearings in a dispute between the Federal Trade Commission and the United States Steel Corporation; part of an epic fight over price-fixing. These hearings gave Paddleford insight into the plight of the American farmer, to which she was already naturally sensitive. She saw that price fixing kept farmers strapped while the steel industry profited.

Meantime, Zimmerman was getting intense about marriage

and wanted Paddleford to relocate. Finally, she yielded on one point; on July 10, 1923, at a small congregational church in Chicago, Paddleford married Lloyd David Zimmerman. Whatever either side's motive for this austere wedding, it wasn't to obtain religious or state sanction to go to bed together. The records show they had spent many nights in the same hotel rooms in a couple of states. As for the other possibility, neither was Paddleford pregnant. Married or not, she was also not ready to move to Texas. Zimmerman accepted the terms, and agreed to let Paddleford keep the marriage a secret from everyone, including her mother, who openly adored Zimm. Paddleford clearly believed that she could lose out on career opportunities if she was not perceived as single, and so she continued to date other men despite her marriage. This pained Zimm greatly, but he dated as well, although not as much as she. "I see your point of view in keeping our marriage a secret, see it very clearly," he wrote to her. Zimm's hope was that his wife would eventually bow to a conventional home life: "For I know there are not going to be any kiddies to occupy your time and attention for a long time at least—but someday, maybe, who knows?" he wrote.

Paddleford had no intention of leaving a city where she was succeeding, at least not until she saw greener pastures. She was sure she had the stuff to be a great writer, one who could achieve wealth and fame, on her own terms. Although she wrote her mother depicting her happy memories of farm life, she was not going home again. "Coming back won't get me anywhere in this little game of being a journalist," she wrote.

Of the publicity accounts Paddleford handled, she enjoyed the Sears work best. Radio station WLS—the call letters stood for World's Largest Store—was housed in the Sherman House

Hotel in the Loop. Radio was a new medium, and Paddleford was on a pioneer team. By early 1924, she had found a place. The announcer George C. Biggar had a weekly broadcast called "Book Farmer," based on current events in agriculture. Of course, this was Paddleford's cornfield. She wrote scripts for Biggar with titles like "What the Farmer Wants to Know," assessing pests and diseases among poultry and sheep after a particularly wet spring.

The research taught Paddleford technical aspects of food production. She was aware this was not creative writing. Of her bosses and listeners she wrote to her parents: "Can't you just see the looks of disgust they'd waste on my little stories if they knew that a girl with the dance fever was the scientific research department?" However, she covered a wide area, everything from the corn market to the shipping of eggs from China, and the increasingly painful issues of tenant farming and sharecropping. She learned to dig for facts.

Many times, she suggested solutions. Typically, during a seed-corn shortage in 1924, her broadcast, "Boys' and Girls' Club to Help Fill Uncle Sam's Seed Bin," advised club members on selecting and drying seed corn and counseled them to market their services at one cent an ear. This story was picked up and published in more than one hundred papers. Occasionally, she got to write about food. In the summer of 1924, she wrote a feature responding to women's dislike of cooking elaborate meals in hot weather. She spun it out, as she would for years: "Hot weather radio menus for the farm dinner are being specially prepared to please the farmer, his wife and the kiddies as they tune in for the regular farm program."

She treated publicity writing casually, creating articles that were on occasion based only loosely on fact. Sometimes, she confessed to Jennie, the stories were "just blah that I made up out of my head." If Paddleford felt guilty about this, it did not show. In this apprenticeship, Paddleford found a voice that listeners could relate to. This skill became measurable when she wrote a kiddie show in which two hosts sang, played games, and read nursery rhymes. She described writing with the idea in mind that the hosts were talking to boys and girls "gathered around the living room in the evening with their nightgowns on ready to jump into bed." With Paddleford's work, that show's listenership more than doubled.

This was the era of the flapper, the young women flat-chested in skimpy sleeveless tunics that reached only to mid-calf, with bobbed hair, thick black eyeliner, and bright lipstick. In her own way, Paddleford incorporated elements of this style into her own look, one that she refined and adapted for the rest of her life. She wore her thick curly hair just below ear length in a wave to frame her long face and wide-set eyes. She often chose dresses with swirling flares and large bows at the back, and, further adding to the flowing effect, shawls. To this assemblage, she added a large tote bag for paper, pads, pencils, and research materials. Topping it all off often enough was a large wide-brimmed hat. She adored the majesty and pageantry of the look she was cultivating: She obsessed about dress patterns, constantly asking Jennie to make over suits or blouses and add the latest collars or sleeves or linings. She was also an inveterate shopper, always on the lookout for a good deal.

Paddleford's work was not without adventure. At a Sears

exhibition related to the Illinois State Fair, held in Springfield in 1924, the Chicago branch's textile department, for which Paddleford occasionally worked, mounted a display of prize quilts that Paddleford had borrowed from farm women. Unfortunately, an official had let gambling concessions at the fair go to members of the mob. When the overall management put a halt to it, the hoodlums retaliated by stealing the quilts. The irate artisans found their best work in the mud, and came after Paddleford. Hems flying, she had to flee by running across the rooftops.

About this time, she met Wheeler McMillen, associate editor of *Farm & Fireside National Farm Journal*, who came to Chicago to make a series of broadcasts at station WLS. On September 8, 1924, McMillen took Paddleford to lunch and asked if she would be interested in a position at *Farm & Fireside*. The monthly magazine, founded in 1878, was published in New York City by Crowell-Collier. It had grown extremely popular with women, and it featured articles on housekeeping, health, and food. At that moment, McMillen confided, the management was not happy with the household editor and he intended to recommend Paddleford when he got home.

The notion suited Paddleford. It also represented a chance to get back to New York. In addition, it was a top editing position for a woman. It entailed a lot of responsibility, writing, editing, and supervising nine departments. These were beauty, better babies, entertainment, experimental kitchen, fancywork (embroidery, crocheting, and knitting), fashion, features, good citizenship, and interior decoration. Paddleford had no doubt she was ready for this, and followed up with a telegram to McMillen in New York: "Will meet all competition presenting qualifications for the position and can show qualities of experience diligence and sympathetic understanding of field that you will find difficult to duplicate."

McMillen responded that he had spoken with the editor-in-chief, George Martin, and that Martin wanted samples of her work and a letter. Paddleford pointed out her experience in agricultural subjects, her degree in journalism, and, probably most important to her future editors, her farm background. Martin invited Paddleford for an interview and hired her. This was before the heyday of the so-called "Seven Sisters" of women's magazines (*Better Homes & Gardens, Family Circle, Good Housekeeping, Ladies' Home Journal, McCall's, Redbook,* and *Woman's Day*), and although some of those magazines were indeed in existence—*McCall's*, for instance, was established in 1880—they had yet to create a successful formula for women's service issues, and had yet to employ staff that consisted in any major way of women.

Before she left Chicago, she visited her family in Kansas. By this time, Zimmerman's place in her life had faded some, although she acknowledged to Jennie that she still loved him best. But she took him into account less and less when making plans. Zimmerman nonetheless stayed in touch, trying to persuade his secret wife to move south and start a family. He made one more desperate try. He had compiled four leatherbound volumes of his favorite love poems, some of them that had been meticulously copied in his own hand, such as "Winter Night" by Gervé Baronti ("Oh crystal-studded winter night/Thou'st tranced my mind in rogue delight"), and Longfellow's "Children's Hour" ("I have you fast in my fortress/And will not let you depart"). Now, like his heart on a plate, he sent them to his distant wife. It didn't work. Paddleford was moving even farther away. Although it might have been hard to leave her close band of journalist friends, the *Farm & Fireside* opportunity was too great to pass up. "I'm my own boss absolutely with all the leeway in the world for trying new things," she wrote to Jennie.

She began her new job in November and swiftly assessed her position as "Head of the Household Division" for *Farm & Fireside*. She diagnosed some significant problems in the structure, chiefly that each of the nine departments she supervised was a fiefdom: No one was working together at all.

"The *Farm & Fireside* kitchen is bigger than the Household Division itself, which is proof enough of its value and incidentally is a good tip to the household editor that something is wrong with the rest of her magazine," Paddleford noted in a letter to Martin and Andrew S. Wing, the managing editor, after a month on the job.

One person Paddleford thought was right was Nell B. Nichols. Nichols, who had graduated from Kansas State five years before Paddleford, was the home economics expert who tested all of the magazine's recipes from her home in Topeka. Nichols grew up on a farm and spoke the language. She knew what the farm women thought about while they worked, and she spent time visiting their households. Such work helped establish an intimate relationship between *Farm & Fireside* and its readers, and created a community of women devoted to Nichols's advice. Her method was virtually a template for what Paddleford later undertook.

In response to what she found in the field, Nichols wrote about clothes washing, ironing, housecleaning, extermination of household pests, and plumbing: the things that weighed on her readers' minds. Other articles focused on cooking, with tips on garnishing and serving meals in addition to the recipes. The recipes were mostly for simple dishes like stews, which Nichols tested herself.

Paddleford admired Nichols's "taking it to the field" approach and pressed her other editors to learn the language of the farm woman, to understand her needs, wants, and desires, and to be able to dispense useful advice on questions ranging from child rearing to interior decoration to cooking. "Personal service builds a reader confidence that nothing can destroy," Paddleford wrote to Wing.

By 1925, Paddleford was revamping her departments and instituting innovations. For instance, Paddleford discovered that rural women often gloried in their skills as cooks but floundered in interior decorating. She perceived this as an opportunity and took a page from Nichols. Some of Paddleford's new articles were "Your Friendly Kitchen," "How to Choose Curtains for Your House," and "These Come Ready Painted," a story about decals. Instead of shooting photographs in a studio, she had a photographer accompany her to take shots of the women she interviewed in their own homes.

Paddleford realized that readers were the best sources for an editorial agenda. One Indiana farm woman told Paddleford, "Farm women are developing a good-looks-consciousness." This proved important in the beauty department, causing a shift in focus from recent college graduates and June brides. Paddleford organized the entertainment pages seasonally. She scheduled articles on a particular holiday for the month before.

Lamb Stew

2 pounds lamb shoulder, trimmed of all fat and sinew
and cut into 1½-inch chunks

Salt and freshly ground black pepper, to taste

2 tablespoons all-purpose flour

2 tablespoons vegetable oil

Boiling water to cover meat

1 medium turnip, diced

1 carrot, diced

1 small onion, diced

1 russet potato, peeled and cut into large dice

Generously season meat with salt and freshly ground black pepper. In a large bowl, toss the meat with the flour.

In a large Dutch oven over medium heat, heat oil and brown meat. When well browned, pour boiling water over meat until nearly ¾ covered. Bring liquid to a simmer and adjust seasoning before covering Dutch oven with parchment paper and then a tight-fitting lid. Over very low heat, keep lamb at a bare simmer until tender, about 1½ hours, or when meat can be cut easily with a spoon. Add turnip, carrot, and onion, and continue to simmer, covered, for 3 to 4 minutes. Add potato and cook until tender, about 6 more minutes. Adjust seasoning.

Yield: 6 servings

Readers wrote letters asking where to buy party supplies, how to make place cards, party favors, and much more. Correspondence files show that boys and girls twelve to twenty years old liked the entertainment pages best and wrote long enthusiastic letters.

In terms of authority alone, the "better babies" section was easiest for Paddleford to align. Founded in 1908 by the Louisiana Congress of Mothers, the National Better Babies Bureau organized baby contests at county, state, and agricultural fairs. Instead of the "beautiful baby" pageants, these were exhibitions of "good teeth, rosy cheeks, and rugged backs." Thus, babies were judged on their wellness. Despite its resemblance to the judging of livestock, many farm parents liked it. The goal was to educate farm parents, most of whom were distant from good pediatric care, on keeping their children healthy. "Hundreds of mothers were stunned by the first realization that their babies were paying the price of prenatal ignorance," she wrote. "Fathers came who could raise livestock but whose babies died at an early age or grew up weak and ailing." Between 1919 and 1925, the magazine's Better Babies department received more than 62,000 requests for expectant-mother literature alone. Paddleford ran letters of appreciation from mothers and photographs of the children.

One department represented the core of Paddleford's plans: features. A voracious reader herself, Paddleford believed that women gravitated to articles written by other women. For the feature pages, she wanted articles about women who were community leaders and whose homes were outstanding. She succeeded. Her stories caught the attention of women who opened the magazine because they were about issues that concerned them the most.

After Paddleford got a managerial handle on her job, she wanted to get word of her improvements to readers. She contacted the State Home Demonstration Leaders, an agricultural organization with many branches. Hearing that an editor at *Farm & Fireside* was interested in the daily farm life of women, members poured letters into Paddleford's in-box.

For example, T. R. Johnson, director of the News Bureau of Purdue University in Indiana, wrote about two sisters, Essie and Fanny McClure. "They are community leaders, use good methods and are successful farm operators, insofar as any of the farmers have been successful in the last few years," he wrote. Paddleford told her bosses her intention was to travel, and she wanted to meet the McClures herself. "I'm against stuff hatched from library reading and seasoned with imagination," she wrote. The two men encouraged Paddleford and said they'd pay her fare.

Paddleford got permission for a thirteen-day exploratory trip. On May 26, 1925, Paddleford left for Chicago. At the Sears, Roebuck store she interviewed twenty-one of the forty department heads, plus the president, the advertising manager, the head of the correspondence department, and the head of the adjustment department. This prodigious work resulted in two articles for *Farm & Fireside*. One, "In a Mountain of Mail I Found a Mine of the Gold and Brass of Human Nature," was not only brilliantly titled but also showed the ways letters expose more about the writers than they would dare speak aloud. Paddleford reported that an elderly farmer wrote to the Sears mail order department for an etiquette book. "I don't like to be taking this up at my age," he wrote, "but my wife has a shine on our banker."

She next went to Indiana to visit the fabled McClures. Paddleford was driven along the trim grass-edged lane leading to their Walnut Grove Farm. A white house stood among flower beds and tall walnut trees on land that had been in the McClure family one hundred years. "Hello there!" A woman greeted Paddleford. The reporter found herself looking into eyes just above the barrel of a gleaming shotgun. "Trying to kill a crow. They're taking all of our young chickens," explained Fanny McClure, younger of the sisters, about five foot five inches tall in blue overalls.

They ambled to a hog barn where Essie was scrubbing cement pens. "Labor is the biggest problem," Essie said. "Men don't like to take orders from women." The McClures' plan was to try to keep hired hands for at least part of the year, but even this proved tricky. Paddleford quickly perceived how the women had learned to do for themselves, noting that they handled hayforks as easily as sewing machines. They cut weeds, sharpened their scythe, harnessed mules, planted and harvested crops, canned produce, fed cattle and hogs, and took rats out of traps. While the sisters finished cleaning the hog house, Paddleford took a ride on Fanny's beloved Indian pony, Red Cap, while her driver and photographer, B. H. Benson, took photographs.

Back at *Farm & Fireside*, Paddleford found herself invigorated; the practice of learning how her readers lived now seemed essential. It was early evidence of her hallmark as a journalist, an unfailing ability to find out what people were eating and who was producing it.

By the end of her first year at the magazine, she had reorganized the departments in her division, made business contacts across the country, and created a niche for her features. On December 18, 1925, she took a train west for Christmas with the family. But not a vacation: she interviewed eighteen people, visited with Kansas home extension experts, met a few farm women in Missouri, and attended an agricultural conference in LaFayette, Indiana.

In De Soto, Missouri, in the Ozarks, she found two more women farmers, Alice Peck and Anne Fisher, who had a fifty-acre spread. Like the McClures, these two women farmed like men. Peck supervised the dairy herd and orchards while Fisher handled the household and poultry end of the business. Their tractor served as the hired man. Their splendid farm and menagerie of pets were forged into classic Paddleford prose.

This sort of scouting gave her more than material for columns, and from it she got a deep understanding of the working-class American women of her era. These gleanings were first put to use in memos to her bosses, Martin and Wing. Some clue to how these two viewed the windmill they had hired comes in a letter from Wing to Paddleford in early 1926. "Started to say 'Clem' but thought it might look too undignified in type. Us editors must cling to our dignity, mustn't we," Wing starts out, quickly undermining his reputation for seriousness. In his two-page note he goes on to implore Paddleford to use her contacts at WLS Radio for information for a story on old-time dances and fiddlers. The letter includes some sketches that *Farm & Fireside* editors Dick Dobson and Russell Lord made of the back of a head with the words "frown from rear" written next to it, and another sketch with a ghastly necktie. "My Gawd the neckties!" Wing breezes on. "The Xmas ties this year were just simply unwearable, seems as though they get worse every year." Winding up, Wing comes back to his point about the WLS contacts:

Now don't get me wrong Miss Paddleford (see I'm not drunk because I can still spell your name, fact is haven't had a drink since, let me see, since last Sunday and then only one, maybe it was three) I'm writing you this looney letter because I just happen to feel that way and because my eyes are hurting me and they don't hurt so much when I type as when I read because I can more or less type with my eyes shut. I am really serious about this spread idea, and also wishing you a good time and a highly satisfactory New Year.

Paddleford was beginning to be recognized as an expert. In October 1926, she attended an event at the Eastern State Exposition in Springfield, Illinois. Seventy household editors and home demonstrators were at the luncheon. She was among the eight guests asked to make a short presentation. Paddleford confided modestly to Martin and Wing, "I did quite a bit of talking but I'm not sure just what about. It seemed to sound all right."

Paddleford made time to interact with farm women every day, which was getting easier because of the mail she received. These women told her what they thought about clothes, schools, politics, the homes they wanted, and their dreams for their children. "This daily inpour of letters has taught me more about the woman of the land than I ever learned in the years I spent growing up in a Kansas farm community," Paddleford wrote.

Given Paddleford's responsibilities, one would wonder where she had the time to brush her teeth, but she wanted to be a consulting editor for another magazine. She sought the approval of officials at Crowell Publishing to apply for a three-month temporary position as consulting editor to a magazine called *Own Your Own Home*. Approval was given with the proviso that Paddleford's name not be used. She was hired at a salary of $35 a week, but before she could assume these tasks, she was called home.

Jennie Paddleford had already been ill for several years, and in October 1926 she had surgery, most likely for stomach cancer. "You were brave to do it all by yourself," Paddleford telegraphed her mother. Back home, Jennie felt good enough to resume her activities. But in January 1927, she was rushed to the hospital for an unknown emergency, and did not recover. On Monday, January 31, 1927, Jennie died.

The death of her greatest source of inspiration affected Paddleford profoundly, which is apparent in what she wrote. "She is gone but her legacy to me is riches that can neither be bought or sold, and into which the question of money enters not at all," Paddleford wrote. "We had little cash money, but we didn't buy our happiness out of the stores. She taught us how to take it firsthand from the farm." People who later met Paddleford described her as full of inner confidence, and for this Paddleford credited her mother.

Jennie's death seemed to evoke a heightened ambition in her daughter. Shortly after returning home to New York, she applied for a position with McFadden Publications, which she did not get, but it left her with two letters of reference that she kept all her life. Her backers were Leo C. Moser, copy editor at Albert Frank & Company, and Glenn Hayes, president of Hayes-Loeb Company. Moser had been a classmate and sometime date (often to the particular annoyance of Lloyd Zimmerman) of Paddleford's at Kansas State, and he had caught up with her later at *Farm & Fireside*, where he had been an editorial manager. Hayes knew Paddleford when she wrote publicity for his company in Chicago.

Moser said:

I have been acquainted with Miss Paddleford's work for a period of nearly five years. She is an able writer of both imaginative and fact material, a combination of abilities which I have found rare among women writers. As an editorial manager of a department of the Crowell Publishing Company, moreover, I have been told that she has initiated changes that have resulted in saving very considerable sums for the company.

If you have an opportunity to secure Miss Paddleford's services for editorial work of any kind, I am sure that you will find that she is conscientious and unusually diligent in her application to the work in hand.

Hayes said:

Miss Clementine Paddleford, whom you inquire about in your letter of the 15th, was in the writer's employ for the better part of three years, during which time she built up for herself a very enviable reputation. She is a writer of exceptional ability, being able to write to a purpose, as well as anyone I have ever known. Her character is above reproach and she is most punctual and reliable in her duties.

Paddleford blazed on, acting on each idea as it occurred to her. She spent the week of June 20, 1927, in Asheville, North Carolina, at the meeting of the American Home Economics

Association. Her objective was new contacts: eleven hundred women from all over the country attended. She held a luncheon for five guests who were important at major corporations and associations such as Kellogg and Kraft. These women would be good sources for years.

In December 1927, Paddleford made her pilgrimage to Kansas. It was the first holiday without Jennie. Perhaps as a result Paddleford spent just three days in Manhattan before hitting the road for work. She visited for two days with Nell Nichols and at each stop met with agricultural office extension workers, attended meetings, and visited farms and kitchens.

By this time she was a member of the American Home Economics Association, Advertising Women of New York, the Woman Pays Club, Pen and Brush Club, American Quill Club, and still the Kansas Authors Club. She visited research laboratories, state universities, and governmental bureaus. She attended all meetings of huge organizations—the Gas Manufacturers Association, and National Electric Light Association, to name two.

After Jennie's death her memos to Martin and Wing became fewer and her tone of upbeat excitement turned concise and strict. She wrote a few freelance articles, for *The Globe Feeder* and *Your Home* magazine. In both of these, in accord with her arrangement to restrict her real name to *Farm & Fireside*, her work appeared under the byline "Clementine Haskin."

Then some vitality returned to Paddleford's personal life. In 1928, she met a woman who would become a lifelong friend and confidante, Alice C. Nichols, a bubbly, birdlike woman with charisma to spare. Although she was no kin to Nell Nichols, the test kitchen expert for *Farm & Fireside*, Alice was also a Kansan, born in Liberal in 1905. Like Paddleford, she showed an interest in journalism at a young age, even creating her own newspaper, *The Nichols Journal,* as a child. After graduating from Kansas State in 1927 with a journalism degree, she worked at *The Kingman Herald,* in Kingman, Kansas. Russell Lord, an editor at *Farm & Fireside,* summoned her to New York in 1928, where she started on the mail desk "reading the slush."

Nichols and Paddleford took to each other immediately. Inspired by her lively new friend, Paddleford bounced back— and her memos to Martin and Wing resumed their detail and vigor.

As her travels increased, Paddleford began to stay in touch with her regular correspondents the only way she could— through chatty letters that were copied and sent to everyone. She called them her "form letters." She also piggybacked assignments, using her *Farm & Fireside*-sponsored trips to her advantage. For instance, while in California in 1928 she wrote an article for *Brighter Homes* magazine, a publication that was essentially a promotional vehicle for its publisher, Glidden, maker of what the cover of the magazine said—in very small type—were "the highest quality of paints, varnishes, lacquers and enamels." This article was about the entertaining style of none other than Clara Bow. "Where a Famous Flapper Folds Her Wings and Rests" has a lead that is pure Paddleford, describing the day's leading entertainer in a way that every woman in every kitchen could relate to. "Clara Bow isn't always a flapper," she wrote. "At home she slips off her flame-colored wings and her screen poses and is just herself." Paddleford's description of the Bow manse in Beverly Hills is equally engaging: "You can see it a mile away, its title roof a red blotch, as daring as Clara's own auburn curls."

Paddleford's interview with Bow is often hilarious, as Bow admits buying a sea-green refrigerator for the color and a set of red pots to placate her cook before acknowledging that her so-called flair for entertaining was actually all about pleasing "the brutes," also known as the men in her life. "I don't know much about cooking," she told Paddleford, "but I do know a lot about men, and I know a lot about that social function they call a 'good square meal.'"

Paddleford was not always as well received as she apparently was by the queen flapper. For instance, while she was on a trip through Madison, Wisconsin, Abby Lillian Marlatt, a staff member of the College of Agriculture at the University of Wisconsin and an old friend of Jennie's, invited Paddleford for dinner. It did not go smoothly, as Paddleford reported to her bosses:

> [Marlatt] doesn't approve of me due to the terrible mistake I made of being honest in regard to my training for the job of household editor. She was shocked, I soon discovered, to know that I wasn't a graduate in Home Economics. I seldom confess the truth, but being an old friend of the family, I banked on a bit of charity in understanding—which I didn't get. I tried to explain that my job was editing and not specialized writing, that we hire specialists to do the special jobs. But this didn't appease her in the least and we battled the point for the evening. She says magazines everywhere are making a damn fool mistake not hiring Home Economics trained women for their staffs. I reminded her with considerable joy, that Katherine Fisher, head of the Household Institute for Good Housekeeping, had taught Latin for 15 years before she took her present job. The eve-

ning was time well spent for me, as I learned never, never, under any circumstance, to again admit that I haven't at least a master's degree in Home Economics. Strange as it seems these Home Economics women can't tell the difference unless I tell 'em. I'm usually cautious to keep my feet on dry land.

When Paddleford returned home, there was more drama. The great Nell Nichols, now busy raising a child in Topeka, untied her apron strings from *Farm & Fireside* in December 1928. Paddleford hoped to hire a woman just to test the recipes and take Nichols's field work for herself. "Instead of one writer providing most of the food and home management articles," she wrote to Martin, "I hope to get this material from personal interviews with farm women, thus giving hard-boiled copy a human interest slant." This plan was one that Paddleford would carry forward in every job. Involving real home cooks in the world of food journalism was quickly becoming her mission.

By the end of the 1920s, Paddleford had a name in journalism. Her adolescent visions of fame and wealth were actually now on the horizon, and ranged around her was a network of farm women to keep her in touch with her roots and sources and to learn from her. She was just past thirty.

· · · CHAPTER 3 · · ·

Rhapsody on a Kitchen Sink

$\mathcal{I}$n the 1930s, food writing in America was not an art. In addition to a handful of short books that existed mainly to show housewives how best to clean chickens, there were two types of newspaper food coverage: restaurant reviews for tourists and the expense account crowd, and recipe pages. The former assessed establishments that many in the country could not afford, and the latter were filled with recipes and time-saving tips written with the sort of excitement that might be generated by advice on darning socks. Food and cooking were portrayed as almost exclusively scientific subjects, and the sun of enthusiasm and passion had not yet risen over the editors. That left a lot of space for sober "how to" advice. As R. W. Apple Jr. of *The New York Times* put it, coverage of food then reflected the belief "that science and technology would solve everything." "Home economics was very well 'formulatized,' or precise," he said.

Not particularly interesting, not evocative, and it did not convey any sense of fun. Paddleford knew that it could be better, and deduced that writing about food and people who were truly enthusiastic about preparing it would make readers both interested and hungry. The adjective that best describes Paddleford, Apple said, is "independent." "And that is a quality that was nourished in the kinds of places where she came from," he asserted.

In the summer of 1930, Paddleford's father remarried. The bride, Araminta Holman, sixty, head of the Kansas State art department, was descended from a pioneer family in Leavenworth, Kansas. She retired from her job when she married Solon Paddleford and spent her time at the Methodist church, teaching Sunday school and working for the women's society. Although the stepmother is remembered by relatives as particularly warm and sunny, it's likely that Paddleford herself never had the chance to get too close to Minty. Her work had become her life, and trips home were becoming rare.

Paddleford was already a powerhouse at *Farm & Fireside*. Her decision to get out in the fields—literally—to learn about her sources' wants and needs had helped her make a name for herself as a professional editor. What she wanted, though, was to be a writer, too—to influence these sources with her words, to lure readers into the kitchen with more than just practical information. Her first step, which she was already muscled for, was to establish a unique voice, one any reader could recognize as "Clementine Paddleford."

The year 1930 was pivotal for her. *Farm & Fireside* was renamed *Country Home* by its publisher and a big push was made to mass-market it, taking it beyond its farm readers. Paddleford had virtually reinvented *Farm & Fireside*'s editorial content. "From 1924 to 1930, when she was woman's editor for us on

Farm & Fireside ... our records show reader response increased 179 percent," wrote Edward P. Seymour, the magazine's advertising manager.

Paddleford, though, was ready to move on. At thirty-two, she applied and was soon selected as director of the church housekeeping bureau of *Christian Herald*, the leading religious newspaper in the country, with an impressive circulation of 200,000 copies a month.

It seems an odd move. Paddleford was never particularly religious. But the publication was well-respected and on the upswing. When Paddleford was hired, the *Christian Herald* was shifting from a weekly to a monthly, and was adding a service department for women. The paper did not hesitate in its choice of whom to hire. "We consulted the food and household advertisers and advertising agents," wrote Godfrey Hammond, the editor. "The woman most frequently recommended had the mouth-filling name—Clementine Paddleford. After talking with ten women, we decided that Miss Paddleford had just the variety of experience, the ability, and the sympathy required."

The job came with a test kitchen to direct and an advertising department to answer to—Paddleford seemed to see a prospect for turning out her own stories. She was bursting with intimate memories of the pleasure of eating: the thrill of a cool glass of tart lemonade on a blisteringly hot day, and coming home from school to the warm yeasty smell of rolls. Like water flowing up in a well, Paddleford's memories of her family meals bubbled up into her reporting. The skill she still needed was learning to describe the season's first strawberries so a reader would have to put down the newspaper and go to market. It would take practice.

Evidence of Paddleford's drive shows in her earliest days at

Christian Herald. From June to October 1930, the first five months of the job, she wrote about forty-three feature stories about food—a vast amount of practice reporting. And the quantity seemed to build quality; Paddleford was learning how to engage readers through prose.

Many of these early columns concerned contests that *Christian Herald* ran for best church suppers, which paid the winner $25—more if it was a Christmas menu. Various brand publicists and home economists were her fellow judges, and occasionally these women would manage to slip their own test kitchen recipes into Paddleford's columns, as was the case with a *Christian Herald* story from October 18, 1930. Called "Meet the Judges," Paddleford had invited readers to "judge the judges" of a church-supper contest. "Joan Rock knows more about making good cakes than anyone else I can name," Paddleford wrote. "And she ought to know all the ins and outs of a cake's anatomy; baking is a part of her everyday work. She can bake anything that requires baking powder. She is the educational director for the Standard Brands, Inc, and Royal Baking Powder is the product she works with most . . . This recipe will turn out a dessert of deliciousness, all snowy inside, its crust a macaroon brown. The frosting tastes even better to me, for it is as smooth as butterfly wings."

Christmas, though, was a subject that seized Paddleford each year. Her readership, church women who had to try to best their previous year's pageant efforts, counted on her to come up with something new when the calendar got down to its last page. "Orange Maries" were one such innovation: a new-fangled take that combined the charm of both baked apples and fruitcake; the orange shells are stuffed with dried fruits—an amusement for a holiday table.

Joan Rock's Coconut Marshmallow Layer Cake

1 cup butter, room temperature

2 cups sugar

6 eggs, separated

2 teaspoons lemon juice

2 teaspoons vanilla extract

4 cups pastry flour

2 tablespoons baking powder

½ teaspoon salt

1½ cups whole milk

Coconut Marshmallow Filling and Frosting (see next page)

Preheat oven to 375 degrees.

In a large bowl, cream butter; add sugar, egg yolks, lemon juice, and vanilla; mix well. Sift flour with baking powder and salt into a separate bowl; add alternately with milk to first mixture. Add egg whites, beaten stiff.

Pour into 3 greased and floured 9-inch layer-cake pans with removable bottoms. Bake for 20 to 25 minutes or until just done and golden brown. Remove from pans and while cooling, prepare the following:

continued on next page

Coconut Marshmallow Filling and Frosting

1½ cups sugar

½ cup water

6 egg whites

¼ cup cream of tartar

6 large marshmallows, finely diced

1 tablespoon lemon juice

10 marshmallows, thinly sliced into rounds

1½ cups fresh grated coconut

In a small pot over medium heat, combine sugar and water and gently swirl the pot to dissolve the sugar without stirring. Raise the heat to medium-high and using a candy thermometer, bring the mixture to soft-ball stage (238 degrees on a candy thermometer), washing down the inside of the pot with a wet pastry brush as needed to keep sugar crystals from forming.

Toward the end of the boiling, start beating the egg whites. In a medium bowl with an electric mixer, beat on low until foamy. Add cream of tartar and then raise speed to medium-high. Beat until stiff, but not dry, peaks form.

Add the diced marshmallows to the sugar syrup, but do not stir. With the mixer running on medium, pour the hot sugar syrup with the marshmallows in a thin stream over the beaten

continued on next page

egg whites. Raise the speed to high and beat until cooled, stiff, and glossy, about 10 minutes. Add lemon juice.

Cool cake and trim the tops if needed to make flat disks. Ice the cake, distributing the icing, sliced marshmallows, and coconut in between each layer, saving enough to garnish the top.

Yield: 12 servings

Other articles showed she was learning to take any subject and find an interesting way to incorporate food. "More Coffee Please," from the spring of 1931, begins a discussion of the perfect ending to any church dinner with these lines: "Good coffee makes the meal. At least, it makes the good meal perfect and the poor meal possible. Ask for a second cup of coffee and the cook is satisfied that all's right with her world."

The story goes on to say a good cup of coffee should be "hot, with a bouquet of aromas lifting from the cup." Instructions were included: "I know women who measure the coffee with the greatest care, but never bother with the water," she wrote. "They know 'just about' how much to put in. I have noticed, too, that the 'just about' makes all the difference in the world." There was stricture that many endorse: "Coffee re-heated gives an evil cooking liquid that might have been brewed out of the Dead Sea after a recipe left by the Witch of Endor."

Still other stories provide a glimpse of Paddleford's future output, when she need not worry about religious themes. In the

Orange Maries

1 tablespoon chopped walnuts

8 large seedless oranges

8 dates, pitted and chopped into ½-inch pieces

2 tablespoons coconut; may use fresh grated or dried shredded unsweetened flakes, plus extra for sprinkling

1 tablespoon raisins

1 egg white, stiffly beaten

1 teaspoon sugar

Preheat oven to 325 degrees.

Lightly toast walnuts in oven 2 to 3 minutes until well browned; set aside.

With a very sharp knife, cut off the tops of oranges and hollow out a small cone-shaped portion of each orange near the top. Then, with the point of the knife trace the inside of the orange, working it around the fruit, removing pulp in one or several large chunks. Drain the fruit "shells" of any pulp and juice. (If you puncture the bottom of the orange while removing fruit, you may patch it effectively with one of the discarded orange "lids" placed upside down in the bottom of the orange.)

continued on next page

Gently slice the removed orange flesh into ½-inch pieces. Place in a medium bowl and mix with dates, coconut, raisins, and toasted walnuts.

Divide mixture evenly among the orange shells and place the oranges in a 13 x 9 x 2-inch glass or other nonreactive baking dish with ½ inch of water in the bottom of the pan. Bake for 45 minutes, until oranges are fragrant; they will be very hot.

Preheat broiler. Fold sugar into beaten egg white to make meringue. While still hot, add to each orange a spoonful of meringue. Sprinkle the meringue with coconut and return the oranges to the broiler to brown. Keep oranges at least 4 to 5 inches from broiler and watch carefully, about 2 minutes. Serve either hot or cold.

Yield: 8 servings

winter of 1931, Paddleford wrote about Etienne Allio, head chef at the Hotel New Yorker, near the city's Penn Station.

I have heard lots of women envy professional cooks because they didn't have to worry about using extra dabs of butter, or have to bother fixing up the cheaper cuts of meat. But chefs have a stricter budget, and hew to the dollar line closer than any church food committee I can name. They may serve breast of guinea chicken under glass with Virginia ham— but what about the guinea wings and giblets and the rest of the bird? If there is any rest they can't throw it out. It has to serve in hash or stew or giblet sauce on toast. Yes, chefs have to think of all these things.

Paddleford's kind of writing pulled readers right in. By tapping into how to make cooking a more cheerful and pleasant task—and by extension how to make meal times fun rather than onerous, Paddleford was devising a genre. "It's the mode for cars to be furnished with all the conveniences of home, from cocktail shakers to ash trays, from beauty kits to dust cloths," she wrote of automobile upholstery in the July 1929 edition of *The Auburn* magazine. Writing on modern church décor in the *Christian Herald* in July 1932, she went for the jugular: "Consider the seating. Or does the very thought bring a 'pain in the neck'? Comfort is important for higher altitudes of mind. But just being physically comfortable isn't enough to ask of the seats, not by any means. They must be built and installed to eliminate squeaks and creaks so annoying to the speaker." In the December 1935 issue of *The American Home*, she tackled the history of Christmas cards. "It was an English gentleman with a capacity for friendship who introduced the high-hearted custom of sending a Christmas card," she wrote. "Mr. Cole, one of the busiest men of his day, suddenly discovered that Christmas 1846 was just around the corner. Jove! Nor a Christmas letter ready for the post! To meet the situation he conceived the idea of sending his greeting printed on a decorated card, an apology of a sort for not writing a personal note."

These stories show the unfolding Paddleford voice, her careful embellishment of details. Instead of merely explaining that Cole hadn't written the traditional greetings of the time, she puts herself in the subject's shoes, imagining the cards as "an apology of a sort" that enables readers to place themselves in a not dishonorable tradition.

Early food stories are notable for her lively, engaging voice as well as for the copious research. In December 1933, for a freelance piece for *The American Home*, she devised a Christmas feast in homage to Charles Dickens, whose descriptions of yuletide food traditions had always bewitched her:

> And how the mouth waters when Dickens talks about dinner. He loved to plunge a carving knife in the breast of a goose and see the 'long expected gush of stuffing issue forth.' He loved to ladle from a steaming tureen the 'clear rich broth in which there are gleaming grains of barley and thin rings of onion and a hint of spice' or to bear in 'a gigantic pudding with a sprig of holly in the top'. He was as eager as a housewife or as Santa Claus, himself, to provide his characters with the comfort of food and drink, which his kindly wisdom knew to be necessary for the tired children of men.

Compared with the scientific tone of food reporting of the day, Paddleford's literary apostrophes were almost revolutionary intellectual scholarship. The article goes on to describe and quote liberally from *The Pickwick Papers*, *Nicholas Nickleby*, *Sketches by Boz*, and, of course, *A Christmas Carol*, and to include several recipes Paddleford adapted from these works. Among them was a spiced cider punch, which she personalized by explaining the ways it related to her own family's traditions. "It was the punch that lighted every eye, for our spiced cider punch is an exciting liquid, a family heirloom. Here is the recipe

Spiced Cider Punch

1¼ pounds dark brown sugar

1 gallon sweet apple cider

1 quart hot black tea

3 sticks cinnamon

1 tablespoon whole allspice

1 tablespoon whole cloves

2 pieces whole mace

½ teaspoon salt

Juice of 5 lemons, about ¾ cup

5 oranges, sliced ¼ inch thick

Mix sugar, cider, tea, spices, and salt in a large pot. Boil 15 minutes. Strain. Add lemon juice and orange slices and serve hot.

Yield: 20 (1-cup) servings

made grandpapa's way. One rule we observed in taking cider punch, no one had a first sip until grandpa gave his toast. He said it like a prayer, 'A merry Christmas to us all, my dears, God bless us!' And we answered as we always do in the words of Little Tim, 'God bless us every one!'"

In the art that conceals art, Paddleford research is presented in the most cheerful and upbeat of tones, as if to ask readers: Instead of all the same-old family recipes, who *wouldn't* want to shake things up and do an old-fashioned English Christmas feast?

In a time when the Depression meant people lost their jobs and enterprises folded daily, Paddleford had an important ally— and genuine fan—in her *Christian Herald* editor, Godfrey Hammond. Correspondence between the two, while always quite professional (nearly all of Hammond's letters to Paddleford are typed and addressed "Miss Paddleford"), also revealed a certain warmth. Hammond sent fond congratulatory memos to Paddleford each time statistics showed a surge in her readership: "Congratulations on a 35 percent increase—this is an especially good showing as you had no money to spend," he wrote in early 1932. Another note in the same year simply said, "Keats wrote 'Ode to a Grecian Urn' but Paddleford wrote 'Rhapsody on a Kitchen Sink.' Daniel A. Poling, president of the Christian Herald Association, wrote to Paddleford in late 1932: "In a hurried conference with Mr. Hammond the other day I learned of the really amazing progress made by your department, the Service Department—an increase of six thousand inquiries in the first ten months of 1932 over the corresponding period of 1931. It is worthy of more than ordinary praise. We all appreciate it—I appreciate it immensely."

Paddleford returned the compliment. In February 1934 she wrote an article in the *Christian Herald* extolling the housekeeping secrets of the Poling household. "Mrs. Poling says: 'Don't tell Dr. Poling you are writing this story for your department. He wouldn't let you print a word of it.' And I didn't, for I knew you would enjoy this intimate picture around the kitchen and dining-room of a most delightful home," Paddleford wrote. The story includes recipes for three dishes—Spanish steak, corn pone, and plum pudding—to serve one hundred guests.

Paddleford also managed a lucrative freelance writing business outside her grueling *Christian Herald* duties. She accepted writing assignments from any publication that interested her, from national magazines such as *Ladies' Home Journal*, for which she wrote mostly about cooking, to industry publications like *Soda Fountain* magazine, for which she devised "Recipes of the Month." If the woman did anything in her spare time besides dream up article ideas, there is scant proof. One coup came in April 1932 when Paddleford pitched an article to H. L. Mencken, editor of *The American Mercury*, an important literary magazine.

" 'Angel food without apologies' or 'Religion by way of the alimentary canal' is an article I would like to do for *The American Mercury*," her overture began, proceeding to outline a story about how church kitchens around the country were run and, most important, the effort involved in serving meals to entire communities. "Cook stoves are doing more religious work than ministers," her letter said. "Hundreds of thousands of churches daily send their palate-tempting incense, the odor of stewed chicken, up the church chimneys of cities and towns throughout these United States. A billion or more church women are persistently and quietly cooking their way into St. Peter's Good Graces." Mencken bought it. He put Paddleford through the editorial mill, cutting her "over-long" manuscript and changing her "rather vague" title to "An Army Travels on Its Belly." What a combination, the iconoclast and the farm girl! Paddleford responded, "I like your title. It has guts and makes 'Angel Food' insipid."

The article appeared October 1932, alongside a story by F. Scott Fitzgerald. Because of a feared conflict with the *Herald*, Paddleford's piece was signed "Clemence Haskin" but it did not escape the watchful eye of her old journalism professor, Charles Rogers, who had kept in touch with his "first student in feature writing." Rogers was proud of having spotted talent before it became known. "I recall how you shed blood all over Manhattan to get something good enough for the *Ladies' Home Journal*, *Pictorial Review*, etc.," he wrote. "You didn't dare even think of the heights of *The Mercury*." How does it feel to be among the immortals of contemporary writers, Miss Haskin?"

While it is remarkable to imagine the work involved in turning out such a great range of stories—images of Paddleford hunched over a desk, pencil in hand plus one behind each ear, legal pad stretched out before her, file folders strewn in heaps around her feet, each one devoted to a different article—Paddleford's personal situation makes the picture even more staggering. In 1931, at the age of thirty-three, Paddleford developed a chronic hoarseness in her throat. This farm girl from Kansas was not one to run to the doctor; she was the type to suffer through all manner of colds and flu if it meant that she didn't have to stop working—she often wrote to Jennie about various maladies she was enduring on her way from one assignment to the next, a stomach bug here, exhaustion there. The throat situation got so bad, though, that Paddleford broke down and went to see a doctor. At worst, she was probably imagining some kind of infection. To her great horror, though, the situation was definitely not one of simple overworked vocal chords or strep throat. Paddleford's doctor came up with the worst possible diagnosis: a tumor, probably cancer.

Paddleford must have thought she was hearing things, too. Serious diagnoses like these are never welcome, of course, but this one was especially surprising given Paddleford's youth and general good health. The timing was horrible: Paddleford had lost her mother, her earliest fan, to cancer just a few years before. She must have thought she was equally doomed—the diagnosis was contrary to logic in so many ways. For one thing, the vast majority of throat cancers are of the squamous cell variety, and these are clearly related to prolonged tobacco and alcohol use; Paddleford was only thirty-three, and though she may have smoked and a drunk a little in her heady college days, she was hardly known as a heavy user of either. Second, laryngeal cancer most often affects people in their fifties and sixties. Today, overall survival figures for head and neck cancer are 45 to 50 percent; in the early 1930s, the odds were much poorer—Paddleford was basically handed a death sentence.

A cancer diagnosis robs a patient of her future. Paddleford probably stood alone in that doctor's office, faced with a fate not much different from that of her mother, only she was so much younger, and had so many plans. Most of her life had been spent building up to this point. That curious little girl with a pen and pad at the train station. The hard-working student. The ambitious career girl holding down three jobs at once. And, now a writer who was just beginning to garner respect. She was on the road to achieving what she had set out to do, and now she might lose it all. That determined woman who sat alone in a sterile doctor's office must have lost her steely veneer for just one moment as she contemplated her future. What next, she must have wondered. With Paddleford, there was, as always, only one answer: Work the pain away.

Instead of retiring to her sick bed, she armed herself with the best weapon in her arsenal: ambition. The patient reported that her doctor gave her a choice of treatments. He told her that if he removed her larynx and vocal cords, he could almost surely cure her (a likely scenario when cancer is caught very early), but that she would never speak again. The second option: He could remove only the infected parts of her larynx, in an operation that was truly avant-garde and performed by only a handful of physicians in the world, but it might not eradicate the cancer. This was far riskier, but Paddleford was hell-bent on continuing in journalism. Without wavering, she chose the second route—confident as always that she was meant to be a reporter, and that nothing like throat cancer was going to stand in her way.

In surgery, a small sterling silver tracheotomy tube, known as a Jackson tube for the laryngologist Chevalier Jackson, who invented it, was inserted to replace the excised section of Paddleford's larynx. The device regulated Paddleford's speech and breathing functions in such a way that to talk, she had to place her finger on a button in her throat so she could blow the air out of her mouth and speak. This is an uncomfortable process—the act of speaking must be entirely premeditated; it's impossible to jump into a conversation when you have to push in a button first. Second, it calls attention to itself, and a reporter's job is to deflect attention from herself. Paddleford was now facing a huge challenge: How could she make a device as obvious disappear? Paddleford likely spent her time recuperating pondering this question. She realized that she would have to be more charismatic, seductive, winsome, and charming than other interviewers—she would have to get a source's eyes to lift above the throat and find her eyes.

But first, she'd have to recover. Two key issues are involved in laryngectomies: speech and swallowing. The ability to regain speech depends upon how much of the vocal mechanism is missing. The more vocal chord is gone—the vocal chords are in the mid-part of the larynx—the more a voice is going to sound croaky, hoarse, and breathy. One never meets a person who knew Paddleford who does not describe the "eerie" nature of her "deep, throaty" voice—it left a definite impression, and not a subtle one. There were additional effects, too. Swimming, which Paddleford so loved, was no longer an option—if she went into a pool, water could easily have gone into the hole in her throat and drowned her.

The upside of this, if there was one, was that of the variety of partial laryngectomies available to patients, Paddleford most likely had a vertical version, which means that her doctors would have taken out a side of her vocal chord but left the epiglottis alone, so that Paddleford could swallow and eat unaided.

In terms of recuperation, within a week of surgery most patients are able to emit some sound, and from there speech improves steadily. Once swelling goes down, in two to four weeks, a patient's speech is even better. Nowadays, a speech therapist would play a big role; in those days, though, at-home therapy was unheard of. Instead, patients stayed in the hospital for quite a long time. Paddleford spent three months in the hospital, dispirited, lonely, and, worst of all, worried she might never work again. She wasn't surprised she had made it through the surgery; she was just annoyed at not being able to do her own version of therapy: hit the pavement and get to writing. Write she could, but it took nearly a year for her to learn to talk above a whisper. Once she was out of the hospital, though, she never experienced a relapse; her throat cancer was gone.

Paddleford ingeniously thought of a trick to camouflage the hole in her throat. She masked it in black velvet ribbon styled as a choker. To a casual observer, Paddleford was sporting a piece of old-fashioned jewelry—an "antique" she never removed, at dinner parties, award ceremonies, in the newsroom—the choker became a permanent part of Paddleford's evolving costume of dramatic, feminine clothing, and it blended right in with her capes and skirts.

The voice was a different problem. Those who knew her described her throaty, low, hoarse sound routinely as off-putting and hard to hear, but also said that once Paddleford got to talking, listening to her became second nature—she really did learn to become engaging with her eyes, and to ask enough interesting questions that sources reported they "forgot" they were talking to someone who had no larynx. Paddleford once said that the only people who dared comment on her voice were taxi drivers, and that eventually she learned to laugh when they recommended various remedies for her "cold" or "laryngitis." Paddleford often responded by assuring them that she "took pineapple," the world's only known source of bromelain, which is thought to be effective for relieving ailments from bronchitis to cancer. To her taxi driver prescribers, she did not acknowledge any problem beyond the garden-variety one. Of her voice, she even developed a kind of optimism: "Actually, it's an asset," she would say with a shrug. "People never forget me."

The emotional part of Paddleford's recovery was worse in some ways than the physical. With Jennie gone and the rest of her family in Kansas, Paddleford had to rely on her friends for support. But self-sufficient as she always was, Paddleford was not used to having to rely on anyone. Expectedly, correspondence saved her—Paddleford was always one for letter writing, and during her convalescence she threw herself into occupying hands and mind keeping up with all her old friends. As far as Kansas went, Paddleford exchanged letters with her father updating him about her health, but there is no record he visited his daughter. One person who came through was Addie Burrell, an African-American woman, the wife of a Pullman porter, who was a personal aide, cook, and maid. She stayed with Paddleford in her apartment at 423 East 52nd Street. The bond the two formed was close; after her recovery, Paddleford found the means to keep Burrell to help her around the house.

If ever there was a time for Lloyd Zimmerman to have appealed to Paddleford, it might have been during her illness. However, the separation was so final that there is no clear record of any correspondence between the two at this time. If he even knew that she had throat cancer, there is no evidence. What is patently clear is that she had fallen out of love with him. With even less fanfare than their secret wedding, Paddleford and Zimmerman officially divorced in 1932. The union was so shaky that they had been married nine years without ever having lived together.

Paddleford's eternally upbeat Kansas sister, Alice Nichols, stepped in. If Nichols was ever fearful for Paddleford, she was careful to be cheerful in her presence. In the privacy of her own diary, though, Nichols fretted Paddleford's circumstances. "Clementine had a perfect breakfast," Nichols wrote in her diary in February 1931, shortly after Paddleford's diagnosis. "Such an admirable person. She is and yet, by the accepted moral standard, condemned—such rot." In April, Nichols reported Paddleford "sounded blue" and "too bad that such an admirable, indefatigable person should have such a misfortune." Nichols described Paddleford coming home from the hospital, on July 19, 1931. "I got there in time for a very delicious dinner prepared by the good Addie," Nichols wrote. She noted further that Paddleford had to return to the doctor a couple of days later to have her tube reinserted. Seven days after her homecoming, though, it appears that the old Paddleford was back: "The courage and gaiety of the woman!" Nichols wrote. "Laughing as always— writing gay, whimsical bits of conversation with a tube in her throat—the whole process of learning to talk to do over again!" In November things were somewhat back to normal. "Dinner with Clementine," Nichols wrote, "nice talk—hope she gets so she can use her new tube. If anyone can, she can."

Nichols's diaries also indicate that Paddleford was not living a monastic existence—soon enough, she felt good enough to take a lover. On July 25, 1931, soon after a mention of Paddleford's having to learn to speak all over again, Nichols writes: "That was a wise move she made on Don. Made him take some contraceptive pills. He was ill for a week and has been most solicitous since." Although there were indeed trials of a male contraceptive pill during this era, what is even more interesting about Nichols's note is that in her own files Paddleford left no information about "Don" or any other male friend in the period of recuperation or even in the entire decade. Paddleford sought to control tightly all personal information about herself while chronicling every last detail of her career.

While adjusting to her new way of communicating orally, Paddleford threw herself back into work to avoid self-pity. Her work at *Christian Herald* continued, but the files show that elsewhere C. P. Haskin, Mrs. Clement Haskin, and Clemence Haskin were filling up columns of type.

Two events in 1936 catapulted Paddleford into new territory. The first was the publication in the *Christian Herald* for May of her article "A Flower for My Mother." This two-and-a-half-page appreciation was by far the most personal material Paddleford had ever published, and it was a heartbreaker. With an illustration of Jennie, a kindly, matronly looking woman with gray-white hair pulled into a bun and a black velvet choker around her neck (quite similar to Paddleford's tube camouflage), are the words: "On Mother's Day, when I lay tribute to her memory, that for more than anything else I thank her for letting me make my own life." The article describes scenes from Paddleford's childhood—Jennie's lilac bushes, her sunflower birthday cake, the time it was so hot in Kansas that Jennie organized an ice cream social to cheer the community up—in loving detail. Without having to try very hard, a reader imagines the strawberry shortcake that felt like love, and the mother who was the backbone of the family. A few sentences leap from the page: "When evil days come, when I feel alone and unnumbered in the city's herds. . . . I hear her say, as plain as print—'Don't whine over evils. Sharpen your teeth on them.'"

The essay was honest and friendly and moving, and it did not go unnoticed. Beatrice Plumb, who worked with Paddleford at *Farm & Fireside*, wrote to her: "You certainly have gone and done it again! This article of yours in May's *Christian Herald* is the best thing you've ever written. Confound you, Clementine, why do you fool with food stuff when you can write real things like this? I am writing this very minute to Godfrey Hammond telling him what a gorgeous thing you have done." Plumb need not have bothered. Hammond himself was already in the line-up of congratulations, sending Paddleford a memo to let her know how much he, too, had enjoyed the personal piece.

Things were looking up for Paddleford. She was forming an increasingly solid relationship with the *New York Herald Tribune* and its Sunday magazine, *This Week*. The *Herald Tribune* was created in 1924 when the *Herald*, founded by James Gordon Bennett in 1835, was bought by the *Tribune*, founded in 1841 by Horace Greeley. Two bigger names in American journalism would be hard to find. As Richard Kluger, a former staff member, wrote in his book about the *Herald Tribune*, *The Paper*, it had "two traditions—polemical and reportorial" to uphold and its reputation in the middle thirties was beyond anything going—it was the most exciting paper put out in the most exciting city in the world. In those days, *The New York Times*, its principal broadsheet rival, was dull looking and dull reading.

At this time the paper was owned by Ogden and Helen Reid. Ogden inherited it from his father, Whitelaw Reid, and his wife had been a social secretary; yet, as Kluger notes, it was Helen Reid who became "the paper's dominant force." Mrs. Reid, according to both Kluger and R. W. Apple Jr., had a reputation for hiring extraordinarily talented women. One was Eugenia Sheppard, who became a legend in the world of fashion—Seventh Avenue and beyond—but she was not hired until 1939. In those days, the female force was Eloise Davison, director of the paper's Home Institute.

The Home Institute was housed on the ninth floor of the *Herald Tribune* building at 230 West 41st Street—it stands today, between 40th and 41st Streets west of Seventh Avenue. At the time, the fourth floor was the place for the Linotype machines and the composing stones, and the second and third housed the presses. The fifth floor was the newsroom, focus of the action. The ninth floor accumulated the components of what we today call "lifestyle" reporting—home furnishings, food, fashion, child rearing. An auditorium was also on the ninth floor, and in time the personnel department ended up there too. The furniture was standard-issue newsroom, rather shabby—oak desks flecked with splintered edges and disintegrating finishes. The lights were grayish and uncertain. It was never air-conditioned. The exception to the worn-out aspect was the kitchen at the core of the Home Institute, which was always furnished with the latest appliances, courtesy of their manufacturers. The kitchen was used to be sure the recipes worked out as described and also to create foods for photo shoots. Top-quality ovens, refrigerators, Mixmasters, fancy knives, new frying pans, and coffee makers and all manner of newfangled gadgets were at hand. It is here that Clementine Paddleford found herself under the direction of Davison.

Eloise Davison was, by all accounts, a strict, small, bird-like woman with pixie-ish looks. Davison never married or had children and, like Paddleford, seemed dedicated to work above all else; at the time, she was in charge of the test kitchen and women's pages, which included food coverage.

Davison's roots were somewhat similar to Paddleford's. She was the product of a Midwestern home economics background, having earned a master's in home economics from Iowa State University in 1924. Davison was also a freelance writer in the home economist mode. An article bearing her name titled "Pots and Pans Are Stored Near the Range" appeared in the July 1935 issue of *McCall's*. Having read Paddleford's *Christian Herald* columns, Davison struck up a friendship and occasionally assigned Paddleford to write stories for the paper. These were more scientifically oriented than Paddleford's usual writing, but their author still managed to inject into the text some lively details and the idea that preparing food was fun.

For example, "More-the-Merrier Menus," published in April 1935, is devoted to banquets and includes three menus, including one for a high school function. "A banquet is a dinner plus," Paddleford wrote. "And the plus is trimming....Cheery as a red bird is the vegetable appetizer in the Junior-Senior menu. This needs a white, yellow, or green garnish for dramatic effect. Arrange the plates with translucent endive in a five-point star. Heap on the appetizer and decorate with half slices of hard-boiled egg in a geometrical design."

Another article a little more than a year later is even more exuberant: "Those Refreshing Melons!" "To be fooled by a melon is the easiest thing on earth," says the text, which then goes on to offer suggestions for choosing summer's bounty. "The best test for the ripeness of a watermelon is to plug it and take a bite. Not a practical plan from the merchants' point of view. Thump and listen is the second best test. . . . A ripe melon emits a muffled sound; the green, a sharp metallic ring."

It was through her relationship with the *Herald Tribune* that Paddleford began contemplating tackling the big time. Shoes or food? Paddleford asked herself. It was 1936, and the country was economically on its knees. Paddleford decided to apply herself and figure out a way to earn some extra money: What did people really need these days? Well, shoes, for one, and food, for another. Paddleford shrewdly decided that of the two, food was more important. After all, everyone had to eat. This would be her ticket.

Watermelon Lemonade

½ cup sugar

¾ cup boiling water

1½ cups finely chopped watermelon

1 cup lemon juice

1 quart carbonated water

Crushed ice

Mint

Dissolve sugar in boiling water. Put watermelon pulp through fine sieve; make sure no seeds get through. Combine strained watermelon juice with lemon juice and add to sugar syrup. Chill thoroughly. At serving time, add carbonated water and pour into tall glasses a quarter filled with crushed ice. Garnish with mint.

Yield: 6 drinks

She persuaded Davison to allow her to take over a small regular food column for the paper, the "market column," based on the seasonal produce and other fresh products in the city's groceries and specialty food shops. This demanded rising early and trawling around town, going from market to market to compare freshness and prices, and scurrying back to an office to write copy that could be published in a timely fashion. It is not hard to imagine reporters eager to shrug off this assignment, but it was the perfect job for Paddleford.

After the appearance of just a handful of columns, Davison noticed how much more widely read the column was—chiefly because Paddleford was able to interject her trademark details into tomato prices. In March 1936, Davison offered Paddleford a staff reporter position as food markets editor of the paper. It required her to write six days a week, articles a half-column long with advice on buying and eating, and it paid $40 a week. Paddleford, in the most important move in her professional career, accepted it. From the standpoint of power, it was a tumble down a hill: she had managed nine departments for *Farm & Fireside* and was now taking over a simple market column. But the publication was the *Herald Tribune*. At the time she took the new title, the paper's food department received 6,077 telephone and letter responses per month. After Paddleford's first month, this rose to 7,429. After Paddleford's first year, the annual total was 78,337, compared with 28,489 in 1935.

Several developments came out of this success. At least one was personal: The friendship between Paddleford and Davison deepened to the point of socializing outside of the office. Davison owned a summer house in Bethel, Connecticut, the birthplace of P. T. Barnum, sixty miles north of New York City. In

1938, Paddleford bought a summer house in Redding, another small town about seven miles southeast of Bethel.

Paddleford's hideaway was a small cape-style bungalow on seventeen acres, not a minor purchase in the Depression. The interior had exposed beams and a big stone fireplace. Paddleford installed a new kitchen. Outside was a flagstone terrace. Paddleford used the house as a place to get away from her job, let her hair down, and relax. The Redding house, while never grand and always quite homey, was a sanctuary from the beginning, and one that she would grow to rely on.

Paddleford continued to write on the side for other publications and to expand her name-recognition among America's cooks. She pounded the pavement for the *Herald Tribune* by day, but on weekends she developed articles for the country's top women's magazines. In the fall of 1938, she wrote for *Better Homes & Gardens*, then as now one of the most widely circulated magazines in the country. "Fry Them Shallow" is a lively article that draws readers to the stove, making them hungry to try "lusciously crisp and crunchy" foods "fried to a tawny gold in deep hot fat." The story has a tone of wry humor in addition to its stovetop tips. "Yet even accomplished cooks are likely to shun the job, complaining that they hate all the bother and mess. As for the amateurs, they get acute panicitis at the very thought of frying anything in a kettle of searing hot fat," Paddleford wrote. "Panicitis" was a term she devised to describe the fears of cooks who are not supremely confident. It was a good way for Paddleford to show that she, too, was just a regular cook who experienced anxiety. In this way, Paddleford distanced herself from the home economists and endeared herself to her readers.

Onion Rings

3 large yellow (sweet) onions

3 cups whole milk

2 cups all-purpose flour

Salt, to taste

3 to 4 cups vegetable oil

Cut onions into ¼-inch slices; separate into rings. Soak 30 minutes in milk. Season flour with salt; dip onion slices into flour to coat completely.

Pour the oil into a deep stock-pot to a depth of ¾ to 1 inch, adding a little more if necessary. Heat to 350 degrees over medium heat. Using tongs, carefully lower onion slices in batches into the hot oil. Fry in batches until golden brown, about 1 to 2 minutes, and remove with a spider or slotted spoon. Drain on a baking sheet lined with paper towels. Season onion rings just before serving with additional salt to taste.

Yield: 4 to 6 side-dish servings

Corn Cakes

1 cup fresh sweet corn kernels
(from about 2 ears of fresh corn)
or well-drained canned corn

1 egg, beaten

¼ cup all-purpose flour

½ teaspoon salt

¼ teaspoon black pepper

Enough vegetable oil to fill a large heavy skillet ½ inch deep

In a medium bowl, combine first 5 ingredients well.

In a large, heavy skillet with sides that should not be more than 2½ inches high, heat oil over medium-low heat until just barely starting to smoke. The fat should be hot enough to brown a bread cube in 40 to 50 seconds. Scoop up by rounded tablespoons and drop into pan; cakes should spread out to about 3 inches in diameter. After about a minute, flip cake and cook a minute more on the other side, or until golden brown. Drain on paper towels.

Yield: 8 corn cakes

By the close of the 1930s, Paddleford's life had once more changed forever. She had survived a life-threatening illness, and had latched on at a most influential newspaper. She was also beginning to reap rewards in the form of plum assignments. In 1939, she was asked to cover the New York World's Fair for the *Herald Tribune*, a thrilling gig. She was beginning to be recognized as an authority in her field; for instance, she received a "Master of Fisheries" degree from the Fishery Council for "excellence in the study of edible fish and shellfish." However, making the most of her job meant getting back on the road and in touch with her subjects. She also needed to remember how to enjoy herself and have a semblance of a personal life in the process. This all lay ahead.

· · · CHAPTER 4 · · ·

It's Always Interesting

Writing was the core at the *New York Herald Tribune*, and pictures and design came next. Editing took a back seat. *The New York Times* was the paper to beat in terms of volume and authority, but the *Tribune* was generally considered "faster, feistier, and funnier."

This was the world Paddleford had longed to inhabit; only she did not arrive at the *Herald Tribune* to apprentice. Although she would not have denied she still had a lot to learn about the daily newspaper business, and although many of her colleagues provided inspiration, Paddleford saw herself as entering 230 West 41st Street to spread her wings and get down to reporting the cultural significance of food. Educated and ambitious, trained in varied journalistic areas, she was going to make the very most of this.

At the time of Paddleford's advent, the paper already had a stable of talented females. No other metropolitan newspaper employed as many female executives—in positions ranging from editor of the Sunday section *Book Week* to assistant advertising manager. Most of the female journalists, though, worked on the ninth floor, headquarters of the Home Institute. A costly promotion booklet from the era described the Home Institute as "central clearing house for the kind of domestic news that's as vital to the career homemaker as the financial and business pages are to her husband." It was also where the test kitchen was. "Up there, you're more likely to catch whiffs of a cake baking in an experimental kitchen oven; or hear the whir of an egg-beater, a vacuum cleaner's hum, a washing machine's swish—all performing under the expert, appraising eyes of trained home economists," the booklet gushes.

This department shows the publishers' wit in demonstrating that "the *Herald Tribune*'s place is largely in the home": It was going to give "more than passing attention to that all-important world behind the front doors of American houses and apartments."

Here Paddleford worked among writers with outsize work ethics just like her own. She also had as much wanderlust as a foreign correspondent and she sought every opportunity to get out from behind her desk. Paddleford habitually mined current news for ways that food could be tied in, and she pitched story ideas to Davison and what by now was a vast network of freelance contacts. More and more this included the Sunday supplement magazine *This Week*. Founded in 1935 as the brainchild of the businessman Euclid M. Covington, whom *Time* magazine referred to as "the pertinacious Kentuckian who got the idea for *This Week* . . . and stuck with it despite discouragement, depression, and doleful predictions of the doubting

Thomases." The magazine was wildly successful. Even when papers didn't do away with their own Sunday magazines, as the *Tribune* did, dailies in cities like Atlanta and Detroit embraced colorful, chatty *This Week*. It was spirited, enthusiastic, and easy to like.

A later editor, William I. Nichols, not related to the two Nicholses already in Paddleford's life, Nell and Alice—was Harvard educated and shrewd. He said *This Week*'s mission was "to recognize the emerging needs of America's exploding mass economy and to create a supermagazine with supercirculation, which would be to communications what superhighways have become to transportation, or supermarkets are to shopping."

Before Nichols arrived in 1943, the head of the editorial division, hired at the start, was the formidable Mrs. William Brown Meloney, Sr., known as Missy, who had been the editorial director of *Herald Tribune*'s own magazine, which ceased publication with the first issue of *This Week*. She had for years directed things on the *Tribune*'s ninth floor. Meloney, who was fifty years old on the occasion of a 1934 *Time* article on the *Tribune*, "was a crack newshawk" who had started work at the Washington Post at age fifteen and became the first woman reporter accredited to the U.S. Senate Press Gallery. *Time* called her "small and indomitable . . . warm, friendly, with large brown eyes and a hawk nose." One of Meloney's major enterprises was the writing and editing of *America's Cook Book*, produced by the Home Institute. The book defined its mission and thus the Institute's: helping women feed their families. "Brides who never before scrambled an egg tell us they could not manage without the book, planned as it is on basic recipes, with the variations easy to remember; experienced home-makers write that it has taught them new tricks of the housekeeper's trade."

Just as Paddleford saw it. It's no wonder that Meloney and then Nichols seized upon Paddleford's work, not to mention her access to a test kitchen and professional recipe testers. Working for both the newspaper and the magazine that the newspaper shared with other major markets was a natural marriage. *This Week* gave Paddleford a national platform for her stories and an expense account, while the Tribune also chipped in on expenses and bills.

By the 1940s, Paddleford's *This Week* stories had evolved from the more generic work into more serious consumer reporting addressed to shoppers' fears and worries. In one such article, "Trapping the Short-Weight Artist," Paddleford tagged along with a "decoy shopper" and noted that one butcher "frequently weighed his thumb when selling chops and steaks" and also that others used false-bottom containers or left more than the recommended fat on meat. Paddleford's stories at this time discussed everything from how to get dinner on the table fast to meeting the challenges presented by wartime.

In "America Makes the Cheese," a piece published in the fall of 1940 in *This Week*, she connected the outbreak of war with the kitchen. Organized like a classic news story, it shows, rather than her often florid techniques, news-gathering abilities. "War has curtailed imports of our favorite foreign cheeses, so American manufacturers skillfully produce domestic types of similar tastes and textures," she wrote. She went on to say that even though "about 52 percent of our imported cheeses come from Italy," the country had a four-month supply of such treats as parmesan, gorgonzola, and romano, but that after that consumers need not worry because "Italian cheeses in all their polysyllabic glory are made in Northern dairy states." Indeed, she said, "few can tell a domestic Provolone from the genuine Italian-made," then offering information on ordering "aromatic cheese masterpieces of America" such as "authentic Bel Paese— New York State made" plus Camembert produced by French cheese makers in America, and tips on how to use these delicacies in recipes.

Homemakers weren't the only ones stretching their materials at this time. Paddleford made good research do double duty. A couple of months before the publication of the "new" cheese primer in *This Week*, a similar story under her byline appeared in the *Tribune*: "Italy's War Cuts Cheese Imports, But America Can Eat Its Own." This highlighted facts unmentioned in *This Week*, such as students at the Minnesota State College of Agriculture who were making "some remarkable Roquefort in limestone caves fronting the Mississippi River near St. Paul." At the end of the story were some recipes plus a coupon similar to the one in *This Week* for information on where to obtain the cheeses. Because *Tribune* readers were likely to have read Paddleford's columns during the week, the Sunday magazine article had to have different content. *This Week*'s longer lead times kept the articles from appearing too close together.

The daily and Sunday bylines and the two paychecks were beginning to make Paddleford a woman of means. Ever the economizer, Paddleford was inherently smart about money. She socked away as much as possible without depriving herself too much. For instance, by December 1940 she had fled her various apartments in Greenwich Village, just north of Washington Square, and moved into a top floor five-room apartment in a townhouse on East 61st Street, Manhattan's Upper East Side. She hired a housekeeper, too.

In 1940 she struck gold with a news story with a major food component: the Republican National Convention in Philadelphia. Were Philadelphia's classic dishes going to captivate pols from around the country? She posited that scrapple, a sausage loaf made of cornmeal mush and leftovers from pork butchering "has a special part to play in that exciting drama of naming a nominee for the greatest office on earth."

Paddleford's column, "Philadelphia Scrapple Welcomes the Delegates" goes to lengths to show how influential the dish was at the convention: "It is Philadelphia scrapple that offers the first warm welcome of this day on breakfast plates—a strengthener for delegates who need a hearty breakfast under their belts to tide them through the bedlam and the oratory of the opening of the National Republican Convention."

In this story Paddleford flexes her skills. First, she applies a conversational voice. "What the deuce?" she writes, not once but twice, imitating the question delegates asked when confronting scrapple at the Bellevue Stratford hotel, convention headquarters. Then she explains the dish, its brief history as it emerged from the tables of the Pennsylvania Dutch, moved into factories that canned the stuff, and sold it nationally as a convenience food. Facts and figures emerge along the way: in winter "the average production is 25,000 pounds of scrapple a day, about 50 percent loaf-molded, the loaves wrapped in cellophane." Thorough she was, too: The story ends with a discussion of other dishes conventioneers were treated to, including one of her personal favorites, Philadelphia pepper pot.

"Philadelphia pepper pot is another hearty dish that will play its little drama on convention dinner menus," she wrote. "This is the soup invented at Valley Forge when Washington ordered his Army cook, 'From nothing you must prepare a great dish. One that is not only warming, strengthening to the body, but inspiring to the flagging spirit of a soldier. It must have him forget his bare feet in the snow, rags, the wind of the north.'" She then describes how pepper pot was made of "scraps from the camp kitchen and a few hundred pounds of tripe which had been sent as donation of some butcher." She concludes that "even if pepper pot is a shade too warming for a summer day"—the convention was held in June—"it has earned its right to the convention mess hall. It is a giver of courage."

Paddleford wound up her Philadelphia report with a flourish, a selection from one of the candidate's wives. Edith Wilk Willkie, wife of Wendell Willkie, the rumply lawyer from Indiana who went on to win the Republican nomination. Not a bad choice, since the Republican Reids, her publishers, were backing Willkie for the nomination. In addition, although Paddleford was unlikely to have known it, Willkie was then involved in a long affair with Irita Van Doren, editor of the *Herald Tribune*'s *Book Week*. "Inquiring about Mr. Willkie's appetite," Paddleford wrote, "his wife said seriously, 'It's as sound as his judgment.'" Sound judgment or not, Willkie lost to Roosevelt.

Philadelphia Pepper Pot

¾ pound honeycomb tripe

2 pounds veal knuckles, about 3 knuckle bones

3 quarts cold water

1 tablespoon salt

1 small bunch parsley

10 whole cloves

16 peppercorns, crushed

3 green bell peppers, ¼-inch dice, about 3½ cups

3 medium onions, ¼-inch dice, 4 to 5 cups

3 tablespoons butter

2 teaspoons vegetable oil

3 medium beets, ¼-inch dice, about 4 cups

1½ cups canned tomatoes,
finely chopped, liquid reserved

⅓ cup uncooked rice

Wash tripe thoroughly; cut into ¼-inch cubes. Place in pot with veal knuckles; add water. Bring slowly to boil over low heat. Simmer 10 minutes; skim fat from surface. Lightly season with salt. Cover pot and cook gently for about 2 hours. Combine parsley and spices in cheesecloth bag;

continued on next page

add to pot. Re-cover pot; continue slow cooking 1 hour; remove bag of spices.

Meanwhile, in a medium skillet sauté peppers in 1 tablespoon of butter and ½ teaspoon olive oil until golden brown, seasoning lightly with salt. Remove from pan and set aside. Repeat process with onions. In same pan, in additional 1½ tablespoons butter and 1 teaspoon of the olive oil, sauté beets until slightly softened, about 3 minutes. Remove from pan and set aside. Deglaze pan with tomatoes and their juices; add this to the soup pot. Then add reserved vegetables to soup mixture along with rice. Cover and simmer 30 minutes. After 10 minutes, check consistency and adjust seasoning: Soup should not be too thick; if the rice is absorbing liquid quickly, add an additional ½ to 1 cup water. Remove veal bones. Skim fat and serve.

Yield: 12 first-course servings or
8 generous main-course servings

continued on next page

Mrs. Willkie's Drop Biscuits

2 cups all-purpose flour, sifted

1 teaspoon baking powder

¾ teaspoon salt

6 tablespoons butter

1 cup cold whole milk

Preheat oven to 450 degrees.

In a large bowl, mix flour, baking powder, and salt. Cut in 4 tablespoons of the butter until well mixed. Add milk gradually, stirring until soft dough is formed.

Measure a heaping spoonful so that the dough is a ball about 1½ inches in diameter, and drop onto ungreased baking sheet. Bake 10 minutes or until golden brown. Melt remaining butter and brush onto the tops of biscuits when they come out of the oven.

Yield: about 16 small biscuits

There was no model for Paddleford's type of story—food tied to cultural happenings, history intermingled with recipes. The *Tribune* realized it had a major talent, and began to give her more and more reporting jobs. By treating food as an important part of world-influencing events, Paddleford was elevating its cultural significance and adding to the paper's value.

In 1940, just four years into her tenure at the paper, Paddleford's work was being critically praised by outsiders. An article in the trade journal *The Northwestern Miller* in February went: "Any time bakers or millers are giving out distinguished service medals, a worthy nominee might be Clementine Paddleford, special writer for the *New York Herald Tribune.* It might be said that she can discover more variety breads, dig up more reasons for eating them, and describe her discoveries in a more hunger-arousing fashion than has been put to paper since Charles Lamb discovered roast pork."

Christmas, as usual, was prime time. In 1940 she decided to pay homage to gingerbread in *This Week*: "Queen Elizabeth introduced the ginger cake to England's Merry Christmas table. A thrifty queen, she viewed the large quantities of ginger root that travelers were bringing to England and thought to put it to new use." While gingerbread came to America with the Puritans, they did not celebrate Christmas and so it was left to the Dutch of New York to revive the Elizabethan tradition.

Paddleford's byline was by now appearing with regularity. She was working as hard as ever, but now she could begin to call her own shots. She traveled all over the country for home economics conventions, and always made sure to link her visits with articles on local cooking.

Her style was also evolving; Paddleford was becoming known for some work that these days would be called over the top. In a column about a crop that is native to, among other places, her native Kansas, beach plums, she wrote: "Down where the sea cries 'hoi-a-loa, hoi-a-loa,' the beach plums take form and the jam makers who know of such matters say the crop promises well."

This verse-like line apparently bowled over Stanley Walker, the *Tribune*'s best-known city editor, who had left there in 1935.

He wrote a poem in response, which *The New Yorker* published in the fall of 1941. "That isn't all that's going on, Miss Paddleford," Walker begins, "In the entrancing world of edibles / Far out in Hawaii, where the sea says 'Whoosh! Whoosh!' / Our little brown brethren, in sarong and leis / Are loading pineapples on the boats— / The big boats that mutter 'Woo! Woo!' / And someday we shall eat them sliced, with kirsch."

Paddleford's travels increased the network of home chefs who wrote her. Just as at the *Christian Herald*, she never failed to respond. In May 1941, right after Mother's Day, Paddleford received a letter from a home economist in Stillwater, Oklahoma, Ruetta D. Blinks. She praised Paddleford for her 1936 story "Pioneer Mother," about Jennie, and let her know that Blinks's minister "paraphrased" the article, "crediting you many times during the sermon." Paddleford responded, of course, and noted to Blinks that "I had letters from all over America when it was written." She also let Blinks know that she had just been in Kansas visiting her dad, and that, while Jennie had passed on, "the lilac hedge is still there."

The core of Paddleford's reporting was the wartime kitchen, with shortages, rationing, and issues of nutrition looming after December 7, 1941. Each Friday her column offered recipes for family dinners that included dishes representative of an ally nation ravaged by war. Each article gave some history of the country, its demographics and typical foods. Recipes were gathered, for example *erwtensoep*, a traditional Dutch sausage-spiked pea soup, and *cochet à la contadine*, a shortcut chicken fricassee from French home cooks. The recipes were compiled into little booklets as part of a "Give a Dime" relief project for refugees; the *Tribune* did the printing and supplied names and locations of

Plumade

6 small black plums, washed, pitted, and quartered

9 cups water

¼ cup sugar

2 2-inch cinnamon sticks

1 lemon rind, grated

3 lemons, juiced

3 oranges, juiced

In a large stockpot over medium-low heat, stew plums in water until very soft and the liquid is a deep rose color, about 15 minutes. Strain juice, return to pot and add to it the sugar and cinnamon. Heat gently until sugar is dissolved, 2 to 3 minutes. Add grated lemon rind and cook three more minutes. Strain again. Stir in lemon and orange juice and serve in tall glasses with chipped ice.

Yield: 10 to 12 servings

stores that sold the ingredients. The yield from the booklet sales was collected and distributed by the *Tribune* to organizations such as the Finnish Consul, the Norwegian Relief Fund, the Belgian Relief Commission, and the Queen Wilhelmina Fund. At the end of six weeks, the program had raised $355.

As another wartime duty Paddleford wrote about tasting beaver, buffalo, muskrat, bear, snake, and whale, all being promoted, in various degree, as alternatives to beef, which was barely available. "Turtle Steak Here to Pinch-Hit for Scarce Beef" she wrote, saying terrapin meat was "red meat in color, but tastes something like veal, only more delicate and sweeter and with an underlying off flavor distinctly its own." Her verdict: turtle was good for stews and broths. Experimentation had its limits, though. When invited to try roasted beetles, Paddleford said it "seemed like going too far" and refused.

Instead, Paddleford focused on such things as "a plan for buying food that can save you up to $5 a week," and another article, which appeared in *This Week* on Pearl Harbor Day, describing a test-kitchen experiment in which sixty-two dehydrated food products were used to create recipes. A year later she did a survey of oils for salads as the "war price of olive oil drops like a bomb in the world's salad bowl" and "tight-fisted budgets turn to the bland vegetable oils." Somewhat more encouraging were stories like "No Rations on Spices," which encouraged readers to perk up breakfast rolls and pies with something other than tightly rationed sugar ("There will be spice in your life in spite of the war"), and "Easy Does It!" an article on a newfangled "regiment of ready-mixes—cakes, breads, muffins, desserts" that make "the doing easy—add water, beat, and bake." These mixes could save the day for the home cook, according to Paddleford, because "war puts premium on leisure." "Women search short cuts to dinner," she wrote. "War dips a deep scoop into sugar bowls" but the boxed goods came with "sugar and spice and everything precious right in the mix."

In the same spirit, Paddleford ventured into other areas. One article was about three Chicago women—a manicurist, an artist, and a sales clerk—who combined resources to take out a mortgage for their own home. "Three Girls Buy a House" was clearly intended to inspire young women during an economic downtime and an acute housing shortage. Another was devoted to encouraging women to learn more about wine. Just "precious few American women we meet can name the chief wine districts or varieties of grapes that make our most popular types of wines," she admonished. "America is vineland bountiful. . . . Last year 100,000,000 gallons of wine were consumed in the United States and over 90 per cent of this was pressed from America's grapes," she wrote. Paddleford's message was don't let "wine snobs confuse us with their patter about vintages" and instead "choose what you please, without ritual." This message prefaced by more than sixty years the advice wine experts such as Andrea Immer, author of *Great Wine Made Simple*, advocate today as wine expertise can intimidate beginners.

In 1943, Paddleford was rewarded for her attention to war's effects on the kitchen by *Independent Woman* magazine. Its article, "Words are Weapons," highlighted the ways in which "America's leading writers are lending their talents to the interpreting of America's war aims to the American people." Alongside the photojournalist Margaret Bourke-White and the anthropologist Margaret Mead was Paddleford. She was commended for her "most entertaining, witty, and wise" reporting and the way in which "she applies her skill and knowledge to the wartime shortages with the same unconquerable humor that illuminates her daily procedure." The writer quoted Paddleford about her beat: "It's always important. It's always interesting. I never find foods or food materials dull."

She also never found them so lucrative. Paddleford no longer had to hustle for freelance assignments, although of course it is a wonder she managed to fit any into her week. At this time Paddleford snared a regular reporting job at *Gourmet*, a glossy independent monthly that called itself "the magazine of good living." It was created in December 1941 by Earle MacAusland, whose widow sold it to Condé Nast publications after his death in 1980. Paddleford wrote a column titled "Food Flashes," devoted to new mail-order delicacies like Perigord truffles, Norwegian Bristling sardines, fresh rabbit meat from Rhinebeck, New York, and "brandy-soaked fruitcakes baked in processed grapefruit shells." Each monthly column listed four or five items, with prices and information on how to order.

The discarded husband, Zimmerman, had by this time taken a job with the Illinois Public Central Utilities Company in Marion, Illinois, and there was no longer any regular contact. It seems that about this time, Paddleford decided as an act of will never to let another man get quite so close to her again. She had a steady stream of dates and escorts, but no one seems to have occupied a special place in her heart. That all began to change, and in a rather unexpected way, in 1942, courtesy of her former Theta Sigma Phi pal Marcelle Laval.

Laval had been busy in the years since Paddleford left Chicago—but unlike Paddleford, she had not pushed romance aside for work. By the end of the 1920s, she had met a young doctor,

Paul Duffé. Although no records of a marriage license have been found, a birth certificate shows a child, a daughter who was named Claire Duffé, was born to them in the summer of 1930. By all accounts, through the 1930s, Laval was a single mother supporting herself as a writer of children's books and, according to Claire, as press agent for the Mohair Indian tribe. Claire says she grew up knowing her father and occasionally spent time with him, but Marcelle was truly her only "parent."

The Theta Sig sisters were extraordinarily close. Letters between the former roommates circulated regularly, and as a result, it became clear to many in this circle by 1942 that Marcelle was dying of cancer, and that Claire, a strong-willed, precocious twelve-year-old whose blue eyes could have been a match for Paddleford's, needed a home.

As Claire would later describe the situation, she "went up on the auction block." Her circumstances, apart from her dying mother, were not tragic; on the contrary, many of the sisters wanted to take her. "Clementine threw her hat in," Claire reported. Surprisingly, single-in-the-city Paddleford quickly appeared to be the one who was in the best position—no husband or children of her own, no impending life crisis, divorce or emotional depression, and she had a very solid financial footing. Her housekeeper, a young Jamaican named Lois Leak, was ready to help. After weighing her choices, Laval apparently made her wish known that Paddleford should have custody of Claire.

Why Paddleford, who had worked so hard to make it as an independent women, with a great job, a steady and enviable income—by the end of the decade she was making $25,000 a year—and a deliberately string-free private life, decided to open herself to a twelve-year-old is one of the great mysteries of her life. A combination of reasons is possible. Having shunned Zimmerman's ardent pleas, Paddleford may have realized that this route would be her only chance to have a child. The advantage Claire had over a foundling infant was that she was barely a child anymore. Her mother's illness meant Claire had needed to grow up fast. She reported that as a child she didn't even like to go off to school and leave her mother alone, and that her usual morning routine involved getting herself up and making breakfast for two before she got out the door, only to come home and prepare dinner for two.

In 1943, Marcelle was still alive, but not doing well. As a trial arrangement, Claire was dispatched from Chicago to spend Christmas with Paddleford. "I came to Clementine and we had a lovely Christmas in Connecticut," Claire remembers, saying that from the moment she got off the train in Redding, Paddleford worked steadily to distinguish the holiday from any the child had previously encountered. One of the things Claire remembers loving: playtime with Paddleford's thirteen-year-old part-Persian cat, Prince Peter, who had been toted from Paddleford's apartment in the city to the country and who welcomed a young playmate with open paws.

At Easter 1944, Claire was again dispatched to Paddleford. This time, the little family spent time in the city, and Paddleford took Claire to Best & Co., a favored Fifth Avenue department store for children of prosperous families. The mission was to get Claire a new Easter suit. "I looked at the price tags," Claire said, "and I whistled, and Clem said, 'You don't do that at Best & Company,' and she bought me the suit." At this point, Claire was attending Kimber Hall Boarding School in Kimberton, Pennsylvania, thirty miles northwest of Philadelphia, a noted institution in its day and the alma mater of Helen Reid of the *Tribune* ownership. The school was a train's ride away from Paddleford, whether she was weekending in Connecticut, as was her habit by this point, or working in the city.

By the time of Marcelle's death in the fall of 1944, Claire had not only accepted the idea of living with Paddleford, but had embraced it. Of Paddleford's world, she said: "If that wasn't heaven enough for a teenage orphan to stumble into." When it came to her feelings for the woman who was in loco parentis, Claire said simply, "She would have been lucky to have escaped me."

When Claire was home from school, Paddleford's old friend Alice Nichols, by then working for the United States Department of Agriculture, was a frequent companion. "Alice was gem," Claire remembers. "She was boisterous." Alice would often meet Claire in the city and ride the train with her to Redding, where Paddleford would have arrived earlier. Nichols had qualities that would endear her to a child. "Alice was afraid of storms, and whenever it would rain she would get into the bedroom closet, which was as big as a carrot stick," Claire recalled. The famed Peter-Pie (also known as Prince Peter and Petey Pie) "was also afraid of storms, so he went in there with her, too."

Paddleford seemed to adopt a role that was motherly in an unthreatening way. Claire recalled a weekend day in Connecticut when she was pitching pennies into a puddle and Paddleford declared "something's wrong with this picture: I am trying to bring money into this household and you are tossing it away!" But Paddleford also had quite a loving touch. As Jennie had, she sent packages of treats to Claire at school. The school had a policy that girls had to share their edible gifts, which Claire says incensed Paddleford, who so loved to hoard her childhood chocolates. To get around it, Paddleford wrote "BOOKS" in bold letters on the boxes. Claire said this only got her into more trouble, as the other students could smell the food as she carried the boxes to her room.

Paddleford put up a protective barrier about Claire to the outside world. To colleagues, she spoke of Claire as her daughter, yet according to those who worked with her she felt no need to explain the circumstances of the child's arrival. This lead to gossip and persistent curiosity: She has a child, but no husband? Is it her natural daughter? But if Paddleford even noticed this, she certainly did not care. The arrangement seems to have given Paddleford a more relaxed attitude toward life, one that surely would have surprised those who assumed from her prodigious output that she worked round-the-clock.

Indeed, photographs from Redding in this period show the country house gave Paddleford a chance to shed her no-nonsense public persona and unwind. One shot shows a woman standing in the woods on a large rock: Her back is arched, her face is tilted toward the sun, her wavy hair is tousled, and her flower-print sundress is worn loose. Here is the picture of a care-free, sexy woman—a far cry from the person who once described herself as "a horse."

In the foreground of the photo is a black cat with a white belly, Dickie the Duke, one of many cherished members of Paddleford's menagerie. "Our cats were allowed everywhere; they ate dinner in bed with us, even," Claire said. Paddleford insisted that all of her guests talk to the cats, too. "If you weren't a cat person, you had to go somewhere else," Claire said. Paddleford clearly appreciated the cats' demeanor as one she favored: aloof, self-possessed, and authoritative.

Others came to the country place. "If I wasn't there, she took dates to Connecticut for the weekend," Claire reported. According to her, Paddleford had "lots of boyfriends" and assigned each a different date night. "Once you got on the list, you were given a night." Paddleford took pains to keep track of her guests' preferences. "For instance, she would write 'doesn't like fish' next to someone's name," Claire said. If Paddleford let anyone truly get close to her, though, she left no trace.

The year 1944 cannot have been easy. Even though Claire was away at boarding school, Paddleford, at the age of forty-six, was now a parent and tied down in a way that she had once so assiduously tried to avoid. In the summer of that year, Paddleford's father died of a stroke in Kansas. Now her only tie to the other Manhattan was her brother, Glenn, and his family, and they were managing the two downtown apartment buildings Solon had left to them both.

As usual, work was the tonic. Paddleford's typical *Tribune* article included a coupon at the end that a reader could return, with a 3-cent stamp, to get leaflets with recipes not given in the story. What was not included was where to get the ingredients for the recipes. Many readers wrote to ask about various "exotic" ingredients, such as Hungarian paprika (which, incidentally, could be purchased at Paprikas Weiss, a Yorkville import shop that Paddleford championed). Finally, when the women's department was receiving hundreds of letters and one thousand telephone calls a day with such questions, the editors began to allow Paddleford to include as many recipes in her stories as could fit, and to include names and locations of shops for ingredients.

As part of this new arrangement, Paddleford had to redouble

her scouting for unusual foods. Some of this inevitably led to invitations to luncheons and dinners staged by press agents and public-relations companies to show off new products. Paddleford rarely went to evening events, preferring dinner at home, a long bath, a glass of wine, and playtime with her cats. She did make exceptions, however, for big-ticket events like the annual dinners of Amis d'Escoffier and Chevaliers du Tastevin, where the town's top chefs and maîtres d'hôtel competed.

By this time, Paddleford was recognized as a phenomenon and the glamorous trappings she dreamed of were trickling in. In 1946, shortly after the end of the war, Paddleford became the only female reporter invited by Air France to fly on their DC-4 to enjoy a two-week tour. As part of an elite group of journalists that included reporters from *The World-Telegram* and *The Newark News*, Paddleford attended twenty-eight receptions held by people and organizations such as the President of France, the Chefs Société du Cent and, most glamorous of all, the Duke and Duchess of Windsor, living in exile.

When she was cooped up in Morningside Heights, this was her fantasy, and it was truly exciting for her. She was star-struck and it came through in her columns. For instance, "Food Editor Finds Many Treats in French Tour" reads: "Maybe it's something we dreamed. But two notebooks filled with scribblings headed Paris, Deauville, Nice, Cannes, Versailles, stand as proof we were there. That and the fact that we are done in gustatorily speaking."

The same column describes meeting the Duke and Duchess for a reception at Cap d'Antibes. For once, food takes a back seat. Sure, Paddleford describes the Champagne ("again and again came the silver trays with fresh glasses of the bubbling Champagne") and the finger sandwiches ("these of three kinds, watercress, smoked salmon, and a savory cheese mixture . . . garnished with a center bouquet of watercress so green as to appear to have been freshly varnished"), but she saves her best words for the hosts, and, no surprise, a pet. "Very much in evidence was a Cairn terrier named Pookie, a well-trained little dog who refused tidbits from a stranger's hands," she wrote.

Paddleford seemed to take advantage of every moment of her trip; while her contemporaries woke late and nursed hangovers, she kept her customary schedule and checked out Parisian fish markets and cheese and pastry shops. Columns waxed rhapsodic about the classic spoon-formed pike quenelle served at La Tour d'Argent ("recipe is given in our leaflet today, although we doubt that any American housewife will take so much trouble ever with a mere fish"), the chocolate soufflé ("tender, steaming hot") at La Jettée, and even the *coq au vin de Bourgogne* served aboard Air France ("no one left as much as a shred on his plate . . . soaking up the last brown drop on a crusty bit of bread"). Still in all, Paddleford wanted to make sure everyone knew her head was not turned. On the plane home, she was overheard saying, "It'll be good to be home where the ice water flows like champagne."

Earlier that year, Paddleford was on another quasi-political mission, this time traveling to Fulton, Missouri, to report on Winston Churchill's visit and the occasion on which he was to deliver his Iron Curtain Speech. "Churchill Enjoys Home-Cooked Missouri Meal" was the title of her spirited story about the "good honest company fare" he was served courtesy of Mrs.

Franc L. McCluer, wife of the Westminster College president, whom Paddleford described as "the alpha and omega of studied calmness" despite the stress. The buffet included Callaway County ham ("plastered . . . with a paste of mustard mixed with brown sugar and spices, then pocked . . . with whole cloves in diamond formation, pineapple juice for the basting"), fried chicken, twice-baked potatoes, asparagus (not fresh, either: "These were turned from the cans, heated, then doused with melted butter and served garnished with sliver-thin slices of green pepper"), hot rolls, olives, celery, sweet pickles, tomato aspic, and, for dessert, angel food cake with ice cream.

Back home, Paddleford fell back into her routine of rising at the break of day, writing for several hours in her small home office, filled with filing cabinets bursting at the seams with folders and scrapbooks of articles, clippings, and correspondence from readers. From time to time Paddleford took a morning break to call about prices and ingredients of products she was describing or to have a shop owner double-check facts. Around 11 A.M., she would head to 41st Street, where the test kitchen was sharpening the recipes. Paddleford would sample their efforts, give notes and corrections, and bustle out the door to a market or an interview.

Around this time Paddleford wrote one of the best articles in her career, one that had a sweeping impact on her life. Published January 12, 1947, in *This Week*, "60,000 Miles of Eating" described the adventures of a salesman from Bowling Green, Kentucky, who in 1935 had begun publishing a list of the best restaurants he found on the road. By 1947, he had "three books with over a million sales every year" to his credit, and had given up sales to become what Paddleford called "America's best-qualified expert on cooking and eating." This was Duncan Hines.

Hines's saga began with a list of his favorite spots and spiraled into an industry that eventually included nine books. Later, in 1958, he sold his name to Procter & Gamble, which immediately used the name for a line of cake mixes. Paddleford briefly gave his history to date, followed by his critical opinions on the best regional food in the country: "Hines calls plain U.S. cooking the best in the world. But he gets mad all over again when he thinks how many small restaurants muff their big opportunity to serve local dishes and turn out poor imitations of big-city hotel food instead." His dislikes involved canned orange juice served in Florida, "misnamed dishes" (when "baby lamb" turns out to be a grown sheep, she wrote, Hines "explodes"), and "overcooked bacon." As far as likes, besides listing New York, San Francisco, and New Orleans as the country's top restaurant cities, recipes for Hines's "12 all-time favorite" were offered to readers who returned a coupon (and ten cents) for a booklet that included black bottom pie from Oklahoma City (he called it "one of those marvelous creations that somehow managed to keep its light under a bushel"—until he circulated a formula for it), buckwheat cakes from the Nixon hotel in Butler, Pennsylvania, crab custard from the Valley Green Lodge in Orick, California, Indian pudding from the famed Toll House in Whitman, Massachusetts (whose chocolate chip cookies became such a sensation that Nabisco, then called the National Biscuit Company, bought the rights to the recipe in 1939), and clam chowder from the Lafayette Hotel in Portland, Maine.

Black Bottom Pie

40 crisp gingersnaps, crushed into fine crumbs (about 2 cups)

6 tablespoons butter, melted

1 cup sugar

1¼ tablespoons cornstarch

2 cups whole milk

4 eggs, separated

1½ ounces unsweetened chocolate (1½ squares)

1 teaspoon vanilla extract

1 envelope (1 tablespoon) unflavored gelatin

¼ cup cold water

¼ teaspoon cream of tartar

2 tablespoons rum (optional)

Preheat oven to 350 degrees.

In a medium bowl, combine crushed gingersnaps and butter. Mix well, and press into 10-inch pie pan. Bake 8 to 10 minutes. Do not allow the crust to color or overbake. When it is first removed from the oven, the crust will feel slightly crumbly, but it will firm upon standing. Cool crust.

continued on next page

Combine ½ cup of the sugar and the cornstarch in a medium heatproof bowl; slowly whisk in milk. Place bowl over small saucepan of simmering water, creating a double boiler. Stir constantly until thickened. Remove bowl from double boiler and set aside.

In another bowl, beat egg yolks well; slowly temper with ½ cup of the hot milk mixture, then gradually stir the rest in. Pour into bowl used as double-boiler top, and place over simmering water, stirring constantly until mixture coats spoon.

Cut chocolate into small pieces into a small bowl; add 1 cup of the hot custard; stir until chocolate is melted. Add vanilla to chocolate mixture; cool slightly and pour into pie shell.

Soften gelatin in water. Pour into remaining hot custard; stir until gelatin is dissolved. Cool until slightly thickened.

Beat egg whites until stiff; gradually add remaining sugar and the cream of tartar, beating constantly; fold into gelatin mixture. Add rum if using; mix well. Pour over chocolate layer in pie shell.

Chill until set, at least 6 hours or overnight. If desired, garnish edge of pie with whipped cream and quartered maraschino cherries. Sprinkle top with chocolate curls if you like.

Yield: 8 servings

Buckwheat Cakes

1 teaspoon active dry yeast

4 cups lukewarm water

2 cups buckwheat flour

1 cup sifted all-purpose flour

½ cup sugar

1½ teaspoons salt

⅛ teaspoon baking soda

3 tablespoons butter, melted

In a small bowl, dissolve yeast in water.

In a large bowl, sift together buckwheat flour, all-purpose flour, sugar, and salt. Whisk yeast and water mixture with flours until smooth. Cover and set in refrigerator overnight.

Just before using, add baking soda. (If in a hurry to use, cover bowl and set in warm place to rise, about 2 hours.) Heat a crêpe or nonstick pan over moderate heat. Brush with melted butter and add ¼ cup of batter, swirling it to coat the pan evenly. Cook until bubbles appear all over. Flip and cook for another moment until done. Repeat with remaining butter and batter. Makes about 18 cakes. Serve with grilled sausages.

Yield: 6 servings

The story about Hines did more than evoke sincere praise from Bill Nichols, the editor of *This Week*. He wrote, referring to "a really stunning Duncan Hines spread." Hines's "traipsing around the country" in search of regional delicacies seems to have struck a spark in Paddleford. Indeed, she re-cut his suit to fit herself.

By 1948, Paddleford had, for once, both personal and professional lives on track. She had chaperoned Claire from orphaned preteen to accomplished high school graduate. She must have been tremendously proud when Claire entered Wellesley College that autumn—quite an accomplishment for a girl whose preteen years were marked by tragedy and uncertainty. Paddleford had done right by her old pal Marcelle Duval, and now she was getting ready to do the most important work of her life. She'd had a brainstorm for a series of columns that would mark her most significant work as a writer, "How America Eats."

The flavor of the columns was local to the bone and each was written to as neat a formula as a novel. Each was set in an American destination of Paddleford's choosing, but she was not a "parachute artist" who plopped down just long enough to use the town as a dateline. Paddleford often stayed a week or more and even if she didn't use all the material she gathered, she saved what she learned for future use. Each article focused on a real person, included his or her specialty, a brief history of how the cook came to make that particular dish, and a recipe or two. The formula was narrow and the tone breathless, as if Paddleford were writing from the trenches—the trenches of the American kitchen.

In an early example, from January 1948, Paddleford told

the story behind the classic New England boiled dinner, one of America's oldest and best known regional meals. She got the recipe from Herman Smith, a writer best known for a cookbook published in 1945 called *Stina: The Story of a Cook*, a memoir with recipes he had learned from his family's Alsatian cook. In keeping with her emerging formula for this series, Paddleford began with a vivid description of the American dish alongside a little history: "The one-plate meal of early New England was the boiled dinner, a twice-a-week joy from the early autumn until the sap rose in the maples. The meal was cooked in the big iron pot swung from the crane and let bubble merrily over the maple log blaze; the pot lid heaved to the rhythm of regular breathing." Then a note or two about the differences between the preparation of the dish in Vermont (with bay leaves and garlic) and Maine (with neither), and then Paddleford turned to give a brief profile of her source. Herman Smith, she wrote, was living in Massachusetts and for a brief period one winter was snowbound. "Nearby friends with a large family who had been locked up together for days to the point of battle, implored him to let them come to his house for dinner, even though the drifts were waist-high . . . ," she wrote. "The idea occurred to Herman to give them the kind of food they would have had when such a predicament was a common lot not merely for days but often for weeks." What works so well in this column is that it's a story-within-a-story: Paddleford has let Smith build a wonderful picture for readers of snowbound delirium that could be cured by a big hot pot. Who wouldn't want to try it out at home for herself one cold evening?

Clementine Paddleford

Clementine Paddleford and her mother, Jennie Paddleford, ca. 1909

Clementine Paddleford sits on the front porch steps of the Blue Valley Farm with her dolls, ca. 1907.

Clementine Paddleford on her horse, White Beauty, ca. 1909

Clementine Paddleford, ca. 1919

Clementine Paddleford standing beside the family car, ca. 1919

Clementine Paddleford, ca. 1931, first known photograph after her throat surgery. The tracheal tube can barely be seen above her scarf.

Clementine Paddleford, ca. 1936. This is the first known photograph after her throat surgery in which the tracheal tube can be seen clearly.

Clementine Paddleford, right, a judge for the Fowl Fashion Shows Finals.
Here she is with the winner, 1950.

Clementine Paddleford, left, at work during the sugaring off party
at Broadlook Farm, Derby Line, Vermont, April 1950

Paul S. Willis, president of Grocery Manufactures of America, Inc., presents Clementine Paddleford with her First Honorable Mention Certificate in the Life Line of America Awards at the GMA's annual luncheon at the Waldorf on November 13, 1950.

Clementine Paddleford in her home office with Prince Peter, ca. 1950

Clementine Paddleford, center, Copenhagen, Denmark, February 1951

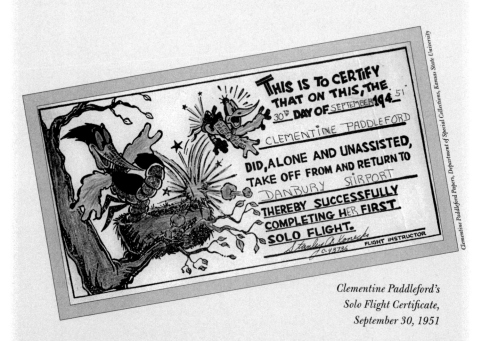

THIS IS TO CERTIFY THAT ON THIS, THE 30TH DAY OF SEPTEMBER 194 51

CLEMENTINE PADDLEFORD

DID, ALONE AND UNASSISTED, TAKE OFF FROM AND RETURN TO

DANBURY AIRPORT

THEREBY SUCCESSFULLY COMPLETING HER FIRST SOLO FLIGHT.

FLIGHT INSTRUCTOR

*Clementine Paddleford's
Solo Flight Certificate,
September 30, 1951*

Here is the picture you requested in the Puerto Rican Public Market Place in Ponce. *I asked for it thinking no other pic might be available.*

Clementine Paddleford in a Puerto Rican public marketplace, Ponce, 1952

Clementine Paddleford and Ken Norris at a dock in Ketchikan, Alaska, 1954

Clementine Paddleford, right, receives an award from Eleanor Roosevelt, left, 1957.

Clementine Paddleford makes at toast at dinner at Vosin, March 11, 1958. Left to right standing: Host, M. Jacques Mercier, director general of the Mercier Champagne Company; John Dennis, Dennis and Huppert, Inc., U.S. importers for Champagne Mercier; Craig Claiborne, The New York Times. *Seated left to right: Mme. Jacques Mercier and Clementine Paddleford.*

New England Boiled Dinner

4 pounds corned beef

½ pound salt pork with a big streak of lean

3 quarts boiling water

½ cup sugar

3 bay leaves

1 clove garlic, peeled

4 medium russet potatoes, peeled

3 yellow turnips, peeled and thickly sliced

8 carrots, scrubbed vigorously

4 white onions, peeled,
leaving a bit of the root end, quartered

6 parsnips, peeled

1 small head cabbage, cored and cut into 8 wedges,
set on wooden skewers

6 small beets, peeled

Wash beef in cold water. Place beef and salt pork in pot with boiling water. Add sugar, bay leaves, and garlic. Simmer, covered, for 4 hours. Thirty minutes before completion of cooking add peeled potatoes, turnips, and carrots. Next add onions and follow with parsnips. If a vegetable

continued on next page

begins to overcook, remove from the broth and hold in a warm spot until needed for serving.

Transfer 2 cups of cooking liquid to another pot and add cabbage and boiling water sufficient to cover cabbage. Cook until just tender.

Dip out another 2 cups of cooking liquid, transfer to a small pot, and cook beets in it until just tender.

Remove corned beef and salt pork from main pot and slice. Arrange the dinner on a warmed platter, corned beef and salt pork slices in the center, the pink and white slices alternating. Slice carrots, beets, and parsnips while hot to ring around the meat. Follow with the potatoes, halved, and the cabbage wedges. Moisten all with any remaining cooking liquid. Accompaniments: English mustard, horseradish for the corned beef; sweetened vinegar for the cabbage and beets. By all means a dish of green tomato pickle. Serve with corn bread squares, split and buttered. No salad, but a big bowl of cottage cheese, sprinkled with caraway.

Yield: 8 large servings

From the beginning it was clear the series would have legs. Another column a year later, January 1949, shows the continuation of the smooth, authoritative, upbeat, and engaging narrative voice Paddleford was cultivating.

From the beginning of "Secret Salad," it's easy to see how the series caught on. "Found: the world's best potato salad, 20 cents a side portion on the Speck's menu—that century-old coffeehouse on Market Street in St. Louis." At last, Paddleford seems to say, I've gone and solved a serious problem for you. This wouldn't be a Paddleford story without some historical detail, which is that Speck's "had been serving up the salad and other hearty German dishes since before the city's great fire in 1849." But oh my, difficulty: the owners wouldn't part with their precious recipe. But victory: one "Thelma R. Lison, home economist for an advertising agency," a Saint Louis gal and one of Paddleford's new contacts, figured out the formula, which of course was provided.

Paddleford now gave herself the title "roving food reporter" and received additional space in the paper and more travel money. Things were meantime changing at the *Tribune*. One change was the departure of Paddleford's longtime boss and sometime champion, Eloise Davison. According to Claire, although Eloise and Paddleford had indeed been friends, by now "she and Clem were spitting at each other all the time." Davison directed Paddleford to attend staff meetings and report on what she had done all week, for instance, an accounting that Paddleford felt she was now above.

Their personal friendship, however, appears not to have suffered too much. Claire reports that one day on East 61st Street, the building's landlord came knocking to tell Paddleford he was planning to sell the building. Paddleford was not at home at the time, but when she returned and got the news, Paddleford became seriously alarmed. "I can't move!" she shouted, and left the apartment. When she returned, she reported triumphantly that she had bought the building—for $15,250, and with a co-owner, Eloise Davison, who presumably chipped in for investment purposes. Despite these ties, Davison, herself

Speck's Potato Salad

6 medium russet potatoes

3 slices thick-cut bacon, finely diced

1 small yellow onion, finely diced

1¼ tablespoons sugar

2 teaspoons salt

¼ teaspoon black pepper

⅔ cup cider vinegar

⅓ cup water

½ teaspoon celery seed

3 tablespoons chopped parsley

Cook potatoes whole and unpeeled in a medium pot of cold, generously salted water over medium-high heat. When water comes to a boil, lower heat to simmer. Cook until just tender, about 25 minutes. Drain potatoes and cool slightly, then peel, using a tea towel. Slice potatoes into rounds about ¼ to ⅓ inch thick.

In a medium skillet over medium heat, cook bacon until just crisp. Add onion to bacon fat and cook 1 minute. Add sugar, salt, and pepper to bacon mixture. Stir in vinegar and water. Cook mixture gently 5 minutes, stirring well.

continued on next page

Pour warm dressing over sliced potatoes and add celery seed and parsley; toss lightly. Taste and adjust seasoning, adding more salt if necessary. Serve warm.

Yield: 6 servings

an ambitious editor, had left the paper by May 1949. She worked first as a home economist and then eventually as "technical consultant" for the University of Tennessee's Home Science Program in India, founded in conjunction with the government. Davison and Paddleford corresponded extensively, Davison writing between bouts of grading papers.

From India, Davison describes the difficulties of finding Paddleford's columns: "Have been reading about your Irish trip in the Trib whenever I can get it which is none too regularly." Another running topic was the state of Davison's Connecticut country house, nicknamed Tops. "I do hope I can rent Tops for two years while I am away," she wrote. "Keep your ear to the ground. As if you had nothing else to do!" She also described things that would interest Paddleford, such as the wedding feasts she attended and the flora. "The 'gul mohr' trees are so beautiful now," she wrote. "They are in full bloom. Have a superb bouquet on the large brass table in my living room. It is made up of bright pom-poms about like large chrysanthemums only a beautiful red (sort of a pinky red) with hollow and large stems."

At work in New York, however, a new sheriff entered the picture. This was Eugenia Sheppard, "with ringleted blond hair, cornflower-blue eyes, and looks that are called cute rather than pretty on a small woman," as Kluger described her in his book

The Paper. Sheppard, a Bryn Mawr graduate from Ohio, had been hired as a fashion reporter in 1941, and she rose to become the daily newspaper world's leading authority on couture. Sheppard was well regarded for two reasons: One was her "unashamedly elitist" taste, meaning that top designers of the day both loved and feared her, and two, she, like Paddleford, treated what was considered a "soft" subject as something worthy of serious effort. "Eugenia Sheppard demanded a standard of journalistic detachment rarely found in women's pages in U.S. newspapers, historically a repository for soft, puffy copy," Kluger explained. "More than anything else, her section was distinguished by good, clear writing."

By 1949, Sheppard had been promoted to women's feature editor, and she supervised the entire ninth floor—"with a competence and independence bordering on the autocratic," Kluger said. Paddleford, though, could no longer be bossed around. Although Sheppard was technically her boss, she and Paddleford were the twin stars of the ninth floor, each with a private secretary and a windowed office. Sheppard was content to let Paddleford chase her beat however she chose—and not to require the increasingly beloved food writer to adhere to any schedule of department meetings. According to Claire, while Paddleford found Eugenia was "cut from the same mold" as Eloise Davison in that she was "carried away with power," she realized that the power was not being wielded over her directly, and the new arrangement was comfortable.

This newfound autonomy came across distinctly in her columns. Setting the stage for more "How America Eats" columns, Paddleford wrote an unusually long and detailed note to her readers in a February 1949 issue of *This Week*, letting them in on what she was up to: "At the request of the editors of *This Week* magazine I've just traveled eight thousand miles from the East Coast to the West, into the South, into big cities, little towns, to see how America eats, what's cooking for dinner," she begins. This reworking of the Duncan Hines story ("The search has already taken him over a million miles, into nine thousand eating places. This year he will cover another 60,000 miles . . .") also serves to display her populist ideals: "I have knocked at kitchen doors, spied into pantries, stayed to eat supper . . . I have interviewed food editors in 24 cities . . . I have shopped corner groceries, specialty food shops, supermarkets, public markets, push carts."

Indeed, the young kid scribbling in her notebook at the depot was grown up, and she seemed to be saying to her readers: Stand on notice, because there will be nothing eaten in this country that I won't make it my business to know about.

If Paddleford had worked like a demon before, she redoubled her efforts for "How America Eats" as if her life depended on it. In addition to raiding pantries from coast to coast, she also began to specialize in another sort of article: Ferreting secret recipes out of top restaurants. Foretastes of this are found in Speck's Potato Salad (page 130), but now she knew that enticing a restaurateur to part with an especially prized unpublished recipe would hook readers into her series. It was the epitome of vicarious experience.

For instance, this gave folks from Manhattan, Kansas, the chance not only to visit San Francisco's Fisherman's Wharf, but also the chance to see it through the bright, shiny, optimistic eyes of their own intrepid reporter. When Paddleford visited the famed Tarantino's Restaurant in March of 1949, she went all out in describing both the place and the food. "I sat in a corner . . . overlooking the harbor, looking into the West, all America at my back. There was Golden Gate Bridge, an arabesque in steel, delicate as spider's webbing against the coming night." A feast for the eyes, but wait until she gets to the restaurant's specialty, the old-fashioned Genoese fisherman's stew known as cioppino, "pronounced cho-PEEN-o . . . a bouillabaisse of sorts": "The dish is made over charcoal braziers, made of whatever the day's catch supplies. It may be shellfish entirely, or seafood and shellfish, the various kinds washed, cleaned, layered in the pot; then a rich garlicky tomato sauce added and the collection cooked." If a reader didn't feel as if he or she was right at Paddleford's elbow, along came this: "Here we give you the recipe exactly as it's made in the Tarantino kitchen. All but the romance: the sight of drying crab nets, the music of water lapping the gray timbers of the pier, the scent of night fog rolling in from the Pacific to enclose the city of hills in a gray wall."

San Francisco was "romantic," but Paddleford also got to give readers some glamour, too. That same year she took them to Lindy's, the famed Broadway hangout. Paddleford wrote about Lindy's cheesecake as if she were Sherlock Holmes. First, she gave readers a taste of the prize: "Proud the cheesecake . . . it stands half a foot tall, it measures one foot across. Its top is shiny as satin and baked to the gold of the frost-tinged oak. . . . Fluffy, velvet soft, the filling dry but not too dry, an extravaganza in richness."

Then she presents the puzzle: "The late Mr. Lindy, full name Leo Lindeman, was a lovable, laughable, unpredictable

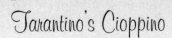

Tarantino's Cioppino

3 sprigs fresh thyme

1 fresh bay leaf

4 cloves garlic, minced

3 tablespoons olive oil

1 medium onion, finely diced

1 green bell pepper, finely diced

1 leek with leaves, finely diced

3 green onions, finely diced

Salt, pepper, and dried red pepper to taste

2 tablespoons tomato paste

1 28-ounce can whole tomatoes, tomatoes minced, juice reserved

2 cups white wine

20 Little Neck clams in the shell, scrubbed, uncooked

4 medium oysters in the shell, scrubbed, uncooked

2 fresh live Dungeness crabs, about 2 pounds each,
or 4 live blue crabs, about 1 pound each

12 large shrimp, shelled, uncooked

Wrap thyme and bay leaf in cheesecloth and secure with string. Set aside. Sauté garlic in olive oil in a large, heavy

continued on next page

pot over medium heat, stirring, until garlic is light golden brown, about 2 minutes. Add onion, pepper, leek, and green onions, season with salt, pepper, and dried red pepper, and cook until softened, about 5 minutes. Add tomato paste, stir, and cook for about 3 minutes, then add chopped canned tomatoes. Add wine, reserved tomato juice, and herb sachet and simmer to reduce by about half. Cover and cook slowly for about 1 hour. Add a little water if necessary; the consistency should be thick and juicy. Check seasoning, adjusting salt and pepper.

Add clams, oysters, and raw crab to the simmering stew and cover, cooking until oysters and clams begin to open, about 5 minutes. Remove oysters and clams to a large serving platter as they open. Season shrimp to taste with salt and add to pot. Simmer, covered, until just cooked through, 2 to 3 minutes.

Discard herb sachet, adjust seasoning, and return oysters and clams to the pot to reheat. Check consistency again, adding a little water if necessary and adjusting the seasoning before serving.

In the kitchen, heap into soup plates, seeing that each bowl has some of each kind of seafood and a big helping of sauce. Garnish with garlic-toast fingers and serve.

Yield: 4 generous servings

little man. If he liked you he would give you virtually anything except the way of the cheesecake." Finally, she emerges, heroic, with a resolution: "Then the impossible happened," she wrote, going on to describe a night when, for no known reason, the restaurateur capitulated. "This is the Lindy cheesecake," Paddleford trumpeted, "beloved by the Broadway celebrities."

The cheesecake recipe was not surrendered for nothing. It was a shrewd choice by Paddleford, and one that paid off in reader response. In a memo to Louella Shouer at *Ladies' Home Journal* about the "How America Eats" series, Paddleford confided that the recipe had been troublesome—but worth it. "Lindy's cheesecake was made and remade," she wrote. "Finally we asked the reluctant chef to come to our kitchen and he made the delicacy while our testers looked on at the step by step procedure. This cake has become the most popular recipe of the hundred published, and no complaints."

There was a payoff for Lindy's, too. Paddleford had by this time acquired enough influence that the mention of a restaurant could easily double its business. For example, in 1949 when she printed the recipe for pecan pie from the tea room of the chic Atlanta department store Rich's, the manager of the store's food division sent her a dozen roses and a note reporting "300% increase in pie sales." Lindy's surely got its due.

Paddleford adored the Creole-influenced cooking in New Orleans, and it showed. After a three-week exploratory stay there, she wrote: "Now I know that no matter what they say about Creole cookery, it isn't exaggerated. It's a cuisine unique, based on the belief that eating should be a pleasure and not a

Lindy's Cheesecake

Filling:

2½ pounds cream cheese, at room temperature

1¾ cups sugar

3 tablespoons all-purpose flour

1½ teaspoons grated orange peel

1½ teaspoons grated lemon peel

Pinch of vanilla bean (inside pulp)

5 eggs

2 egg yolks

¼ cup heavy cream

In a large bowl, combine cheese, sugar, flour, grated peels, and vanilla. Beat in eggs and egg yolks, one at a time, stirring after each addition. Stir in cream and combine thoroughly.

continued on next page

Pastry:

1 cup sifted all-purpose flour

¼ cup sugar

1 teaspoon grated lemon peel

Pinch of vanilla bean (inside pulp)

1 egg yolk

½ cup butter

Preheat oven to 400 degrees. In a large bowl, combine flour, sugar, lemon peel, and vanilla. Make a well in the center and add egg yolk and butter. Work together quickly with hands until well blended. Wrap ball in waxed paper and chill thoroughly in refrigerator, about 1 hour.

Roll out to ⅛-inch thick and place over oiled bottom of 9-inch springform cake pan. Trim overflow dough by running a rolling pin over sharp edge. Reserve trimmings.

Bake for 20 minutes, or until a light gold. Cool.

Reset oven to 500 degrees to preheat. Butter sides of cake form and snap over base. Roll remaining dough ⅛-inch thick and press inside the band. Fill form with cheese mixture and bake for 10 minutes. Reduce temperature to 250 degrees and bake 1 hour. Let the cake cool for at least 2 hours before cutting.

Yield: 12 servings

task to be hurried through, that food and drink are fine things to be talked about, and that recipes are meant to be shared. Such a variety of recipes and each with some distinctive touch. . . ."

Paddleford credited the great food of New Orleans to its French influence, calling the city the "Little Paris of America," and to the geography that allowed such delicacies as tabasco peppers and a unique variety of mustard seed to flourish. The coastal site, the bayous and backwaters produce "an abundance of fish, many of which are found but rarely anywhere else" for the city's menus, including "crawfish and river shrimp, soft shell turtles, red fish, sheeps head, terrapin, black fish, sting ray."

Her greatest triumph in the Crescent City, though, was winning the trust of the Alciatore family, owners of the historic French Quarter restaurant Antoine's, established in 1840 and often described as the oldest family-run eating place in the country. When she finally ate there, it did not disappoint. "Next to going to heaven to dine on ambrosia is going to New Orleans to eat at Antoine's," she wrote in 1948. Apparently the family thought as highly of her. Having corresponded for ten years with Roy Alciatore, grandson of the original Antoine, Paddleford finally persuaded him to part with not one but ten signature recipes that had previously been secrets for more than a century. "Nowhere else in the world is eating so surrounded by mystery, by legend; restaurant of a thousand dishes, and each a guarded secret, that is, until now."

Before giving the recipes, though, Paddleford uncharacteristically warned of complications. "But have patience, take care," she wrote. "A majority of Antoine's specialties require a ritual too involved to be practical for home use. Home cooks lack the necessary seasonings, stock pots, and sauces to produce master-

Oeufs Sardou

8 artichokes, stems peeled and trimmed,
tough outer leaves removed

16 anchovy fillets

8 eggs, poached

1 cup Antoine's Hollandaise Sauce (see next page)

½ cup chopped cooked ham

1 tablespoon glacé de viande or rich beef stock

4 slices truffle (optional)

Cook artichokes in boiling salted water until tender, about 20 minutes. Remove petals and choke; reserve bottoms. Place bottoms on baking pan and put 2 anchovy fillets on each. Run under low broiler heat to keep warm.

Have poached eggs ready and warm on the side. Have warm Hollandaise at hand.

Now assemble the dish: on each artichoke, over the anchovy fillet, place a poached egg. Cover with Hollandaise sauce. Sprinkled chopped ham over, and a few drops of the glacé de viande over ham and sauce. Place one slice of truffle on the very top. Serve immediately.

Yield: 4 servings

continued on next page

Antoine's Hollandaise Sauce

2 tablespoons tarragon vinegar

1 tablespoon water

1 tablespoon minced onion

3 peppercorns

4 egg yolks

1 cup clarified butter (see note below)

Juice of ¼ lemon

Salt, to taste

In saucepan place vinegar, water, onion, and peppercorns. Cook over very low heat to reduce to 1 teaspoon. Remove peppercorns. Cool.

Place egg yolks and the cooled, reduced vinegar in a medium metal bowl over a medium pan of water on a very low simmer and whisk until lemon-colored. Whisking constantly, drizzle in the butter, adding the lemon juice at the end. Season with salt to taste. Serve immediately.

Note: To clarify butter, slowly melt butter. Let stand until clear part can be skimmed off easily and reserve.

Yield: 4 servings

Oysters Rockefeller

2 large leaves butter lettuce

5 tablespoons butter, melted

⅓ cup fresh spinach, very finely minced

2 tablespoons finely minced onion

2 teaspoons finely minced celery

3 tablespoons fine dry bread crumbs

½ to 1 tablespoon finely minced fresh herbs,
such as chervil, tarragon, parsley,
and chives, combined

¼ teaspoon anchovy paste

¼ teaspoon salt

Few grains pepper

Rock salt, for serving

12 oysters on half shell

Gently wilt leaves of just rinsed (damp) butter lettuce over low heat in a dry sauté pan, turning once or twice. Pat dry and mince.

In a medium bowl, combine melted butter with lettuce, spinach, onion, celery, crumbs, herbs, anchovy paste, salt, and pepper. Mix well, set aside.

continued on next page

Put rock salt into 2 pie plates and set 6 oysters in shells into each pan, using rock salt to hold them level. Place spoonfuls of spinach-herb mixture on each oyster. Broil until thoroughly heated. Serve immediately.

Yield: 4 servings

pieces." The recipe for the restaurant's famed pommes soufflé is intimidating: "If the puff does not develop that is just too bad; start over from scratch," she advised. Such flourishes only put flashing lights around her great coup.

Despite attention to detail, the Paddleford name occasionally appeared over a blooper. Perhaps the worst gaffe of her career came in the autumn of 1949, in a "How America Eats" column about East Hampton, New York, a founding family, and its clam chowder. At the home of Jeannette Edwards Rattray, whose husband ran the *East Hampton Star* and whose family traced its Long Island roots to 1648, Paddleford was served a Manhattan-style chowder "thick enough to catch with a fork but always served with a spoon and big pilot crackers." No problem there, but the recipe for another treat, soft molasses cookies, was a different story. The recipe's ingredients did not include molasses. The *Herald Tribune* office was flooded with letters.

"*This Week* has over 10,000,000 circulation so you can imagine the mess I'm in," Paddleford wrote to Mrs. Rattray, with a certain amount of amour-propre. "Also had to write the women editors of twenty-six newspapers in which *This Week* appears. The time that story was being okayed one of the girls who tests and rechecks the recipes was on vacation: the girl I work with on

Great-Grandma Joan Hunting's
Soft Molasses Cookies

½ cup evaporated milk

1 teaspoon white vinegar

½ cup butter, at room temperature

½ cup sugar

1 cup molasses

2 eggs

2 teaspoons ground ginger

1¾ teaspoons baking soda

Pinch salt

3 cups sifted all-purpose flour

3 tablespoons sugar, for sprinkling

Sour the milk: Add vinegar and allow to sit at room temperature for at least 30 minutes but not more than an hour.

Preheat oven to 400 degrees. Grease and flour a cookie sheet.

In a medium bowl using an electric mixer, cream butter with ½ cup sugar until thoroughly blended, 1 to 2 minutes. Mix in molasses, eggs, ginger, baking soda, and salt; stir to combine. Stir in flour.

continued on next page

Drop batter from teaspoon onto prepared cookie sheet, placing cookies 1½ inches apart. Sprinkle with sugar. Bake about 8 minutes, rotating pan once during baking.

Yield: about 40 small cookies

This Week was having pneumonia." Molasses had appeared in the original copy, but somehow dropped out, unnoticed to any of the checkers at the *Herald Tribune*, where the test kitchen was, or *This Week*, which printed the story. "If anyone had doubts that 'How America Eats' series wasn't being read—they can now change their minds. Have just signed 72 letters for to-day's mail and still they come," she said. Despite this embarrass-ment and the time-consuming correction process—the recipe was subsequently reprinted in its entirety—Paddleford was cool. "I didn't miss the 'lasses," she confessed, "a few ingredients mean little to me. What I watch for is if the copy reads pretty."

Indeed, sometimes Paddleford intentionally stretched the truth for the sake of her "pretty" copy. In a story about food she enjoyed at the Dobbs House, a Dallas restaurant she holed up in when a flight out was delayed, she reported a story told to her by the restaurant's manager, Frank Stevenson, as if it had happened to her. The tale involved two stranded travelers "who left com-pletely satisfied after a dish of buttermilk and cornsticks." To Stevenson, to whom she sent the copy for recipe approval, as was her custom, she wrote: "Copy of the piece is attached a bit fictionalized in the opening but you may remember telling me [the story of the travelers]."

Paddleford had by now become an industry. She had her

own secretary at the paper, Helen Marshall, a bird of a woman in thick glasses, whose sole responsibilities were to help coordinate Paddleford's schedule and decode her handwriting. Coordinating must not have been easy, as Paddleford had two offices. She was everywhere, and of course, eventually a member of the press attracts press coverage of her own.

"Her Passion is Food," the only full-length profile of Clementine Paddleford published, appeared in the April 30, 1949, edition of *The Saturday Evening Post*. It ran with exactly one photograph: Paddleford "preparing steak in her New York apartment" is the caption under a shot of the subject kneeling before her fireplace, tongs in hand, grasping a giant T-bone and placing it on a rack. "Meet Clementine Paddleford, a personality as improbable as her name," wrote the reporter Josef Israels II. "While others woo the nation's eaters with complicated recipes, she keeps readers drooling by just telling them how good things taste." The story is full of lively anecdotes and details, from the Gimbel's umbrella department to the throat cancer to the "short-lived marriage to Lloyd Zimmerman, an engineer who had too much traveling to do" to the "quantities of black coffee alternately from a French drip pot and an Italian espresso machine" with which Paddleford fueled her work habits. Even her process was laid bare: "For fifteen years, seven days a week, Miss Paddleford has devoted the better part of the hours from 5 A.M. until late in the evening to tasting, testing, eating, talking, reading and writing about food. It takes her from 5 A.M. until 11 A.M. to turn out the first draft of her daily *Herald Tribune* column. She writes on white bond paper—no other color will do—in a long-hand pencil scrawl, using a sort of personal shorthand with most words left hurriedly unfinished. This is intelligible only to Helen

Marshall, her secretary, who turns it into typescript acceptable to the printers."

The story is filled with important details—such the attraction of her work to more than homemakers. "George Cornish, managing editor of the *Herald Tribune*, says that "Miss Paddleford is unusually valuable to his paper because, unlike most food writers, fully half of her readers are masculine. There was spectacular male as well as female response to a cooky column that started out: 'Open your mouth and shut your eyes. Like it? That's a cooky from the blue tin. Memories crowd in—a stone cooky jar that held the most enticing smell in the world.'"

The article's coup is the way it spelled out what made Paddleford so popular. Sure, Israels noted her trip to France—she had bona fide reach, and international clout and reputation—and the way she exploded the Alciatore recipes—she had guts and perseverance. What was magical was much more than those attributes, though, and Israels knew it: "Clementine is just as apt to devote her space to the 'little old lady' who cooks jellies in a tiny Ninth Avenue store or the one who peddles horseradish on an East Side street corner." The fact that she was utterly democratic in her tastes, able to appreciate what a home cook could do as well as what a trained French chef could, is what made her, at fifty years old, a legend in her own time.

All the Sights and Smells of the Country

Did you hear the one about Clem's trip to Idlewild? According to the gang who in the early 1950s lunched in the ninth-floor test kitchen at the *Herald Tribune*, it went like this. Paddleford heard airlines touting the quality of their meals, and was of course interested in learning more. One airline, no one could remember which, invited the influential food writer out to what was then clumsily known as the New York International Airport at Idlewild, Queens, to show her the skillful chefs, the ingenious devices to load the food into the airborne galleys, and to let her learn at first hand how delicious everything was. So the airline sent a limousine to 41st Street to pick up Paddleford, and she was ferried out to what is now J.F.K. Airport to poke into it all.

Sometime in the afternoon there was quite a dust-up—the limo driver could not locate Paddleford. Nervous, he called the *Trib* and asked where she was, mentioning which hangar he'd be waiting at. The women in the office tittered: Old Clem kidnapped? Lost? Was she stuck on a plane or in a hangar or trapped someplace? Mercifully, no. Paddleford was found, according to legend, sleeping peacefully, propped against a tree at the edge of the tarmac. Word was, she'd had an extra gin and tonic with lunch, and airport security was finally deployed to find her. Reunited with the driver, she boarded the limo for home.

Paddleford was good copy, in print or over coffee. Joan Cook, a ninth-floor reporter on the parent and child beat, said Paddleford told this one on herself. Paddleford had a former lover who lay dying in Bellevue Hospital. "Clem was not made of rock," Cook reminded her friends, saying that Paddleford went to the formidable old hospital in the afternoons to visit the discarded dear one. According to the story, the guy asked her to bury him at the Redding house, underneath an apple tree where he and she "had spent so many happy hours." According to Cook, when the man died, Paddleford attended to the cremation, taking the urn of ashes to her country home. In time, she got a shovel and dug a hole under the tree. At that point, Paddleford reported that Claire stepped in to say: "You can't just go out and dig a hole and bury ashes. You have to have some kind of permit." Paddleford thought this probably had a ring of truth. So she then took the urn and put it on a shelf "next to the bottle of bourbon," as Cook explained, where she and her lover "had spent so many happy hours."

These stories were widely circulated through the *Trib* staff, and while some of them may have been burnished by time, they show how larger-than-life their subject had become. (Whatever doubts may be raised about the vision of Paddleford with her foot on the shovel under the apple tree, a 1950 death certificate for one Bruno West was preserved among her papers. Claire recalled being at the Redding farm once when some highball glasses inexplicably broke and she and Paddleford decided West's ghost was probably behind it. Claire said that she and Paddleford would look at each other and say "Bruno!") Paddleford had become a bona fide brand by this time, world famous, and everyone working at the *Trib* and *This Week*, across town in the Graybar Building on Lexington Avenue, was aware of her clout.

Paddleford was a particular presence among the close-knit group of women who spent their work days on the *Trib*'s ninth floor. At this point the editorial part of the ninth floor had ceased to be called the Home Institute, although "Home Institute" was still used as a label above extra material added to the back pages in the *Herald Tribune* edition of *This Week*. A sleeker model had slid into the area, now called Women's Features, and with it a new cast of characters.

In addition to Paddleford, by 1952 Eugenia Sheppard's posse included Helen Carleton, a super-chic garment-district reporter and photo stylist; the reporters Guin Hall, Harriet Morrison, Harriet Jean Anderson and Joan Cook; Pat Doyle, Sheppard's secretary, and Helen Marshall, Paddleford's; and Bea Meyers, a fact checker. Among the more amazing reportorial hires made by Sheppard was Denise McCluggage, like Paddleford a Kansan, but one who loped across the room like a cowboy in sling-back pumps. She later became a pioneer female sportswriter with a specialty in auto racing and went on to become a racing driver herself. In 2006, she became the first journalist inducted into the Automotive Hall of Fame. What the petite fashionista Sheppard or the omnivorous Kansan Paddleford would have thought of their former colleague is unguessable.

Closer to Paddleford's domain were Joyce Jones, a home economist in her early twenties who had recently replaced Anne Pappas in the job of testing the recipes that ran in Paddleford's column, and Helen Cloudy, a test kitchen helper and general office assistant in her early fifties. In July 1952, in anticipation of Cook's impending maternity leave and with an eye on the continued medical leave of Cleora Forth, the editor for the Home Institute material for *This Week*, Sheppard hired Betsy Wade, a new graduate of the Columbia Journalism School, as a desk person and reporter.

Wade, now seventy-eight and retired, junkets around the country giving seminars and lectures to students and other audiences about feminist issues in the newsroom. More than fifty years ago, four years after her time at the *Trib*, she became the first woman to be hired by the *New York Times* as a copy editor. At the *Times* for almost forty-five years, she was a union activist and a moving force in the sex-discrimination lawsuit filed against the paper in 1974. Wade credits Paddleford with giving her tools to help open the *Times* doors. Though she rose to be head of the foreign copy desk at the *Times*, Wade's first editing assignment there was in Women's News.

Shortly after Wade arrived at the *Trib*, her stepmother, an old friend of Tracy Samuels, Paddleford's sorority sister from Chicago, asked Samuels to drop a line to Paddleford about the new *Trib* employee. Within days, Paddleford emerged from her hideaway into the outside office and stood over Wade's desk. "I understand you are a friend of Tracy Samuels," Paddleford said.

According to Wade, she replied that Samuels was a friend of her father's and stepmother's and was a frequent guest at their home. "Tracy Samuels is the best person in the world, and I'm so delighted that you're here," Paddleford replied. "If I can do a thing to help you, let me know."

Paddleford kept her word and then some. "Clementine wasn't just invaluable to me in my career," Wade says, "she was invaluable to me forever." Paddleford gave the young reporter a priceless break. When out of town on assignment, she had to leave the Friday market basket column to someone in the office because it could not be written in advance. As Wade describes it, it covered "how much perishable foods like lettuce and bananas cost that week and that kind of thing." Bypassing Harriet Jean Anderson, an established food reporter, Paddleford specified that Wade would assume this chore. Sheppard had already been giving Wade bylines on her features, but to fill in for the mighty Paddleford—even with just the prices of lettuce and bananas—under her own byline gave her a valuable stepping stone to the future. "That is what Clem Paddleford did for her friends' children," Wade said. "And I think that there was a very strong aura about those children who came from this Chicago group."

Indeed, if Paddleford had an appropriate opportunity, she was always willing to lob it in Wade's direction. "Once my own photograph was used alongside a Paddleford article about tomatoes," Wade reports. "Clem could call the shots on things like that, and there I am in a photo by the women's department photographer Joe Engels, holding toothpicks with little tomatoes."

By this time, Paddleford had become an innovator to the home cook, introducing her to such exotica as, well, the Caesar salad—a novel idea in 1952. At that time it was a delicacy reserved for the country's top dining rooms, including the Gourmet Room in the downtown Cincinnati Terrace-Hilton Hotel.

"Ohio does more sophisticated eating than any other state in the United States outside California," Paddleford said in the opener of her April 13, 1952, column. The manager of the restaurant even compared the "really beautiful, almost as beautiful" view of downtown Cincinnati to that from the famed Rainbow Room at Rockefeller Center in New York, where he had first trained. It was here that the Caesar salad was presented to Paddleford, and lovingly passed on, very likely for the first time, to her readers: "The ingredients are never mixed in advance—this salad must always be made at the table," she explained.

Paddleford may have been generous both to her subjects who boasted the Cincinnati view and to her junior colleagues in newspaper work, but she was tough when it came to results.

If she assigned a job to a subordinate, she expected perfection. The home economist Jones recalls Paddleford's grueling attention to detail. Jones, now Joyce Crosby, laughed, groaned and held her head in her home in Augusta, Maine, when she remembered a recipe for Swiss Pear Bread from Elsie Gerber of Green County, Wisconsin, that she had to test no fewer than six times.

Paddleford had included a stop in the area northwest of Chicago known as "Little Switzerland" as part of the "How America Eats" series; Gerber was the cook she was spotlighting. Local dessert cheeses were the high point of the meal at Gerber's house, Paddleford wrote ("these laid out on grape leaves; the Bleu, Camembert, Liederkranz and Neufchatel") but Gerber also did a major dessert, a "dried pear bread . . . almost as fruity as fruitcake."

Jones found the concoction, studded with five kinds of dried

Caesar Salad

½ teaspoon salt, or more to taste

1 large clove garlic

5 anchovy fillets, minced, about 2 teaspoons

Juice of 2 lemons, about ¼ cup

5 drops Worcestershire sauce

2 eggs, at room temperature, coddled for 2 to 3 minutes to taste

1 cup garlic oil (see below)

2 heads romaine lettuce

4 tablespoons finely grated parmesan cheese

Croutons, sautéed in garlic oil (see recipe)

Freshly ground black pepper, to taste

For the garlic oil:

1 cup olive oil

3 cloves garlic, smashed with the side of a knife

For the croutons:

1 baguette, crust removed, cut into 16 cubes

Remaining ⅔ cup garlic oil

continued on next page

To make garlic oil, let olive oil and garlic sit together at room temperature for several hours or overnight before removing the garlic.

Over medium heat in a medium skillet, fry bread cubes in garlic oil until well scented and golden.

Sprinkle salt with a generous hand over the inside of a wooden bowl. Rub with cut clove of garlic. Add minced anchovies, lemon juice, Worcestershire sauce, and egg, mixing to combine and then drizzle ⅓ cup garlic oil to bowl, and blend with whisk, breaking up the cooked egg white if chunky.

Break heads of washed and dried lettuce into fair-sized lengths (about 2 inches), dropping into bowl. Add parmesan cheese and croutons. Toss to combine all ingredients, adjusting seasoning and adding freshly ground black pepper to taste.

Yield: 4 large servings

fruits and four aromatic spices, difficult to replicate—the dough was sticky, it had to stand overnight, the fruits became soggy, etc.—and she failed several times to produce something that Paddleford accepted. Undeterred and unwilling to abandon the recipe though she had many others from this kitchen, the boss kept Jones at the task until the cake came to satisfactorily resemble what Paddleford had eaten on her reporting trip.

"There was a Swiss pear bread we made six times," Paddleford told an editor at *Ladies' Home Journal*, whom she hoped to

Swiss Pear Bread

1½ cups dried pears (if not available, double the dried apples)

1½ cups dried apples

1 cup dried currants

1¼ cups seedless raisins

⅓ cup pitted prunes

1 teaspoon finely diced candied citron

2 tablespoons butter, plus 1½ tablespoons

½ tablespoon anise seed

¼ teaspoon ground cloves

½ teaspoon ground cinnamon

½ teaspoon ground nutmeg

½ cup sugar

½ cup walnuts, whole or chopped

½ package active dry yeast

2 cups warm water

¾ teaspoon salt

4 to 5 cups sifted all-purpose flour

Put dried pears and apples into a pot with water to barely cover and bring to a low simmer, cooking over low heat

continued on next page

until very tender. Combine while hot with currants and raisins. Cook prunes in water to cover until soft; add to hot cooked fruit mixture. Add citron, 2 tablespoons of the butter, the spices, and ¾ of the sugar while mixture is still hot. Let stand overnight.

In the morning, if any water remains, drain it. Then add nuts to the fruit mixture. Dissolve yeast in ⅛ cup of the warm water and let stand 5 minutes without stirring. Then mix thoroughly and add 1½ tablespoons of butter, salt, the remaining sugar, and the rest of the warm water. Let stand until the mixture bubbles. Mix in enough flour to make a stiff dough. Keep stirring in additional flour as long as it's possible (about 4 cups).

Turn dough out on floured surface and work in enough more flour to prevent sticking (it might take 1 cup). Let dough rise until doubled in bulk. Pinch off 3 pieces the size of a golf ball. Add fruit-nut mixture to remainder of dough. Work fruit into dough by kneading until there are no streaks of white left. The dough will be quite sticky. Divide into 3 portions. Shape into narrow loaves. If it's still too sticky, add more flour, working in well. Using a generous sprinkling of flour on the board and rolling pin, roll each of the small pieces of dough into a very thin sheet, so thin there are likely be some holes. Wrap a sheet of this plain dough around each loaf. Make it uneven so that the dark fruited roll shows through gaps and holes.

continued on next page

Let rise in a warm place until nearly doubled in bulk, about 1 hour.

Preheat oven to 375 degrees. Bake for about 20 minutes, until the dough has come up, then reduce heat to 325 degrees. Continue baking for 25 to 40 minutes more.

Yield: 3 loaves

entice into writing a feature about her "How America Eats" series. "Finally a loaf was sent to the Swiss homemaker in Wisconsin for her opinion. She told us in a hurry where we made the mistake; a little matter of technique."

Perhaps because of her tenacity, and no doubt because of her obvious influence in the world—"she had authority, she had lots of people working for her, she was able to be what she wanted to be," Wade said—the younger women enjoyed working with Paddleford. That said, they knew very little about her beyond what they saw in the office.

"I don't think she mixed the office with her private life," Wade said. "She did not socialize with any of the young girls in the gang, did not eat lunch with them, never invited any of them over to her house. I had high regard for Clem but I don't suppose she and I passed more than five hundred words that weren't directly related to work."

By this time, Paddleford was making $28,000 a year, she had cars that the paper hired to fetch her and take her to interviews, and she had a flow of visitors ranging from food and kitchen equipment manufacturers to restaurant press people.

Observing Paddleford's comings and goings and her roster of colorful guests was a popular office sport. One Wade recalls vividly was Peter Schlumbohm, the German-born American chemist who created the Chemex coffeemaker in the early 1940s. "He would come up to the kitchen and set up his coffee-making contraption and put in his filter," Wade said. "It made much better coffee; he kept saying it never touched metal and that was the difference. So when he was coming to show some modification of it to Clem, he would go back into her office and they would talk." Schlumbohm's invention, based on the notion that "a coffeepot should not be a steam engine," as he once explained it to *Time* magazine, went on to make him millions before he died in 1962 at age sixty-six of a heart attack. Wade believed he was probably not just a source but eventually became a friend of Paddleford's because his incursions into the test kitchen would otherwise have been excessive.

Paddleford's private office was back on the 40th Street side of the building. Marshall sat close to the department entrance, near the 41st Street set-back, where she clattered a rickety standard typewriter and coped with two phones, assuring Paddleford uninterrupted time to write, or talk to the cat she brought to work. Sometimes when Paddleford had to explain illegible copy changes, she would swish out to Marshall's desk, her scarf flowing, sheaves of paper, pencils and sometimes recipes in hand. When she spoke, she bent over Marshall to be heard, keeping one hand free to press a middle finger on her throat tube at each breath. Sometimes crises erupted, but mostly the Paddleford-Marshall exchanges were modulated and always conducted with an eye on the deadlines.

One exception involved the Delmarva Chicken Festival.

First held for the chicken producers of the Eastern Shore—Delaware, Maryland, and Virginia, where such chicken biggies as Purdue and Tyson still maintain branches—the party, which was a lot like a state fair, began in 1949 in Snow Hill, Maryland, where it is still held today.

In the spring of 1953, Paddleford was invited to cover this fete, the highlight of which was to be the frying of tons of chicken in what was dubbed "the world's largest frying pan." She was really engaged. "Clementine had gotten a car and driver to go down there," Wade said, "and she came back late in the afternoon, my guess would be around 4, 4:15. And she was as excited as I'd ever seen her. She had found herself a story. It was full of people preparing chickens by their own recipes. I suspect it was something that she recognized from her childhood. She was just atwitter. And she came in to the desk of her secretary Helen Marshall, which was immediately inside the doorway. She said 'Oh, Helen, oh, I just had the best time and it's such a good story and I didn't have a photographer with me, but I found a freelance photographer down there and I just told him I would buy whatever he had inside his camera sight unseen.' And Helen said, 'Oh that was smart, Clem.' And Clem handed her the yellow box of cut film and said, 'Take it down to the lab right away and see if you can get something developed.' Then she went in her office and her cape was flapping and she sat down and pulled out notes, I guess. And in a very short time Joe Engels, the photographer, came upstairs and made Clem as upset as she had been happy. He said to her: 'Clem for god's sake there's not a goddamn thing on that film. You bought yourself nothing!'

"Helen Marshall looked up from her desk and you could see her wig rising on her head," Wade said. "And she said, 'that's what I thought when I opened the box.' And I just looked at Helen Marshall and thought: I'm not going to say anything. Clem is going to have to be the one to tell her that she opened the box of undeveloped film and destroyed it with daylight. I think Clem eventually called up the public relations person and they sent her up a picture of a giant frying pan or something of that nature. They would be findable. The conversation between Helen and Clem after that was back in Clem's office."

This event fed one more Clem tale into the chatter of one ninth floor routine: Four days a week, Cook, Doyle, Jones, Wade, and Cloudy, and sometimes McCluggage, gathered in the test kitchen to eat lunch, with the participants taking turns bringing tunafish salad, liverwurst, bologna, probably the humblest fare that passed through there. Sharing lunch was a major money-saver, but it also made for a companionable time. When Cloudy and Jones were finished with their testing or marketing for the morning they would clean up and set up for lunch. "We'd all come into the kitchen and sit around the island in the middle, and eat our sandwiches and drink iced tea or lemonade," Wade recalled. "And after that we played canasta for the rest of our lunch hour." In these sessions, if Paddleford was out of the office, she was sometimes a topic of conversation—and not always favorable. "We made fun of her writing," Wade says. "We laughed because a lot of it was overdrawn, but she knew what she was doing and she knew what she could get away with—which was practically everything." At that point, the paper's copy editors offered little resistance to Paddleford's often florid prose.

Stanley Alpern, who joined the *Trib* as a twenty-one-year-old copy boy in 1948, was one of the souls who had to deal with this. "It was highly unusual for one so young to become a copy reader—the average age of my seventeen colleagues on the copy desk must have been about fifty," Alpern reports. "Copy readers are, or were then, usually former reporters who settle down to a desk job in mid-career. The American Newspaper Guild, our trade union, had inserted a clause in the N.Y.H.T. contract specifying that copy boys (or girls) should be given one-year try-outs on the copy desk, when feasible, and I was the first one chosen." As low man on the totem pole, Alpern was given the job of cleaning up Paddleford's copy and putting a headline on the column. "She was already an N.Y.H.T. institution," Alpern recalls. "I was flattered to be so trusted, but actually it was not an assignment that any copy reader coveted. It was not easy to edit Clementine's prose." This was not only because the subject of food was considered far less exciting than hard news, but also because her copy contained words and phrases beyond the realm of the *Trib* stylebook. Alpern remembers wrestling with Paddleford's grammar and spelling, but unlike her editors at *This Week*, he does not recall her coming to the desk to complain about changes.

"Sometimes it was to her detriment that they didn't go after her a little harder," Wade said. "I had a friend working at *This Week* in an internship and he said to me, 'she really is strange.' And I said, "what do you mean?" and he said that she wrote in a sentence that 'the children were happy as a guinea.' And he said, 'What do you suppose she meant? Do you think she meant a guinea hen? She couldn't possibly mean an Italian.' And I said, "I don't think so." And he said well, I think 'happy as a guinea' went into *This Week*."

For all their good-humored gossip, the younger staff members admired Paddleford, and recognized her bigheartedness.

"She wasn't looking for followers or for anyone who was going to make her life better or different," Wade said.

True indeed, Paddleford was getting all she had hoped out of her career by this point. By the early 1950s writing awards were just rolling in, the most frequent of which were the dozens from the New York Newspaper Women's Club, and also from commercial organizations such as the Grocery Manufacturers Association.

In early 1950, Martin Weldon, a reporter for WCBS radio and a contributor to *The New Yorker* magazine, spent the better part of a week trailing Paddleford for a profile of the Home Institute. Instead of treating Weldon as a nuisance, Paddleford embraced his presence and allowed him unlimited access to the goings-on; she even chronicled his time in the kitchen. "Anne Pappas let him help mix the batter for French crullers," the account began. "Eugenia Sheppard, women's features editor, took him along on a photographing binge, something to do with sleeveless dresses. . . . Ann Pringle gave him a detailed report of Macy's mid-winter furniture show. . . . Guin Hall introduced him to the newest equipment in the Home Institute laboratory . . . we took him for cocktails with Edna Cast, the date lady here from Mecca, Calif., with new date products to show." The crowning touch here was that Paddleford signed off and let Weldon write the rest of the column. "If this Martin Weldon wants really to wear the other man's shoes, let him wear our No. 7s and write today's yardage," Paddleford wrote.

Weldon's postscript is a send-up of typical ninth-floor activities, from cruller-making ("Well, the batter stayed up and I thought I passed with flying crullers, but when I started offering the bake around, everybody got busy on long-distance calls") to

Crullers

3½ cups sifted all-purpose flour

4 teaspoons baking powder

¼ teaspoon baking soda

¼ teaspoon salt

1 teaspoon ground nutmeg

⅛ teaspoon ground ginger

½ cup egg yolks, about 6 extra-large egg yolks

½ cup buttermilk or sour milk

½ cup half-and-half

1 cup sugar

1 to 2 quarts vegetable oil

Sift flour, baking powder, baking soda, salt, and spices into a large bowl. Beat yolks in a large bowl; mix with buttermilk and half-and-half. Add sugar and stir until well blended. Add sifted dry ingredients and beat until almost smooth.

Turn a portion at a time onto a lightly floured surface and roll or pat out to ½-inch thickness. Cut with a 3-inch doughnut cutter, or use a 3-inch biscuit cutter, then make a hole in the center of each round with a 1-inch cutter or the end of a wooden spoon handle.

continued on next page

In a heavy 6-quart pot filled no more than halfway with oil, heat oil to 365 degrees. Fry doughnuts 45 seconds to 1 minute on each side, until golden brown. Drain on paper bags.

Yield: 2 dozen crullers

tasting the newest product from the venerable Schrafft's chain of bakeries and restaurants, which was Fresh Strawberry Buttercream Roll ("Helen Cloudy, the Home Institute maid, looked at me for a long minute. 'It's the custom around here,' she said, 'to taste these new foods, not to finish them right down to the end.'") Weldon wrote that he left his tour with "a lot of respect for the way the gals of this department rush from fashion show or hot stove to typewriter to deadline," before urging readers to tune in to his radio broadcast to learn if the reporter's "own 10½s fit him after this breathless week in the pounding pumps of twelve women."

Paddleford must surely have enjoyed this, but it provided no day off: The column's sidebar features a recipe for a "money saving dish" meant to take advantage of the remains of the "gala cuts of pork" that were cooked in the preceding holidays. "Now homemakers are thinking of pork as ever but the more thrifty of the cuts . . . rich in nourishment, ace high in appeal, but easy on the dollar." Move over, Weldon, because you can't turn the head of Paddleford if she's looking after her penny-pinching home cooks. She gave them sweet-sour spareribs, devised by the test-kitchen cooks.

Another reporter took at look at Paddleford's life. In December 1954, Catherine Royer profiled Paddleford on a show for the Voice of America, "Women in the Free World." The title

Sweet-Sour Spareribs

2 pounds pork spareribs, about 16 pieces 4 inches long

Salt

1 tablespoon vegetable oil

About 1½ cups water

¼ cup raisins

½ teaspoon salt

2 green peppers, cored and thinly sliced

1½ teaspoons cornstarch

¼ cup sugar

¼ cup cider vinegar

1 teaspoon soy sauce

Season ribs generously with salt. In a large Dutch oven over medium heat, heat oil and brown ribs in batches, about 5 minutes to a side. Add ½ cup of water, the raisins, and salt. Return all ribs to Dutch oven, cover tightly, and cook over very low heat for 20 minutes, turning once about halfway through. Add green pepper slices, stir in cornstarch blended with sugar, the vinegar, and 1 cup of water. Cover and continue cooking over low heat for 30 minutes, turning once about halfway through. After 10 minutes have passed, add

continued on next page

soy sauce and continue to cook over gentle heat, using a spoon to baste the ribs. The liquid will slowly reduce, so add more water as needed to prevent drying. The ribs are finished when tender, glazed, and slightly saucy.

Yield: 4 appetizer servings

of the segment: "A Country Girl Whom Misfortune Stirred to Great Achievement." Royer focused on Paddleford's bout with throat cancer. "As she sought ways to pick up the thread of her life," Royer said, "a friend offered her a newspaper job at a modest figure, as Food Markets Editor at the New York *Herald Tribune*'s Home Institute. She put all the sights and smells of the country into it."

Pushing forward, Paddleford now had the aid of an established serial column. By 1951, the "How America Eats" series was three years old, and it had attracted a serious following in both of its publications, *This Week* and the *Trib*. One big reason was that Paddleford aggressively sought to publish the kind of unglamorous recipes we now consider comfort food. There she was with managing caterer for the Des Moines, Iowa, Women's Club, whose job, in a throwback to Paddleford's days covering all those church supper planners for the *Christian Herald*, entailed planning a weekly luncheon for four hundred from October to May. Edith Davison, "a home economics graduate of Iowa State College," provided her prize recipe for macaroni and cheese. (Her appearance, incidentally, is not an example of nepotism on Paddleford's part; this Davison was not related to Paddleford's pal Eloise Davison, coincidentally herself a 1924 home economics

Souffléd Macaroni and Cheese

1½ cups scalded whole milk

1 cup soft bread crumbs

1½ cups grated cheddar cheese

1 cup cooked macaroni

3 eggs, separated

¼ cup diced pimientos

1 tablespoon chopped parsley

1 tablespoon grated onion

1 teaspoon salt

3 tablespoons butter, melted

Preheat oven to 350 degrees. Grease a casserole.

Pour milk over soft bread crumbs; add cheese. Cover and let stand until cheese melts. Add macaroni. Combine and add beaten egg yolks, pimiento, parsley, onion, salt, and butter. Beat egg whites until stiff but not dry and fold into mixture.

Pour into prepared casserole. Bake uncovered for 25 to 35 minutes.

Yield: 4 entrée servings

graduate of Iowa State College.) This version of the old familiar was "almost a souffle, but easier to handle." Down home dinner-on-a-busy-weeknight fare, that was Paddleford's meat, and she knew it.

Far from shunning these commonplace dishes, Paddleford's readers ate them up and came back for more. Paddleford gave herself a little back-patting in her Christmas Day column that year, posing the question, how do we know this column is well read? "Never a week but somebody is writing, 'I lost that most marvelous recipe for the Philadelphia sticky buns,' or again it's the prize angel cake baked by the Governor's wife of Oregon, Mrs. Douglas McKay." As a holiday gift to her fans, she printed "tied with ribbons of citron, all a-sparkle with sugar, perfumed with spice" the "eight best-loved recipes of a three-year journey crisscrossing the states, stopping at home kitchens, at roadside inns to gather food lore and famous regional dishes," which included both the sticky buns and the green goddess salad dressing originated in the kitchen of San Francisco's Palace Hotel.

Of the latter, she wrote in her confident, confidential mode: "You have heard, of course, of the Green Goddess Dressing? This originated at the Palace but today there are as many versions of the Goddess as ways to make apple pie. Here's the original recipe."

Paddleford created good copy for local papers, too. A 1952 trip to Florida and Puerto Rico was typical. The *Florida Times-Union*, in Jacksonville, published pictures of Paddleford interviewing the region's "most celebrated cooks," while the *Tampa Morning Tribune* reported that she came to town "with the 14 sharp pencils and pliable notebooks which make her an annual customer for the year's largest handbags." *El Mundo,* San Juan's

Green Goddess Dressing

4 anchovy fillets, finely minced

2 tablespoons minced onion

1 tablespoon parsley, very finely chopped

1 tablespoon tarragon, very finely chopped

4 teaspoons chives, very thinly sliced

1 tablespoon tarragon vinegar

1½ cups mayonnaise, preferably homemade

Salt, to taste

Combine anchovy, onion, parsley, tarragon, chives, and tarragon vinegar in a medium bowl. Add mayonnaise; gently whisk together until combined. Season with salt to taste. Serve over greens tossed together in a salad bowl rubbed with a cut clove of garlic.

Yield: 1¾ cups

Philadelphia Sticky Buns

1¼ cups whole milk

1 package active dry yeast

¼ cup warm water

5 cups sifted all-purpose flour

1½ teaspoons salt

¾ cup plus 1 tablespoon sugar

½ cup shortening

2 eggs

¼ cup butter or margarine, at room temperature

½ cup packed brown sugar

2 teaspoons ground cinnamon

½ cup chopped walnuts

½ cup raisins or dried currants

2 cups corn syrup

Scald milk; cool to lukewarm. Dissolve yeast in water in a large bowl and add milk. Make a sponge by adding 2 cups of the flour, the salt, and the 1 tablespoon sugar, beating until smooth. Set aside in a warm place.

In a large bowl, whip shortening until light. Whip in the ¾ cup sugar. Add eggs, one at a time, beating each in thor-

continued on next page

oughly. Gradually beat this mixture into the bubbly sponge. Stir in remaining flour, or enough to make a soft dough.

Cover and let rise in a warm place until doubled in bulk, 1 to 1½ hours. Divide dough in half and roll each portion to ¼-inch thickness. Spread with butter. Combine brown sugar and cinnamon and sprinkle over dough. Scatter on the nuts and currants and dribble with 1 cup of the syrup. Roll each piece as for a jelly roll. Cut each roll into 1½-inch lengths, about 12 pieces per roll. Grease 2 deep 9-inch-square pans well with ½ cup syrup each. Stand buns on cut end in pans.

Cover and let rise until doubled in bulk, 1 to 1½ hours. Top buns with remaining syrup.

Preheat oven to 350 degrees. Bake for 30 to 40 minutes, or until brown. Turn out of pans immediately.

Yield: 2 dozen buns

Fritas de Bacalao (Cod Fritters)

2½ cups sifted all-purpose flour

2 teaspoons double-acting baking powder

1 cup plus 3 tablespoons water

½ teaspoon salt

2 tablespoons butter, melted

1 clove garlic, minced

2 cups fresh codfish, shredded and seasoned
generously to taste with salt or ½ pound salt cod,
soaked in a bowl of water in the refrigerator
for 24 hours, with the water changed several times

2 quarts vegetable oil

Sift flour and baking powder into a large bowl; add water and salt and mix well. Add melted butter and minced garlic; blend thoroughly. The batter will have a fairly thick, sticky, bread-dough-like texture.

If using fresh codfish, salt the batter. If using salt cod, remove from water and simmer in fresh water. As it begins to boil, remove from the heat and drain. Remove any skin and bones and shred the fish.

In a deep pot, heat vegetable oil to 350 degrees. With two spoons loosely form walnut-size balls; make sure there are

continued on next page

pieces of cod in each ball. Drop balls in hot fat and fry in batches until deep golden brown and cooked through, 4 to 5 minutes.

Yield: about 30 fritters

leading daily, in one day printed two stories about her visit: "Clementine Paddleford Recibe Informes Sobre Platos Nativos" and "La Experta de *Herald Tribune* Busca Recetas en Puerto Rico."

She may have been getting around the globe a little more, but she always made sure that she swung through her home state of Kansas at regular intervals, not because she had much family there that she was close to (although she certainly had plenty of old friends who were happy to welcome this newly minted media star). It was because she truly believed in the wholesomeness of the food of the Midwest. She returned to it again and again. "Today I hear much criticism regarding food in the Middle West," a Kansas column began. "The complaints come usually from tourists who pass through at sixty miles an hour, eating en route in public places, and seldom at the best. I doubt these scorners have ever sat down as a guest at a family table." To prove her point, she offers a specialty from the Orville Burtis Ranch in Ashland Bottoms. "Crowd supper parties were a frequent event. Mrs. Burtis would make stew or maybe a tub full of chili. Either dish has a rib-sticking quality that makes you young beyond your time. The meat was taken from her well-stocked thirty-foot locker, and it was home-grown steer beef."

For all her adherence to her personal principles about food, Paddleford was rewarded with an ever-increasing audience—

Chili

1 pound dry red kidney beans

4 quarts cold water

5 cups tomato juice

1 tablespoon salt

2½ pounds ground chuck

1 tablespoon plus 2 teaspoons vegetable oil

3 tablespoons chili powder

1 large onion, grated, about 2 cups

Rinse beans; cover with cold water and soak overnight in heavy 6-quart casserole. Cover beans and simmer in their soaking water 1½ to 2 hours, or until they are tender, adding tomato juice from time to time to keep beans covered as liquid boils away. If tomato juice runs out, add more water if necessary to keep liquid an inch above the beans. Add ½ tablespoon of the salt.

Divide meat into batches. In a large skillet over medium heat, heat ½ tablespoon of the vegetable oil and brown meat, stirring the next batch into the earlier one. Divide chili powder evenly among batches and stir continuously

continued on next page

until evenly browned. After all the meat is browned, add remaining salt. Remove beef from heat.

In the remaining 2 teaspoons vegetable oil, sauté onions until golden. Add beef and onion to casserole of beans. Cook mixture over low heat, stirring continuously, about 10 minutes longer. Serve with rolls or crackers.

Yield: 8 generous servings

and an ever-increasing group of advertisers who wanted to associate their products with her well-received words and formulas. Her employers certainly knew how to work this to their advantage. The *Trib* in particular heavily promoted their star. An ad in June 1950 urged readers "a trifle tired of the usual table d'hote" to get "a daily dash of Clementine Paddleford's exciting column of culinary scoops in the *Herald Tribune* every day," which was guaranteed to "convert you into an amateur Escoffier overnight." The ad copy bragged: "Miss Paddleford literally travels the world to bring you news."

The paper's newsletter publicized her awards, too, while giving a little nod to the advertisers who paid the paper's bills. "That isn't our Clementine's flying carpet draped around her shoulders," ran the copy in yet another promotional piece, this one dated June 1, 1951. "That was just part of her garb on November 13th last, when Paul S. Willis, President of Grocery Manufacturers of America, Inc, presented her with the First Honorable Mention Certificate in the Life Line of America Awards—at the GMA's annual luncheon at the Waldorf. The award was one for best interpretation of essential processes and services on food from farm to table." A few years later, the promotion department had a field day when Paddleford's appearance at the tenth annual meeting of food editors, held in Chicago, was written up in *Time* magazine in October 1953.

Time wrote: "The New York *Herald Tribune*'s Clementine Paddleford, whose Sunday *This Week* column appears all over the U.S., reported that housewives in her home territory, Manhattan, Kansas, are turning to gourmet dishes barely a step behind amateur cooks in her adopted town. 'Everybody wants to do a flame cooking,' said she. 'And in Chicago, they want the flame three feet high. I always look for a fire escape.'

"Other food trends noted by columnist Paddleford: the elimination of an appetizer at dinner parties ('It's no disgrace at all to serve dinner without a first course'); filling guests awaiting dinner with cold soup from a cocktail shaker; casserole dishes that 'don't spoil if the crowd gets a little high.'"

By the 1950s, Paddleford's authority was widely acknowledged. This was in part because of her research and travel, but also because of her journalistic voice, close to the scene and ever speaking directly to her audience. It still retained its buoyancy and fanciful adjectives, but something had changed: More practice and the evolution of her own personal style with the times meant that Paddleford's copy, while still containing some exotic adjectives, now benefited from a top coat of sophisticated, polished professionalism. She sounded less awestruck and more "this is the way it's done."

Now she was able to visit the homes not just of women her tipsters had alerted her about but to choose people and recipes to profile that interested her personally. Her reasoning must have been that if she found a food subject compelling enough, she could make her readers see exactly how and why. She turned out to be right, as was the case with her column about Robert P. Tristram Coffin's lobster stew. Paddleford had made Dr. Coffin's acquaintance during her travels in Maine, a state whose understated beauty and glorious natural food resources held a special place in her heart. Coffin, age sixty-one in 1953, was not only the Pierce Professor of English at Bowdoin College, just down the road from a working farm on the Kennebec River that Paddleford had herself purchased the year before, but he was also a poet and writer who had won the Pulitzer Prize for his work of poems *Strange Holiness* (Macmillan, 1935). Pretty distinguished company for a Kansas farm girl, a fact hardly lost on the reporter herself.

"Hearing that I was in Maine to collect lobster recipes, Dr. Coffin invited me for dinner at his saltwater farm in Pennellville, a few miles out of Brunswick . . . 'About the recipe, Dr. Coffin,' I had my pencil in hand. 'You must know the history of each lobster you cook,' said my host."

One triumph of this article is that it takes what was a hard to find and expensive ingredient, fresh lobster, and makes it seem as down-to-earth as a burger on the grill, something anyone could prepare at any time. It not only demystifies lobster, but suggests that preparing it is almost a poetic duty. Even if a reader in someplace like Minneapolis could never get her claws on a Maine lobster, she could at least savor its description.

By June 1951, according to a feature called "Sidelines" in *This Week*, Paddleford had published twenty-one installments of her "How America Eats" series, flown more than twelve thousand miles, and visited fifteen states. Duncan Hines was probably lurching against his cake mixes. What came next was natural: travel abroad.

Dr. Coffin's Lobster Stew

4 cups Maine seawater or 4 cups fresh water with 2 tablespoons
salt, plus additional salt to taste

6 medium lobsters (about 1¼ pounds each)

1 stick butter

3 pints milk

1 pint cream

Bring 2 cups water to a boil in a 10- to 12-quart pot with a tight-fitting lid. Lay in 3 lobsters on their backs, shell side down, to steam in their own juices. Cover and steam over high heat 7 or 8 minutes. Remove from pot and repeat with remaining saltwater and lobsters. The meat will be slightly underdone; pick it from shell while hot. Remove intestinal vein and lungs. Chop meat into large bite-size chunks.

Melt butter in a large pot over low heat and add lobster meat; sauté gently for 2 to 3 minutes. Add the milk, stirring clockwise constantly to keep the mixture from coagulating; bring almost to a froth but not to a boil, then add the cream and once again bring almost to a froth. Check the meat for doneness; if not quite cooked through, allow to simmer for a few additional minutes. Remove from heat. Season to taste. Serve immediately.

Yield: 6 servings

She became a frequent guest of newly expanded airline routes. In 1951 Air France flew her to Paris, Florence, and Rome on an ingenious mission: to learn "how Americans eat abroad." The stories filed from Denmark, Brazil, Italy, and elsewhere were similar to those in the "How America Eats" series, but they were less vigorously promoted. R. W. Apple Jr., whose own exotic datelines were followed closely by readers, noted that Paddleford was a weaker reporter away from home. Her wide-eyed approach left no margin for a commanding voice. Whereas her work on the regional American foodways was airtight with authority, the Europe-based columns would today be called gee-whiz journalism.

"Spring they say is when you fall in love," she rhapsodized from Copenhagen in 1951. "Then and there we fell in love with a country that makes joyous with flowers. No Danish table is completely set without at least one daffodil. Spread over the stalls and pavement were snowdrops, primroses, anemones, lilies-of-the-valley, baskets of sweet-scented violets—everywhere the bold tulip: red and yellow." She was there as one of ten American food editors invited by the Danish government. Paddleford wrote about pastries on the train from Copenhagen to the countryside; the 178 varieties of "smørrebrød," or open-faced sandwiches, served at Oskar Davidsen's restaurant; a visit with bleu cheese makers; and the curried eel at the Hotel D'Agleterre. Readers could get the recipe for the later, she wrote, via the sideline import company of a writer for a Copenhagen newspaper who was based on Madison Avenue in New York.

Three "news" stories, that is to say, articles about markets and economics that contained no recipes, were filed from this trip, all thickly buttered with wonder and awe. "The Nielsens are a family of four, and for food and household expenses they pay the equivalent of 300 kroner a month, or just about a third of the average worker's income which is around 9,000 kroner, or $1,260," she wrote, before noting that the mother "shops daily, foraging to take advantage of the good buys and to serve the perishables fresh"—partly because "she hasn't a refrigerator."

The jewel crowning Paddleford's work abroad in that decade was her trip to England for the coronation of Queen Elizabeth II in 1953. The correspondence to organize this enterprise created a file two inches thick, but the venture would yield eleven articles for the *Herald Tribune*, in addition to several for *This Week*, plus her monthly "Food Flashes" column for *Gourmet*. Paddleford was a whirlwind in a city that was overrun with correspondents.

The venerable food halls of Harrods in Knightsbridge got their innings in *Gourmet*. "I have visited most of the outstanding food stores of our larger cities and a few on the Continent, but I have never before seen anything equal to Harrods," she wrote. List after list of the fish, fowl, game, jams, and pies sweet and savory are proffered before a brief history of this emporium, which was 104 years old in 1953.

Perhaps the most inspired of what Paddleford called her "English series" is the piece in *This Week* about the coronation meal itself. Although not one of the select eight hundred invited guests (these consisted historically of people "representing the trade guilds of the City"), Paddleford scored interviews with both Lindsay R. Ring, general manager of Ring & Brymer, "the firm which has catered these Lord Mayor Coronation parties since the crowning of Victoria in 1837," and Arthur Edwards, the chief steward of the Lord Mayor of London, charged with arranging the banquet tables for the new Queen. Edwards is pictured in *This Week*, a tall, slim figure who resembles a white-haired, pointy-featured version of Vincent Price as he stands somewhat spookily above a table with a gigantic fruit arrangement and an ice sculpture of the Queen on horseback.

All the details of the six-course menu are provided (Queen Victoria had more than one hundred dishes, Paddleford noted), from the turtle soup ("Once the huge turtles weighing 150 to 250 pounds were imported by the captains of Her Majesty's ships returning from the West Indies. Now the big fellows come dressed and frozen") to the beef course consisting of "Aberdeen Angus steers . . . fattened in Scotland and properly aged" that were roasted at Mansion House and "carried sputtering hot, to Guildhall, four blocks away," to the traditional orange jelly–based dessert called Maids of Honor. "The 'Maids,' Mr. Ring told me, were first baked at the order of Henry VIII to please Anne Boleyn."

Files from the English trip provide a glimpse into a well organized machine of food journalism. The copious correspondence includes letters to and from Ring & Brymer; Huntley & Palmers, the cookie and cake manufacturers, who supplied Paddleford with special coronation tins for illustrations and gave her a bakery tour; and notes exchanged with Edith Walker, an official of the emergency meals division of the London Ministry of Food. She was referred to Paddleford by one of her frequent escorts, Bush Barnum, an advertising executive for the Glass Container Manufacturers Institute.

Paddleford came to know Barnum through her work, but he was also a man about town. He was included, along with Fred Astaire, Miles Davis, and Douglas Fairbanks Jr., in *Esquire* magazine's 1960 list of America's best dressed men. The citation said Barnum "graduated from Colgate in 1933, resides in Gramercy Park in one of Manhattan's most desirable apartments, and has

Maids of Honor

¾ cup whole blanched almonds

1 14-ounce package prepared puff pastry

½ cup sugar

2 egg yolks, beaten

2 tablespoons heavy cream

1 tablespoon all-purpose flour

Grated peel of 1 lemon

1 large egg

1 teaspoon water

Preheat oven to 350 degrees.

Roast nuts on a baking sheet in oven until golden, 10 to 12 minutes.

Cool and process until fine in a spice grinder. Set aside.

Turn oven up to 400 degrees. Line 12 tart pans 2½ to 3 inches across with pastry. Alternatively, you can bake the tarts free-form by placing 12 2-inch to 3-inch squares of pastry on a sheet pan. In a medium bowl, combine nuts, sugar, egg yolks, cream, flour, and lemon peel in order given. Distribute the filling evenly into pastry shells or centers of squares.

continued on next page

Make an egg wash by beating the whole egg with the teaspoon of water. Brush tarts with egg wash. Bake for 20 to
25 minutes. Cool and remove from pans.

Yield: 12 tarts

been a Bernard Weatherhill—$260 and up per three-piece suit—
customer for more than a decade." Barnum offered to help con-
nect Walker and Paddleford ("I think Miss Walker has both
charm and ability, and that you might find a talk with her on
Britain's plans for emergency feeding interesting and worth-
while," he advised). Paddleford took the advice and seemed to
develop a warm relationship with Walker.

After the trip, she wrote to Walker: "When you come again to
the States, and of course you will, be sure to contact me in advance
of your visit. I'd love to take you to some of the interesting dining
spots here. Or a weekend in Connecticut where I have a small
house. You would like Connecticut; it is not too different from the
English countryside in Kent." In thanks for the time Walker spent
entertaining her, Paddleford gave her a *Gourmet* subscription.

The vast English correspondence seems to have been divided between Helen Marshall, who typed most of the letters to
Ring & Brymer, and Anna Marie Doherty, Paddleford's home
secretary, who handled Walker. Even two secretaries were not
quite enough. In a thank-you letter to Walker, she apologized for
a delay, saying that when she got back "as usual, I would be
months catching up with my mail."

Some letters took precedence, of course—especially those
passed along by her boss at *This Week*, Bill Nichols. A Mr. G. C.

Vandegrift of Philadelphia had written to Nichols questioning a caption for a picture showing "Elizabethan serving wenches," the table implements that were on display in London's Gore Hotel. The missive found its way to Paddleford via Joan Rattner, Paddleford's copy editor there, who asked Paddleford: "Can you give him any kind of answer as to where you got terms?"

Paddleford hopped to it, providing Vandegrift with the contact information he would need. "I am the writer of this Coronation article and was in London to get the facts for the story," she began. "I interviewed Robin Howard, owner of the Gore Hotel, whose idea it was to set up the Elizabethan dining room and made a study of that period: food, decorations, table utensils, everything in keeping. If you will write to him I know that he can answer your questions, for he spent more than year doing research of that period to have his dining room authentic in every detail."

Rattner had inherited the editing of the "How America Eats" columns from her predecessor at *This Week*, Mary Lyons, in the early 1950s. She was a logical choice because she had spent about six months at the Home Institute before moving on to the Sunday supplement. Paddleford, she said, was hardly ever in the *This Week* office, conducting virtually all of her business there over the phone. Crucially, there was no test kitchen at *This Week*. Recipes for *This Week* were tested in the *Trib* kitchens or, on rare occasions, in the kitchens of freelance testers Paddleford employed in a pinch. Paddleford's issues with her *This Week* editors were all about words and for that, the phone would suffice.

"Mary was a very sweet, lovely person," Rattner, now Joan Rattner Heilman, a book author, recalls, "but I challenged Clementine more. She had some really weird sentence structure sometimes and if I made any changes in that sentence structure she would get really angry. She wanted things exactly as she wrote it. *Exactly as she wrote it.*" Rattner says that when she got to *This Week*, Paddleford was already a star and had the affect, behavior, and physical appearance of "a very strange woman," in part because of her voice. "It was a voice like you never heard in your life, a very hoarse whisper," Rattner says. Added to that were her unusual clothes. "She always wore a huge cape, kind of a beige-brown." Rattner emphasizes that Nichols was very pleased at having Paddleford, strange or not, on his staff. "Respectful is the word for the relationship between Clementine and Bill," she recalled. "He didn't know her very well, to tell you the truth," she says, but he was "very proud" of her, "she was a well-known person, an authority in her field."

"Her recipes were pretty darn good; I still use them," Rattner says.

Paddleford's "How America Eats" columns were on full boil, the author a seemingly inexhaustible source of ideas for what to cover next. For instance, Paddleford met Commander Winfield G. Knopf of the Navy, an officer aboard the aircraft carrier Leyte, at a small dinner in Manhattan. His ship was at the Brooklyn Navy Yard for an equipment overhaul. No unsuspecting table companion was left unmolested and soon, Paddleford had arranged for a tour of the vessel. Once aboard the "floating city," Paddleford discovered a lesson in economy, reporting that the Leyte saved the Navy money because its cooks studied their garbage to determine what was not consumed, and then struck those items from future menus. The cooks reported that they gave three choices of meats, at least four vegetables, and six salads per day. Hits included such stick-to-your ribs classics as hamburger pie, fried shrimp, pizza, and chicken cacciatore.

As she had done years before with her *Farm & Fireside* editors Martin and Wing, Paddleford took up the habit of sending Nichols memos of her travels—and of how she was spending *This Week*'s money.

One trip to the Pacific Northwest in 1956 yielded a whopper memo of more than thirty-five pages in which Paddleford updated her boss on the minutiae of her findings. Observations included the fact that "buffet-style entertaining is replacing sit-down dinner," "the diet trend is everywhere," and "husbands [are] helping with meal preparation—more so in cities and where women work outside the home."

One detail from this trip that she found less inspiring: "Outside big cities highballs and cocktails belong only before dinner or on party occasions. After life in New York and weekend living nearby I was surprised, yes and disappointed, that seldom, almost never, did anyone suggest a 'drink,' 'Won't you have a drink,' meant coffee, tea, or lemonade." This kind of note, a "data dump" in today's newsroom parlance, is usually written by a reporter eager to show that the travel expenses are worth the cost; it's difficult to imagine that Nichols would have cared in the case of his ace food writer, but these memos certainly didn't diminish his estimation of her as earning her paycheck.

When not roaming the land, Paddleford was meantime fighting hard to maintain a semblance of a personal life. Receiving a letter in the 1950s from Helen Hostetter, a professor of journalism at her alma mater, she responded to a question about job satisfaction. The up sides: "Life is never dull" and also "That my work is fun. That few people are allowed to plan their own schedules, articles & go where they please no questions asked."

The drawback: "No time for friends or quiet weekends in the sun at my Connecticut hilltop."

Paddleford distributed her limited spare time on her own priorities, but her choices now reflected her income. Weekends and evenings went to air navigation classes at New York University, where she enrolled in 1953. She wrote about this to Louise Swanson, a source from Flushing, Queens, whose husband was general manager of S. B. Thomas, a Manhattan bakery opened in 1847, today a huge enterprise whose leading brand is Thomas' English Muffins. Mrs. Swanson's son also had a tracheotomy tube. Paddleford wrote that flying was a singular pleasure. "I hope that he has found, as I have, that a breathing tube need not spoil one's life in any way, except that you can't go swimming, and tennis is too strenuous a game for me," she wrote. "So, I have taken up flying for recreation. I don't fly well but at least have my student's license and am studying Navigation to try for my Pilot's License this next summer."

Her flying did improve, when she had time for her instruction. Paddleford wrote to her cousin Alice Paddleford Wood, whose family was to visit New York in the late summer of 1954, she would not be able to see them: "I'm so very disappointed, Alice, that your visit here is timed almost exactly to my trip to Alaska . . . to do a series of articles on salmon fishing and canning," she wrote. "This had been a year of travel: to Brazil on coffee, Central America on bananas, France on wine—now Alaska . . . Maybe some day I can fly up and visit you. I'm getting pretty good now at finding my way. For a long time I was constantly getting lost—I'm not much good on directions."

Spatial relations did present her with problems: In 1952,

she filled out a questionnaire from a publicity company that wanted to accommodate her needs. It asked whether she preferred horizontal or vertical photographs. She responded that she couldn't remember which was which, but that she liked this kind, and then she drew a vertical rectangle on the questionnaire.

Connecticut was still her main place for relaxation. Weekends there were now spent with friends like Barnum and Alice Nichols. Claire had grown up, finished school, and, thanks to Paddleford, was engaged to be married. Through one of her contacts from her Danish food reporting, Paddleford had introduced the young Wellesley grad, then interning at the *Herald Tribune* in the photography department, to a handsome young Danish soldier named John Jorgensen. They wed in November 1952. That year, seemingly as a wedding present, Paddleford purchased a one hundred fifty-acre farm with a rambling house near Bath, Maine—not far from the one owned by Dr. Robert Coffin that she had so admired—for the young couple. She insisted that she, too, would use the house for vacations, perhaps so they would not feel beholden.

Claire reports that she fell so in love with the farm that she often dreamed of it while riding the subway in New York, and that one day while out buying shoes she realized it would be just as easy to do the things she needed to do in Maine as in Manhattan. "Just like that, we picked up and moved," she says. By 1956, the Jorgensens were in Maine full time and set about becoming locals, beginning a steady stream of improvements to the farmhouse, adding new rooms and buildings across the property, and keeping goats. Their first child, Mark, was born in July that year. Today, he lives on the farm and runs a landscaping business.

He, too, has added buildings to the farm, including converting the property's stable into a garage to shelter Paddleford's

1960 Studebaker Lark convertible, the car she once used to tool around in Connecticut. As it happened, she seldom visited the house in Maine, though she often met the Jorgensens in Connecticut for family time and at holidays.

Paddleford, now in her middle fifties, was wearing out some. In the fall of 1956 she reported in a memo to Nichols that she was suffering back pain and "battle fatigue" from fighting her *Trib* editors for more space for food versus fashion, and also from the occasional skirmish for column inches versus colleagues like Guin Hall and Isabel McGovern. Some of this may have been exaggerated, because in the same letter she also said she was insisting the paper give her an assistant to stave off becoming "a basket case." Nichols presumably would be an ally in this effort.

A couple of weeks later, Paddleford reported in a letter to Hilda Hamlin of Northampton, Massachusetts, who had become a steady correspondent in the late 1940s, that her doctor had suggested a brief hospitalization, presumably for the back. Instead, she decided to check into the Waldorf-Astoria with her cat Pussy Willow. "My ailment—back muscles that wouldn't function," she wrote. "I was immobilized for a few days." After four days being waited on and afraid that Pussy Willow would escape the room, Paddleford checked out and returned to work, apparently feeling well enough to resume travel.

A trip to New Orleans in December 1957 had more to do with official *This Week* business than with reporting on the place Paddleford acknowledged was a great favorite. A detailed letter to Nichols notes she was a guest of both Wesson Oil and of its advertising company, the Fitzgerald Agency. Paddleford's letter reveals more of herself than she ordinarily let out, acknowledging that constant chaperoning by various officials left her "exhausted just being pleasant" because "twenty-four hours is about my limit on that." A dinner companion, the wife of the ad agency's vice president, she related, "drank too much and left with the shrimp," although "she is old family New Orleans society, so it didn't matter."

The sponsors of the trip had crucial business in mind in inviting the prominent editor. In the same way that electric range manufacturers were battling to change the basic cooking instruction "turn off the gas" to "remove from the heat," the oil companies sought to get their generic phrases imbedded in the language. Vegetable oils were burgeoning, with competing versions and competing labels. For instance, Kraft called its product "all-purpose oil," while Lever Brothers identified its liquid Spry as "liquid shortening." Wesson was trying to persuade Paddleford, and in turn *This Week*, to use its generic version, "vegetable oil." By flying the reporter down, wining and dining her and putting her up in what she described as a suite "furnished with antiques of the seventeenth and eighteenth centuries" that went for the then-exorbitant rate of $68 a night, they succeeded. But there may have been an iron fist in the lavish glove: Wesson had apparently threatened to pull its advertising. This is referred to in correspondence from George Beveridge, *This Week*'s Atlanta-based advertising director, who wrote to Nichols of Paddleford's visit: "It is rare and wonderful and hasn't she done us a lot of good! I really think that this is now all settled and in the respectable way in which we would like to have it settled."

Nichols forwarded Beveridge's letter to Paddleford with a note that read: "Here are happy words from N.O." Whatever her role as a diplomat, Paddleford didn't come away with nothing, publishing a column about a wonderful dinner at Brennan's, a newer and beloved restaurant in the French Quarter, where the owner, Ella Brennan, sent over a bottle of 1953 Pomeroy Champagne "as I have known Ella fairly well and had written about their restaurant at its very beginning." In return, Paddleford carried a recipe for Brennan's shrimp bisque.

This piece of give-and-take is an example of everyday business in the life of Paddleford, who at this point was a star. As proof, she rounded out 1957 as the recipient of one of five awards given at the annual Front Page Dinner Dance of the New York Newspaper Women's Club. The emcee of the evening was Steve Allen, the keynote speaker Governor W. Averell Harriman. A fellow recipient, for her series of reports about the conditions in the Soviet Union in her column, carried in the *New York Post*, was Eleanor Roosevelt. Lustrous company indeed for Paddleford, who won "for her prediction about the changing eating habits of the American people"—yet another of her trend stories.

Occasionally, though, Paddleford delved into unusual territory—away from trends and practical home cooking matters and into customs and ceremonies. A 1957 column about "traditional Jewish sweets" baked in the home of Mrs. Norman Less of Cleveland, Ohio, is a perfect example. Less served hamantaschen, the tri-cornered jam-filled cookie served at Purim.

"I asked the reason for Purim," Paddleford wrote. "Mrs. Less explained it has been celebrated for around 2,400 years. It's on this day the Book of Esther is read aloud to Jewish congregations in commemoration of her successful appeal to Ahasuerus, the ancient Persian Emperor, to save her people from the mass death planned by the Grand Vizier, Haman." Paddleford did something smart with this column: reminded readers they needn't be Jewish to enjoy a good cookie. "But we like them just any time," she wrote, depicting the Less family's love of playing bridge and the fervent requests of their friends to bring hamantaschen over "just

Hamantaschen

Dough:

2½ cups sifted flour

½ teaspoon salt

½ pound butter, room temperature

3 egg yolks

3 tablespoons white vinegar

3 tablespoons cold water

In a medium bowl, combine 1½ cups of the flour, salt, and butter, rubbing butter into flour with fingers.

In a separate bowl, mix egg yolks with a fork. Add vinegar and water. Sift the remaining 1 cup flour into the egg mixture, mixing together lightly. Combine the mixtures and blend well with a fork. Store, covered, in the refrigerator 6 hours or overnight.

When ready to use, the dough will be sticky; work quickly while it is cold. Preheat oven to 400 degrees. Pick off dough the size of a walnut and roll on a well-floured surface into a 3¼-inch round. Place a level teaspoon of filling in a center. Pinch the sides together, forming 1 closed triangle over the

continued on next page

filling. Cut the pinched edges about ¼ inch deep at ½-inch intervals to give a scalloped top when baked. Place on an ungreased baking sheet. Bake for 20 minutes, or until browned.

Yield: 25 hamantaschen

Poppy-Seed Filling:

¾ cup ground or whole poppy seeds

½ cup whole milk

¼ cup honey

2 tablespoons chopped pecans

2 tablespoons sugar

⅛ teaspoon ground cinnamon

Place seeds in a fine strainer and run water through it again and again; if using whole poppy seeds, grind in coffee grinder. Place in top of double boiler with milk and cook over hot water until milk is absorbed; the filling will have thickened considerably. Add honey, pecans, sugar, and cinnamon. Cook about 4 minutes, stirring until sugar is dissolved and honey is blended. Cool, cover, and store in refrigerator.

Yield: about 2 cups

continued on next page

Apricot Filling:

1 cup dried apricots

¾ cup water

¾ cup sugar

Wash apricots. Chop coarsely. Place in small saucepan, add water, and cook over low heat until very soft, adding more water if necessary. Add sugar and heat, stirring constantly, until fruit comes to a boil, about 12 minutes. Cool, cover, and store in refrigerator.

Yield: about 2 cups

The filling in these two recipes is more than enough for the 25 turnovers in the pastry recipe. The poppy filling will keep for three days in the refrigerator and the apricot for two weeks.

any time." An accompanying photograph showed Less baking with her grandchildren, Laurel and Richard Kronenberg; another showed a platter of hamantaschen on a lace tablecloth. "Mother was delighted and she liked being in the limelight after Clementine's article was published," Jacqueline Kronenberg, Less's daughter, now a retired preschool teacher in suburban Cleveland, said. In addition, her mother received letters asking about the tablecloth, and the letters, as well as the recipe, are still in the family.

Sometimes "How America Eats" columns took readers to less homey events. Paddleford visited Washington, D.C., at least twice in six years to investigate. In 1951 she profiled Mary Turner, for twenty-seven years director of the Home Service Bureau of the Potomac Electric Power Company; in this position Turner supervised the cooking classes that the company sponsored for hundreds and hundreds of women over the years. Paddleford made the bold statement that Turner "has done more, perhaps, than any other one person to influence the eating habits of cross-country America" because "all of these years she had taught women cooking, the tried and true and things brand-new" and her "influence has been nation-wide."

Turner was indeed a powerful person, the kind of home economics wizard who might have earlier misjudged a young Paddleford because she lacked a home ec degree. There was nothing but love between the two, though, when Paddleford visited Turner at home; Paddleford displays a pitch-perfect ear for the life of a capital hostess. In that city, she notes, "women come, women go. They come from every state in the Union, live for a period, then home again to show the neighbors how it's done."

What Paddleford wanted from Turner was a glimpse into what it was like to be a fixed star in an ever-changing galaxy, and as usual she honed in with her most important question: " 'Is there any one food belonging especially to Washington?' we wanted to know. 'Yes, the blue crab of the Chesapeake,' " was Turner's reply before offering up her own favorite recipe.

The second time Paddleford hit the capital was in 1957, when she was among the journalists invited to cover the unveiling of the "Senate salad," an event theoretically created by senators from seven states to tout their regional produce. Paddleford joined the "movie and TV cameras" in the Senate Dining Room in Washington in June 1957 for this one. "The salad recipe was

All the Sights and Smells of the Country   197

Casserole of Baked Crab Imperial

2 cups whole milk

3 tablespoons butter

2 tablespoons all-purpose flour

1 teaspoon salt

⅛ teaspoon black pepper

Dash cayenne

1 egg yolk, beaten

2 tablespoons sherry

1 cup soft bread crumbs

2 tablespoons minced fresh parsley

1 tablespoon minced onion

1 pound jumbo lump crabmeat

¼ cup toasted buttered bread crumbs

1 teaspoon sweet paprika

Preheat oven to 400 degrees.

In a small pan, warm milk over low heat. Meanwhile, in a medium pan over low heat, melt butter. Whisk in flour, raising heat slightly, and continue to cook until blended, about 2 minutes. Gradually whisk in warmed milk and seasonings and bring to a low simmer, stirring constantly, until

continued on next page

thickened, about 2 minutes. Gradually add egg yolk, tempering to prevent scrambling, and continue cooking 2 minutes more. Remove pan from heat. Add sherry, soft bread crumbs, parsley, and onion; mix gently. Season to taste with additional salt and pepper. Add crabmeat.

Pour into well-greased shallow 1½-quart casserole. Top with buttered crumbs and sprinkle with paprika. Bake 20 to 25 minutes. Serve with green salad and toasted bread, if you like.

Yield: 4 entrée or 6 appetizer servings

made in conference with seven states trying to mix garden wares. The problem was which state would give what?" The solution: tomatoes from New Jersey, California lettuce and avocados, watercress from West Virginia, grapefruit and romaine from Arizona, "little green onions" from Texas, and celery from Louisiana.

The final ingredient? "Nobody argued when Senator Margaret Chase Smith announced, 'Maine adds the lobster.' And beautiful it was with the claw pieces laid in a wide band over the top and more sweet lobster lumps waiting the fork interwoven through the greens." It turns out, Paddleford reported, that the official salad was a lot like one that Smith made for her family at home. "Senator Smith likes to serve the salad along with a steaming baked Maine potato. Dessert, I asked? Vanilla ice cream with fresh strawberry sauce. 'It's an old wives' tale,' Senator Smith said, 'that lobster and ice cream are incompatible.'" Paddleford pointed out to her readers not from Maine that they would find

Senate Salad

1 cup bite-size pieces butter lettuce

1 cup bite-size pieces romaine or escarole

½ cup bite-size pieces watercress

1½ cups diced fresh lobster meat

1 cup diced celery

½ cup thinly sliced green onions (green and white parts)

2 medium tomatoes, cubed

1 medium avocado, peeled, pitted, and cubed

5 large pimento-stuffed olives, sliced

8 or 12 segments from half a grapefruit

Salt and pepper, to taste

Combine lettuces and make a bed on 4 individual plates. Place the ingredients in rows or separate piles on the lettuce. Season with salt and pepper. Pass with Senate salad dressing.

Yield: 4 entrée salads

continued on next page

Senate Salad Dressing

½ cup olive oil

1 tablespoon plus 2 teaspoons white wine vinegar

1 small clove garlic, chopped

3 hard-cooked eggs, finely chopped

½ cup mayonnaise

1 tablespoon thinly sliced chives

½ teaspoon salt

Combine oil and vinegar and whisk in remaining ingredients.

Yield: 2 cups dressing

the recipe "an adjustable salad—instead of lobster, use chicken or shrimp, or crab meat. Or leave out the extras and make it a salad of greens."

Interviewing senators was big fun for Paddleford, and the chance to do turns like this one enhanced her profile as a reporter. Another less generic piece of work that separated the likes of Paddleford from other reporters, this time for reasons not of power but of restrained sentimentality, was her 1936 article "A Flower for My Mother." Though portions of it had already been published, Paddleford had kept the manuscript active and had worked on it, slowly and steadily, over the years. In 1958, she again took up that work in earnest, turning it into a longer essay. She sent a copy of the manuscript to Bill Nichols with a somewhat disingenuous cover letter. "Here is 'A Flower for My Mother' written out of my head and very quickly," she wrote. "This was first conceived as a 'Most Interesting Person' story for the *Reader's Digest*, but never completed, just put into outline form. I think this is oversentimental, but it's my general idea of the theme. You like it or you don't. Let me know soon."

It is clear that Paddleford hoped Nichols would choose a part for *This Week*, and described some additions she might make if he was interested, such as: "We had the only bathroom in a few hundred miles. All the children within a twenty-mile radius were invited to come on Saturdays and take turns at the tub." Nichols seized the piece and printed a great deal of it in two consecutive issues, May 18 and May 25, 1958, no revisions necessary.

It was an unqualified success, bringing hundreds of letters to *This Week*, such as one from Lawrence Thompson of Miami, whose parents were born in the Blue Valley. The town of Stockdale had been virtually demolished by 1957—it had been flooded to make way for the Tuttle Creek Dam in 1962—and when Paddleford replied to Thompson, she said: "I was in the valley only last August. It was all in ruin and gave me a heartache. I doubt, even with the dam opening delayed, that I will ever go back."

A Flower for My Mother was published by Henry Holt as a slim book bound in lilac purple, with an afterword by Nichols speaking of America's "No. 1 food editor."

The dedication is "To Jenny Jorgensen who is named for my mother." This second child of Claire's had just been born and Paddleford was clearly delighted at the arrival of a soul who would carry forward a name from the precious days in Kansas. If you can find it in the used-book market, this book is distilled Paddleford and in many ways less sentimental than its author believed. It was also more popular, perhaps, than she knew. A story published in the *Manhattan Mercury*, a Kansas daily, in May 1959, includes the following anecdote: "Not long ago a demonstration of [Paddleford's] fame came up in a column syndicated by Leonard Lyons. He was quoting Ernest Hemingway who was telling of his experience in autograph signing. The author remarked that once when he stopped in a small Italian village, residents quickly bought out every Hemingway book in the local store for autographing. Then they bought other books for him to sign. 'I was signing all sorts of books,' he said, 'from Galileo to Clementine Paddleford.'" The true collectors' item, then, might be *A Flower for My Mother* autographed by . . . Hemingway.

After all these years on top of her game, Paddleford had no intention of slowing down. But now this journalist, who had always extended an arm to help others, found herself with a powerful rival who had landed at the *Trib*'s competition, *The New York Times*.

Craig Claiborne was hired as a food writer for *The New York Times* in 1957, at the age of thirty-seven. He quickly became the restaurant reviewer, and ultimately the paper's chief food editor. He shared some background with fifty-nine-year-old Paddleford. Claiborne was born in the Mississippi Delta town of Sunflower, where he, like Paddleford, had an especially close relationship with his mother that in his case showed up in a love of cooking. Instead of feeding a farm and helping run a grocery, Claiborne's mother ran a boarding house. Claiborne's upbringing also informed his palate, especially his relationship with a succession of excellent black cooks who managed his mother's dining room and taught her son about food.

"I loved to 'pick' at foods that appealed to my sense of sight," he wrote in his memoir *A Feast Made for Laughter*, published in 1982, "crisp, browned bits of fried chicken that fell to the bottom of a serving dish; the crisp tail ends of fish that clung to the sides of a deep-fat fryer; the burnt edges of toast that were trimmed away; the remnants of pulp from squeezed lemons and oranges, the partly burnt crusts of pies."

Unlike Paddleford's, however, Claiborne's childhood was traumatic: *A Feast* details "many memories of pain," as the writer Roy Reed described in a book review, that Claiborne endured as "a man haunted by the memory of a hovering mother, a man of once-excessive appetite for drink and sex, a man tormented for years by early poverty, early fears and early homosexual guilt." The book details the shame Claiborne felt over a childhood spent in hatred of the sports that boys were expected to like, and includes a confession of sexual abuse by his father.

In his memoir, as the food writer Betty Fussell so aptly stated, Claiborne detailed himself as a man "in the Twain tradition of the picaresque rube who alternates between chutzpah and shame," a man who managed to escape the Delta in a yeoman's and then an ensign's uniform, first stationed in Morocco and then in Okinawa. Out of the service for good in 1953, Claiborne decided to follow his passion for food; he enrolled under the G.I. Bill in l'Ecole Hotelière de la Societé Suisse des Hoteliers in Lausanne, Switzerland. There he learned how to cook and, more important, appreciate the intricacies and traditions of fine French food. Upon returning to America, he landed a job writing about restaurants for *Gourmet*. He got through the final hurdle at *The New York Times* courtesy of a lucky Mississippi State connection—an irony, since Claiborne had felt unworthy as a young man at not having gotten into the famous university in Oxford. He thus became in 1957 "the first male food editor in a journalistic world dominated by women," as Fussell put it, in what was only a slight overstatement.

Claiborne came to stardom not as a food writer in the tradition of Paddleford, who was the hero to home cooks, but as a restaurant reviewer. His main objective was to codify restaurant atmosphere and food in a way that gave readers a good idea of how they might like to spend their money while on the town, and his public proved quite grateful. As a result, Claiborne earned a reputation as a bon vivant and a quasi-celebrity, the kind filled with great anecdotes about everyone's favorite restaurants—and once he even got arrested for drunken driving, in a story made humorous because he liked to tell it on himself.

Something about Claiborne vexed Paddleford, according to Claire Jorgensen. When asked about any journalist Paddleford might have considered a rival, Jorgensen cited only him. What she could not answer, though, was why Paddleford disdained a person from a similarly meager rural background who shared her zest for food.

A couple of reasons are possible. One is that Claiborne's earliest articles for the *Times* seem to show him nipping at Paddleford's heels. For example, in December 1965, Claiborne wrote about Paprikas Weiss, the Hungarian food importing business that had long been a favored source of Paddleford's. Claiborne wrote about the place, which by then had been in business for seventy-nine years in May 1966, as if he were the first to discover it, lauding its "special dumpling machine" used to make galuska, a side dish, served buttered, with goulash (the goulash recipe of the shop's second generation owner, Mrs. Alexander Weiss, is also given). This column appeared only about five months after Paddleford wrote in her regular column in the *Herald Tribune* that Paprikas Weiss had announced that the Hungarian goulash was coming to market in cans, a product she liked enough to recommend. The similarity of these two stories cannot have sat well.

Another factor is the emergence of the *Times* as a threat to the *Trib* itself. When Paddleford joined the *Trib*, it was by far the more exciting paper. By the late 1950s, however, its quality could not make up for its serious financial losses. The *Times* had one thing the *Trib* did not: its own Sunday magazine, which became a juggernaut for advertisers. "The *Times* ate the *Herald Tribune*, basically, because they managed to get a pile of money out of that Sunday magazine in co-op ads that were paid for by manufacturers," Betsy Wade explained. "Huge, huge ads. But the *Herald Tribune* got thinner and thinner and thinner and sadder." Shrewd as she was, Paddleford could not have mistaken this trend, and for all the job offers begging her to come do publicity work, there is no record of the *Times*'s ever knocking on her door. At this time, there were plenty of defections from the *Trib* to the *Times*, but not its biggest female stars: not Paddleford and not Eugenia Sheppard.

So Paddleford had to live with the emergence of Claiborne. However Paddleford may have been irritated by Claiborne's presence on "her" turf, she need not have worried about losing her audience. At this time, she was the grande dame of food writing, and everyone, including Claiborne, knew it. In his memoir, published fifteen years after Paddleford's death, Claiborne writes about coming onto the New York City restaurant scene in the late 1950s and finding it "a hick town." "The only much-read and much-quoted critic in town was Clementine Paddleford, a well-meaning soul whose prose was so lush it could have been harvested like hay and baled," he wrote. "The truth of the matter was, however, that Clementine Paddleford would not have been able to distinguish skillfully scrambled eggs from a third-rate omelet. I am not at all sure that she ever cooked a serious meal in her life. But she had a readership that was estimated at the time of her death as 12 million."

While Claiborne had youth on his side, he clearly misjudged Paddleford and misunderstood her mission. She never saw herself as a critic of the restaurant world; at least 90 percent of the "How America Eats" series, all 845 columns of it, are about the regional specialties of American home cooks. Her legacy is the definition of "regional American food," left in what is essentially map form, detailing the dishes, ingredients, and culinary customs and ceremonies of home cooks from Alaska to New York. "How America Eats" is a primer for understanding the foundation of American food—it shows how immigrant cooks adapted their old-fashioned, time-honored recipes with what they found in their new homes. In compiling the material, Paddleford's intention was to help home cooks figure out, using each other for inspiration, what to cook for dinner—and to tell the stories behind the original recipes. Of key importance is that Paddleford, unlike Claiborne, was *not* an expert cook—the kind of work she did, and the kind of legacy she left, was not something for the elite. It would not take an expert cook, after all, to translate the stories of home cooks and to show how they made their recipes. What it took was an expert writer who understood the magical way in which good food transforms ordinary meal-times. And at that, no one could rival the sixty-two-year-old Paddleford.

CHAPTER 6

What Men Eat on Submarines

$\mathcal{G}$rowing up on her family's farm in the Blue Valley of Kansas, Clementine Paddleford had outsize dreams—of becoming a famous writer and traveling the world, of being a household name, of being rich. At age sixty-two in 1960, she had achieved all of this. Where was there left to go? Thirty feet below sea level in a narrow steel tube, of course.

In July 1960, Clementine Paddleford did something that she likely never dreamed she would. She boarded the USS *Shipjack*, then the fastest nuclear submarine in the world, docked in the Thames River in Connecticut, for a day-long stay that included a submerging in Long Island Sound. Paddleford was as on-mission as ever, but this was unlike anything she had ever been on. As she climbed aboard, gripping the hem of her skirt as it threatened to swirl over her head, she must have looked a fright. "I had asked for it—a dive to the ocean floor," she would later report (in *This Week* on July 10, 1960). "The wind rushed at me like a mad bull. I clung to a one-rope rail, walked the narrow ramp from State Pier, New London, Conn., to the curved top of a mighty whale. It looked like a whale, but it was a different kind of fish."

The naval cadets all smiling and greeting her warmly must have found this curmudgeonly older woman, a food writer nonetheless, quite an amusement—here was Paddleford, thick gray fringe of bangs framing her wide-open face, cape draped over shoulders, notebook in hand. If she seemed silly to the young men in uniform, she could not have cared less.

"I had come aboard . . . to see how America eats in what the crew call 'our underwater hotel,'" but even for one willing to go to extremes, she couldn't help but find the experience harrowing. "I was clothed in darkness—and in gooseflesh. 'Who cares,' I thought to myself, 'what men eat on submarines?'" She was bound to have felt uneasy among the most powerful weapons the world had ever seen.

Still, she stood by the Navy chefs as they showed her around the tight quarters and narrow passageways of the six-foot-by-nine-foot "capsule kitchen" where they prepared three meals a day for seventy-five to one hundred men. Despite her protestations, Paddleford cared deeply about what men ate on submarines—and perhaps more important she understood that spending time on such a vessel would give readers an unexpectedly delicious vicarious thrill. Masking her fear as much as possible, she witnessed what likely was both the most unusual kitchen she'd ever been in and the most organized. No fish was left flipping around: From storage solutions—"Everything is compressed, even flour, always a bulky item aboard a ship, has been compressed to one-fourth its normal volume without loss of quality"—to various convenience-based innovations—"a one-

pound can of dehydrated orange juice crystals which will recon-
stitute to a one gallon beverage, with a space saving of 75
percent"—to the touchy issue of garbage disposal—"It is packed
in sacks weighted down, put in a projector like a miniature tor-
pedo tube, and fired out to the fish."

The *Skipjack* column attests to her ingenuity. In it, she an-
swers every question a reader didn't know he had about culinary
life on a submarine. The two recipes Paddleford picked to use
"are in quantity amounts, with the thought that these might be
useful when planning a community meal"—brownies to feed
eighty, and hamburger pie for one hundred. Whether or not her
readers ever put those mammoth recipes to use, they had to
admire Paddleford's willingness to go to any length to report
on food.

Maybe it was her swirly-twirly clothing, or maybe it was her
florid prose that morphed mushrooms into umbrellas, or maybe
her generally eccentric attitude—by this point Paddleford had
well earned what the writer David Kamp referred to in his 2006
book about the rise of American food culture, *The United States
of Arugula,* as a reputation for being an "endearingly loopy"
character. Still, boarding the *Skipjack* was no publicity stunt.

It had taken her more than a year of finagling to get clearance
to board the *Skipjack,* and she had worked so hard for the story
that her tenacity impressed her friend James Beard. In a letter to
Helen Evans Brown, the noted Californian chef and food writer,
in December 1959, Beard wrote: "Clementine was down here the
other night for her annual story-getting session. She was in fine
form and is hoping now to go out for a cruise on an atomic submarine to see how they all eat. She is surely the getting-aroundest
person I have ever known, except for Eleanor Roosevelt."

A careful observer might have noted, though, that despite the splashiness of the *Skipjack* article, Paddleford was not traveling as much as usual—the breakneck pace of the early years of "How America Eats" had slowed to the point that she spent a whole month—mid-August through mid-September of 1960—without a dateline on her columns.

Resting a bit on her oars meant that Paddleford devoted her articles to perennial seasonal classics: "Summer Salads, All Dressed Up" was about innovations in the salad dressing aisle and required little more than a trip to the supermarket and a call to some publicists. "Less than a decade ago salad dressings exceptional numbered under a hundred," she wrote. "Today there must be 20 big firms with complete lines of any kind of dressing you care to name. Some of these are ready mix packaged in envelopes, others ready to serve, to pour from the bottle. Why should a woman ever turn a hand to making salad dressing with such choice unlimited?" She goes on to tell the story behind the development of Wishbone's, Kraft's, and General Foods' lines of dressings, and to give three salad recipes, including a chicken-avocado version, that readers should try.

Later that month she turned her attention to "the many splendored squash," offering up a primer on "the Buffalo Bills of the vegetable bin" that "gallop into market with tough, hard exteriors hiding hearts of gold." As usual, she dipped her toe into the gourds' history ("The word squash comes from the Massachusetts Indian word Askutasquash. Spanish explorers took squash back to the old world . . . Navigators used a hollowed out calabash squash to sight the stars") before suggesting six ways, including the comfort food staple of a casserole of baked summer squash and cheese, to enjoy the stuff.

As summer wound down, the *Tribune* column of September 16, 1960, was given over to the country's "bountiful harvest of grapes" for which September through November is the big season. Here she elaborates on the several kinds of table grapes sold in markets ("starting with the little Perlette from Coachella Valley, then that red grape the Cardinal, followed by the flame Tokay and Red Emperor and finally the Almenia, a pale green grape"). Four recipes are included, from a humble grape cobbler to an haute hollandaise-topped trout Vernonique; these were "treasured recipes from the *Herald Tribune*'s Kitchen Collection"— repeats—since Paddleford hadn't visited any new kitchens.

A brief break was certainly permissible for someone like Paddleford. Moreover, at this point in history she was one of the few people that America trusted for cooking advice. But to keep herself on top, she'd need something more enduring than a newspaper column. It would be the publication of *How America Eats*, a collection of columns written for *This Week* between 1948 and 1960, that put the frosting on her career.

How America Eats was long in the making—the columns spanned twelve years of Paddleford's career, and the publication of the book took years instead of the months that it might take to produce a cookbook today. The process began in 1957 when Paddleford sold the rights to her column collection to Charles Scribner's—the same publishing house that in 1937 delivered to eager homemakers the seminal *America's Cookbook*, compiled by the Home Institute of the *New York Herald Tribune* with a foreword by Mrs. William Brown Meloney. Scribner's was experienced in handling and marketing cookbooks; as usual, Paddleford chose her collaborators wisely—and the Scribner people were pleased, too.

Chicken Avocado Salad

3 cups cooked chicken, in large chunks

1 teaspoon grated onion

½ cup diced celery

2 tablespoons light cream

½ cup mayonnaise (preferably homemade)

¾ teaspoon salt

Dash of black pepper

1 tablespoon lemon juice

1 medium avocado, peeled, pitted, and diced

In a large bowl, combine chicken, onion, and celery. In a small bowl, blend cream with mayonnaise, salt, pepper, and lemon juice. Toss to taste with chicken mixture—you may not need all the dressing. Lightly toss in avocado. Chill.

Yield: 4 servings

Escalloped Squash Casserole

1½ to 2 pounds yellow summer squash,
6 to 8 squash

1 medium onion, chopped

Salt, to taste

1½ cups white sauce, hot (see next page)

1 cup grated cheddar cheese

2 eggs, lightly beaten

1 cup dry bread crumbs

1 cup butter, melted

2 tablespoons grated parmesan cheese

Preheat oven to 325 degrees.

Slice squash into rounds ½-inch thick. Combine with on-ion. Place in boiling salted water to cover. Simmer 2 to 3 minutes, or until crisp-tender. Drain well. Combine hot white sauce and cheddar cheese: stir until cheese melts. Stir small amount of hot mixture into eggs; add to remain-ing sauce. Fold in squash.

Turn into a baking dish 10 inches by 10 inches, or any pan that will hold all of the squash in a layer 3 inches deep or less. Combine bread crumbs and butter; sprinkle over

continued on next page

squash mixture. Sprinkle with grated parmesan cheese. Bake, uncovered, 35 to 40 minutes, or until lightly browned.

Yield: 6 servings

White Sauce

1½ tablespoons butter

1½ tablespoons all-purpose flour

1½ cups hot milk

Salt, to taste

In a small, heavy saucepan, melt butter over low heat. Stir in flour with a wooden spoon. Continue stirring and cook for about 2 minutes; do not let the flour brown or color. Gradually whisk in hot milk, a little at a time, waiting after each addition for all milk to be absorbed. Bring to a simmer to thicken and salt to taste.

Trout Veronique

6 trout fillets, about 6 ounces each, from 3 fish

4 cups dry white wine

2 lemons, thinly sliced into rounds

Salt

12 to 18 seedless green grapes, each sliced into 4 rounds

1½ cups Hollandaise Sauce (see next page)

Preheat broiler.

In 1 or 2 heatproof baking dishes or a nonreactive roasting pan large enough to hold the 6 fillet pieces in a single layer, bring the wine and lemon slices to a gentle simmer; do not boil. Season fillets to taste with salt. Slide fillets into simmering liquid, cover pan with foil, and remove from heat. Check for doneness in 2 or 3 minutes. Gently remove fillets when still slightly underdone and pink and place them skin-side down on a heatproof platter.

Distribute grape pieces over top of fillets and pour about 4 tablespoons of the sauce on each. Place under the broiler until golden brown, 3 to 4 minutes.

Yield: 6 servings

continued on next page

Hollandaise Sauce

1 cup butter, clarified

2 tablespoons white wine vinegar

1 tablespoon water

1 tablespoon minced onion

3 peppercorns

4 egg yolks

Juice of ¼ lemon

Salt

To clarify butter: Slowly melt butter. Let stand until clear part can be skimmed off easily. Reserve.

In a small saucepan place vinegar, water, onion, and peppercorns. Cook over very low heat to reduce liquid to 1 teaspoon. Remove peppercorns. Cool.

Put egg yolks and reduced vinegar in a medium metal bowl over a medium pan of water on a very low simmer and whisk constantly until it is lemon-colored. Continue to whisk while slowly drizzling in clarified butter. Add lemon juice at the end and then salt to taste. Adjust the texture if necessary by adding a little water; the sauce should be pourable but still fairly thick. Pour over fillets immediately.

Yield: about 2 cups

"I was delighted to hear from William Nichols that you will be able to take time off this summer to devote yourself entirely to *How America Eats*," Burroughs Mitchell, an editor at Scribner's, wrote to Paddleford in early June 1957. "I am writing now just to tell you that our interest and confidence in the book haven't lessened in the least, and to remind you that we are ready to pay an advance any time you want it." The advance, $1,500, was deposited into Paddleford's account at Chase Manhattan later that summer, and indeed there were two months in the autumn of 1957 when Isabel McGovern and Guin Hall wrote all of the food articles for the *Herald Tribune* in Paddleford's stead, although there was no mention of her absence in the paper and her byline continued to appear sporadically in *This Week*, in columns filed in advance.

The so-called sabbatical was put to good use. Finally Paddleford's columns were organized geographically. When the book went into the stores in time for Christmas 1960 at $10 a copy, it was an immediate hit. Most of the credit goes to the variety of recipes, of course, but there was also an especially winning foreword, a short essay by Paddleford describing not only what readers would find inside but also laying out her assessment of eating in America. It is arguably the most stirring writing of her career, the kind of muscular prose that hooks readers and drags them along on what Paddleford called a "voyage of discovery" into the world of food.

"This book has been twelve years in the writing," it begins, establishing immediately the fact that shoe-leather reporting and serious scholarship have been involved. Next, Paddleford lays out her methodology: "It was in January 1948 I started crisscrossing the United States as roving Food Editor for *This Week*

Magazine—my assignment, tell 'How America Eats.' I have traveled by train, plane, automobile, by mule back, on foot—in all over 800,000 miles," she asserts. That is more than three times the distance from the earth to the moon, all in the service of food, over twelve years.

"I have ranged from the lobster pots of Maine to the vineyards of California, from the sugar shanties of Vermont to the salmon canneries in Alaska," she writes. "I have collected these recipes from a wide variety of kitchens: farm kitchens, apartment kitchenettes, governors' mansions, hamburger diners, tea rooms and from the finest restaurants with great chefs in charge. I have eaten with crews on fishing boats and enjoyed slum gullion at a Hobo Convention. I have eaten many regional specialties I had never eaten before—cioppino on Fisherman's Wharf in San Francisco, Alaskan King Crab of the North Pacific in Seattle, mango ice cream in Tampa, chawed on cuts of fresh sugar cane in Louisiana, eaten roasted young goat in San Antonio, and roasted fresh truffles flown in from Italy at the Four Seasons in New York."

What was left to explain was quality control: How did Paddleford ensure, with all the foods she had tasted, that each recipe was the genuine article? Paddleford plunges in: "This book is based on personal interviews with more than 2,000 of the country's best cooks. And I have eaten every dish in the book at the table where I found it. I have eaten each dish again when the recipes were tested by home economists in *This Week*'s kitchen."

Of course, *This Week*'s office had no ovens and no home economists; the *Herald Tribune* provided both. Rather than explicate the arcane financial arrangements between the magazine and the newspaper, Paddleford simplified them. For instance, it would not have been a selling point for people reading *This Week* in, say, the *Cincinnati Enquirer*, to learn that the recipes were tested at the *New York Herald Tribune*. Because the finances meant that the ninth-floor domain at the *Trib* was as much the *This Week* kitchen as the *Trib* kitchen, readers of the book were not being deceived. This situation merely highlights the murkiness of the *This Week–Herald Tribune* relationship. For instance, some editors who worked only on the *Herald Tribune* edition were paid by *This Week* in its corporate guise as the United Newspapers Magazine Corporation; however, they also got small *Herald Tribune* payments for picture layouts and other work for the beefed-up edition distributed with the *Herald Tribune*. National advertisers in *This Week* who were based in New York thought that their ads appeared everywhere in the same plump magazine they saw in New York; however, the national advertisers who were based in Cincinnati would have seen their ads in a rather thinner magazine. No one lied exactly, but no one strained to tell the truth.

Further in her introduction to *How America Eats*, Paddleford meets the question of the title: How does America eat? And at this point, her question reaches the rich, rotund level where her writing has always been: America, she said, eats on the fat of the land, in every language.

"For the most part, however," she continues, "even with the increasingly popular trend toward foreign foods, the dishes come to the table with an American accent. From the very beginning, American dishes came from many countries, made from recipes German, Swedish, Italian, ad infinitum. . . . In some regions these dishes have kept their original character. But more often, over the years, they have been mixed and Americanized.

"The pioneer mother created dishes with foods available. These we call regional. It is these, perhaps, I have given the greatest emphasis here. However, I am not given to food favorites, hold no food prejudices. Good food is good food, wherever you find it. Many of these recipes were salvaged from batter-splashed, hand-written notebooks. The great majority had never been printed until they appeared in *This Week*. They are word-of-mouth hand-downs from mother to daughter. To get such recipes takes ever-lasting patience, and a dash of effrontery, too."

Here is likely the first published definition of regional American food; before that, there was considered to be no such thing—food was French or Italian or German, but never, ever American. It took Paddleford to come along and explain how a dish like Hungarian goulash, if it was made in someplace like Cincinnati, was just as American as it was Magyar.

In this book, Paddleford documented the way in which immigrants influenced the American table, and she did this by spending quality time in the kitchens of people like Mrs. Norvin H. Vaughan, who every Christmas baked traditional German sweets like *schokoladeplatzchen* (pronounced as shokoladepletzheeyen, or little chocolate drops); Mrs. Eliot Fletcher, who hailed from a family of cigar makers who left Cuba for Tampa and served up a killer Spanish *boliche* (eye roast stuffed with olives, lime juice, ham, and garlic); Mrs. Carl Stewart, the former food editor of the *Des Moines Register*, who made vinegary barbecued pork; and Mrs. Thomas W. Jensen of Salt Lake City, whose apple dumplings put those of her eight daughters-in-law to shame.

Clementine Paddleford, 1958

Clementine Paddleford interviewing a worker at Sunkist Growers, January 1959

The Hot Dog Society of America

Be it hereby known unto the entire World of Gastronomy that

Clementine Paddleford

of

New York Herald Tribune

is a duly elected and certified Charter Member of the Hot Dog Society of America, for unalterable loyalty to the creed that this most traditional and succulent of all American delicacies deserves a lofty place in the hall of fame of earthly cuisine, and for indefatigable, selfless service in spreading this symbol of joy throughout all mankind and for the infinite taste and wisdom in choosing this dish to relish above all others; and has thereby earned all rights and privileges entitled to a bonafide hot dog gourmet, including the inevitable respect accorded a person of obvious epicurean discrimination.

Be it so inscribed on this *29* day of *May* in the year *1961* for the National Hot Dog and Sausage Council:

Red Skelton
Chairman

*Clementine Paddleford's certificate as Charter Member of
the Hot Dog Society of America, May 29, 1961*

*A sample of the approximately seven hundred
menus in the Clementine Paddleford Papers.
Front cover of menu, Le Château Richelieu,
New York, April 15, 1963.*

*Inside page of the Le Château Richelieu
menu, April 15, 1963. Signatures of
those attending the dinner.*

T. Norman Palmer, president of the Society of Gourmets for the Leisure Arts, presents Clementine Paddleford (center) with an award as Lillian Ross (right) looks on, March 1964.

Clementine Paddleford, third from left, receives approximately 35,000 recipes in her Cook Young Recipe Swap, 1965.

Clementine Paddleford is greeted by an old friend—Mr. DeSoto, president of the Olive Association, Seville, Spain, October 1965.

Get well card to Clementine Paddleford from conference goers, prior to her death in 1967

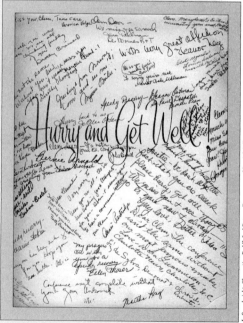

Signatures of conference goers on a get well card they sent to Clementine Paddleford in 1967

Clementine Paddleford relaxing on a screened porch on a hot July day, ca. 1952

Clementine Paddleford (left) talks to two women on a beach, ca. 1955.

Silhouette of Clementine Paddleford, ca. 1954.
Photographer: Arthur J. Daley, who died February 1987.

Clementine Paddleford, wearing a polished cotton dress, examines several products, including Dorset Chicken Gumbo Soup, Extendo (Good Housekeeping Seal of Approval), and Cassava Lace (Au Gourmet brand by Meyer and Lange), ca. 1949.

Clementine Paddleford interviewing an unknown man, ca. 1953

Clementine Paddleford in her New York Herald Tribune *office reading correspondence from Marion C. Dennis, ca. 1955*

Clementine Paddleford, right, and two other women enjoy a meal of clams, ca. 1955.

Passenger Clementine Paddleford rides sidesaddle aboard a scooter, ca. 1965.

Caricature of Clementine Paddleford by Dick Kirshbaum, Food Editor, Newark News, while in France in 1946

Schokoladeplatzchen
(Little Chocolate Drops)

¾ cup blanched almonds

3 egg whites

⅛ teaspoon salt

½ cup sugar

4 ounces German sweet chocolate, finely grated

Preheat oven to 275 degrees.

In two batches, process almonds in food processor until nuts are a fine powdery mixture; take care not to overprocess. Remove any large pieces of nuts that remain. In a large bowl, beat egg whites with salt to firm, moist peaks. Add sugar slowly, beating constantly, until mixture becomes slightly glossy. After adding last of sugar, beat 2 minutes more. Fold in processed almonds and grated chocolate.

Drop by heaping teaspoonfuls onto a lightly greased baking sheet. Bake 35 to 40 minutes, or until dry enough to remove from sheet.

Yield: about 50 cookies

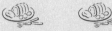

Boliche

8 strips salt pork, each strip about 1 inch by 3 inches by ¼ inch

3½- to 4-pound brisket of beef

8 strips ham, each strip about 1 inch by 3 inches by ¼ inch

32 pimiento-stuffed olives

4 cloves garlic, finely chopped and crushed
to a paste-like consistency

4 tablespoons olive oil

¼ cup lime juice

½ cup white wine

¼ cup chopped parsley

1 cup coarsely chopped onions

1 teaspoon salt

2 cups homemade beef stock or canned low-sodium consommé

Simmer salt pork in water for about 2 minutes; remove and set aside. Remove silver skin and fat from beef and wipe with damp cloth or paper towels.

Take a sharp, slender knife and, holding it at a 45-degree angle from meat, make 16 deep incisions, wide enough to accommodate the strips of pork and ham, almost through the meat from end to end. Fill incisions with strips of salt

continued on next page

pork and ham. Make 8 more incisions and fill with olives. Force fillings in with fingers. Mix garlic with 1 tablespoon oil, rub over meat. Place in shallow pan. Squeeze lime juice over meat; add wine, parsley, onions, and salt. Let meat stand, covered, in this marinade in the refrigerator at least 8 hours or overnight. Turn occasionally so that all sides are marinated.

When ready to cook, preheat oven to 325 degrees. Remove meat from marinade, scraping off all onions. Reserve marinade. Pat brisket dry. Brown on both sides in 3 tablespoons of oil in a Dutch oven with a tight lid. Pour marinade back over meat, adding beef stock, enough to cover meat about halfway. Cover tightly. Bring to a simmer. Remove from stovetop and place in oven for 3½ to 4 hours, or until fork-tender. Remove meat, skim excess fat from gravy, and strain into bowl, or purée with the onions. Slice meat across grain in ½-inch slices and serve on warm platter.

Yield: 6 to 8 servings

Apple Dumplings

1 cup sifted all-purpose flour

2 teaspoons baking powder

¼ teaspoon salt

2 eggs

⅓ cup light cream

2 cups boiling water

3 medium apples, peeled, cored, and cut into 12 slices each
(about 6 cups sliced apples)

¼ cup butter

½ cup sugar

1 teaspoon lemon juice

Into a medium bowl, sift flour, baking powder, and salt together. Beat eggs and light cream together; add flour mixture. Whisk together.

In a shallow saucepan 10 to 12 inches in diameter, combine water, apples, butter, sugar, and lemon juice; bring to a boil and allow sugar to dissolve. Allow apples to cook 2 to 3 minutes more, or until slightly softened.

Form dumplings with 2 spoons using about ¾ tablespoon batter for each, yielding about 18 dumplings. As each

continued on next page

dumpling is formed, drop it into sauce in between the apples. Cover pan. Cook over low heat for about 5 minutes. Remove from heat and let sit for 5 to 10 minutes to absorb most of the remaining liquid. Serve just warm and still juicy with plain cream, whipped cream, or lemon sauce.

Yield: 6 servings

These are all regular people, cooks who show us that home cooking is what is meant by "American food." In each chapter of *How America Eats*, Paddleford gives pronouncements about what she's found in a particular region. For example, "New England dishes are as devoid of fuss and feathers as a Puritan's hat." She also paints vivid pictures of the cooks she meets, spicing them with her dry wit. Take this line: "In Bethel, Vermont, I met a princess, a wonderful woman, the late Anna Maria Schwartzenberg. She invited me to dinner to try her pot roast. All the way there I kept saying to myself, 'What a crazy idea to go to Vermont to eat a Viennese pot roast.' What was good enough for Grandma is good enough for me, I thought. For my New England grandma and her league certainly could go to bat any day with one of those fellows in a tall white hat—French, Viennese, or a Princess for that matter."

Once again, Paddleford gives her opinion, an opinion that today would be taken as fact, that where a dish is eaten and where it originated are different things and should both be treated with respect, whether it's pot roast in Vermont, pot roast in Vienna, or pot roast in Kansas. Paddleford's compellingly readable style is straightforward, authoritative, breezy, and obviously infused with a grand passion for food. In her, readers meet a writer who spun gold from the simple wisdom of American recipes. Without actually saying "melting pot," Paddleford created a portrait of the distinct phenomenon that is American food: We are a melting pot culture and our food is tied not to one tradition but to many. This is an idea we take utterly for granted today but that was not yet a cliché in Paddleford's day.

The book was reviewed—uniformly glowingly—all over the country. In these reviews, different aspects of Paddleford's mission and methodology were highlighted. For instance, in North Carolina's *Chapel Hill Weekly*, Paddleford is referred to as "the eminence in the sift-and-fold-in set," and praised for her desire to "leave no Stollen unturned," her willingness to "give credit where credit is due—to the hundreds of housewives all over America," and her inclusion with each recipe of "an interesting report on the hows and whys of the sleuthing that took Miss Paddleford from one home to the next, from plate to sate."

The Sunday Patriot-News of Harrisburg, Pennsylvania, no surprise, took special note of the recipes included from the home state: "Residents of Central Pennsylvania with their Pennsylvania Dutch background will read with special interest the pages of the book which tell of Miss Paddleford's visit to Hershey, Kutztown, Hungerford, and Allentown. The recipes she gives for sauerbraten, sweet sour beans, and bombeera fillas, among others will strike a familiar note. And of course there is the inevitable and tasty shoo-fly pie in its three variations—wet, dry, and cake-type."

House of Schwartzenberg Pot Roast

3½ to 4 pounds chuck roast

Salt and pepper, to taste

2 tablespoons vegetable oil

1 carrot

1 stalk celery

8 small sprigs parsley

1 bay leaf

2 tablespoons butter

1 medium onion, sliced

3 shallots

3 medium tomatoes, peeled and cut into large dice

2 cups beef stock

2 cups white or red wine

½ cup cognac or whisky

⅓ cup dry sherry wine

1 medium head green cabbage, cut into 8 wedges

3 tablespoons heavy cream

continued on next page

Preheat oven to 325 degrees.

Wipe meat with clean cloth or paper towel, sprinkle generously all over with salt and pepper and allow to come to room temperature. Heat vegetable oil in a Dutch oven or casserole over medium heat. Sear the meat on all sides to a deep golden brown. Then add carrot, celery, parsley, and bay leaf.

In a separate pan, melt butter. Add onion and shallots and sauté until golden. Add to meat with tomatoes, beef stock, wine, cognac, and sherry. Cover tightly and bring to slow simmer.

Put casserole in oven and continue to cook for 3½ hours, or until meat is fork-tender. About 10 to 15 minutes before it's done, add cabbage and re-cover. When cabbage is just tender, remove meat and cabbage to a warm platter. If liquid remaining is more than 3 cups, reduce to roughly that amount, strain, then return to a simmer. Add cream and stir well; adjust seasoning.

Yield: 8 servings

Sauerbraten

Marinade:

1½ cups cider vinegar

½ cup red wine

1 cup water

12 peppercorns

2 tablespoons sugar

2 large onions, peeled and sliced

4 bay leaves

12 whole cloves

1 teaspoon mustard seed

2 teaspoons salt

3½- to 4-pound round or rump of beef

2 tablespoons all-purpose flour

1½ teaspoons salt

Dash pepper

¼ cup vegetable oil

1 onion, sliced

½ teaspoon mustard seeds

6 whole cloves

½ teaspoon peppercorns

continued on next page

⅓ cup all-purpose flour

⅓ cup finely crushed gingersnaps, about 7 cookies

Two to 4 days before serving, combine marinade ingredients in a large plastic bag. Place beef in this mixture and let stand for two to four days in the refrigerator. At the end of marinating remove meat and dry on paper towels.

Combine the 2 tablespoons flour, salt, and pepper and coat meat on all sides with this mixture. Brown on all sides in vegetable oil in Dutch oven. Strain marinade and add to meat with additional sliced onion, mustard seeds, cloves, and peppercorns. Cover and simmer 3½ hours, or until meat is fork tender. Remove meat to heated platter, slicing beforehand, if desired. Strain liquid from pot. Mix the ⅓ cup flour and crushed gingersnaps in Dutch oven and slowly re-add liquid. Simmer, stirring constantly, until thickened. Pour some of this gravy over meat. Serve remainder at table.

Yield: 6 to 8 servings

The Orlando Evening Star reprinted the book's recipe for lime chiffon pie from an area woman, along with the advice that the book is "well worth the ten bucks it sells for" thanks to "regional recipes and pleasant little human interest stories about the people and places" from "probably the best known food writer in the world."

The Berkeley Daily Gazette in California went further. After writing a brief review of the book, the reporter Ken Carnahan came back with a second column on the subject. "I told you about a new cookbook called *How America Eats* in my Christmas check list but I didn't really tell you enough about it," he begins. "Clementine Paddleford, who writes the weekly column about food for *This Week* magazine, has written a cookbook which is not only full of excellent recipes but which really gives a picture of life in our United States."

The reach of *How America Eats* is difficult to calibrate, given the recent history of publishing houses. (In 1978 Scribner's merged with Atheneum to become The Scribner Book Companies, which in turn merged into Macmillan in 1984, which was purchased by Simon & Schuster in 1994. At that time, only the trade and reference book operations bore the Scribner name. The former imprint, now simply "Scribner," was retained by Simon & Schuster; the reference books went to Thomson Gale in 1999.) What patchy records there are for this title, housed today with the Scribner's archives at Princeton University, indicate that it was a hit: one thousand copies were made for a first print run; these sold out and another thirty-two hundred were ordered; a third printing was for five thousand more. The Cookbook Guild had sold an additional five thousand copies by 1962. The title became a Book of the Month Club selection, and The Escoffiers, Inc., used the book as a mailing for their Gourmet and Travel Book Club.

Other valuable outlets existed, too: *How America Eats* was distributed by American Mineral Spirits Company, a subsidiary of the Pure Oil Company (which no longer exists), which often printed books in special leather-bound editions as gifts for executives and clients. The Scribner's archive also shows that a representative from the Dole Corporation wrote to inquire about using the book as a premium with their products, but that Paddleford rejected the idea because she felt this commercial association might cheapen her work. Nevertheless, the publication of a second edition shows that publishers considered it solid material.

The reason is clear. Carnahan, in Berkeley, was able to express succinctly not only Paddleford's appeal as a writer but also her significance: She was using food to tell the stories of our lives. He recognized her work as the embodiment of the philosophy of Jean-Anthelme Brillat-Savarin, the French lawyer, politician, and author of what is perhaps the most noted gastronomic tome, *Physiologie du goût* (*The Physiology of Taste*), published in 1825. Brillat Savarin's most famous and quoted mot is: "Tell me what you eat, and I will tell you what you are." Paddleford's work did that: She knew that what women chose to make for dinner in their own homes and even the foods they fantasized about, such as the cheesecake from Lindy's restaurant on Broadway spoke volumes about what they considered important. Nowadays the preparation of food is exalted as artistry, but in Paddleford's day it was barely paid attention to; what you ate for dinner was not considered a mirror of your soul.

Even in this exciting time, Paddleford managed to turn out her regular columns—some of them groundbreaking. A February 1960 column titled "Happy Cooks of Napa Valley" for *This Week* was set in St. Helena, California, at the home of two wine-making brothers whose father, owner of a fruit packing business, had bought for them the oldest winery in the valley, Charles Krug, established in 1861. The brothers were Peter and Robert Mondavi. "One important thing I learned in this two hours of sight-seeing—fine wines of the world are the result of infinite care and an in-born respect for the wine itself," Paddleford wrote before detailing a meal prepared by the sisters-in-law Blanche Mondavi and Marjorie Mondavi: prosciutto-wrapped pineapple cubes ("a delicious hors d'oeuvre; one you may like to try") and salmon gnocchi in shrimp sauce.

As usual, Paddleford was ahead of her time—this time in recognizing the charms of the Mondavis. Today, of course, Robert Mondavi, aged ninety-four, is considered a pioneer of the California wine industry, an innovator in the technical improvements and the positive marketing of American wines. He split from his brother and Krug in 1965 and established the winery that bears his name, now among one of the most successful in America. One of his chief accomplishments was advocating labeling wines by the grape variety instead of some fanciful name.

Back in 1960, he was a young buck trying to make his father proud. After Paddleford had recognized his family's potential in print, he sent her a note offering his "heartfelt thanks for being again mentioned in your distinguished column," calling her visit "one of the real high lights of our year" and requesting the pleasure of her company "at any future time you may be out our way."

Another Paddleford subject who would go on to become a food-world luminary was Paul Keene, a farmer from Central Pennsylvania. Keene was an organic farmer who got started in the mid-1940s, when the idea of growing crops without chemical fertilizers and insecticides was "viewed as eccentric, if not downright un-American," as Margalit Fox put it in Keene's obit in *The New York Times* in 2005. Keene operated Walnut Acres Farm, which produced and packaged an array of foods available in health food stores and by mail order—including their signature apple butter, called Apple Essence, which was cooked in iron kettle over an open fire. It was this product that caught Paddleford's attention.

She mentioned Apple Essence, sold for a dollar a quart, in a column, and the rest was history: "Miss Paddleford rhapsodized, and Walnut Acres was inundated with letters and visits from eager customers," Fox reported. By 1994 Keene's annual sales totaled nearly $8 million. In 2000, Walnut Acres was acquired by the Hain Celestial Group, a natural-foods conglomerate.

As she was bringing the Mondavis and Keenes to world attention, Paddleford was aware that she was no longer the only serious food reporter in town. Two blocks north, at *The New York Times*, Craig Claiborne was hot on Paddleford's heels, assimilating her beat into his as a food writer. The forewarning of Claiborne's gradual eclipse of Paddleford came in a review of *How America Eats*, this one published in *Playbill* magazine in 1961. The review in the magazine theatergoers get wrapped in with their programs was by Barbara Kafka. Kafka, today a noted food writer and author of five major cookbooks, began her career as a student of James Beard, eventually becoming an assistant and, later in his life, adviser. Early in her career, when the *Playbill* review was written, Kafka had heard many tales about Paddleford from her friend Beard.

"Well, of course one knew about her," Kafka reports. "I never met her personally. But there were wonderful stories." One tale Beard told her involved flying: "Although she was a licensed pilot, she had no idea of navigation and she flew around using a roadmap which she kept on her lap."

As a result of her own career and her association with Beard, Kafka was familiar with Paddleford's mission, and in her review, laid it out plainly: "Some of the best recipes are not usually found in books; they are found in the Sunday editions of good newspapers and, as Clementine Paddleford, food writer for *This*

Week and the *Herald Tribune*, would contend, in old family collections. These sources tell us what America eats and what it has traditionally eaten."

However, the review goes on to extol not just *How America Eats* but another new cookbook based on collected recipes of the nation's cooks: *The New York Times Cookbook*, published in 1961 carrying Craig Claiborne's name as author. "The recipes, as readers of the *Times* will know, are easy to follow, sound and interesting," Kafka writes. "The *Times* tells us that America, at least New York, is a lot more sophisticated than she used to be and draws recipes from all over the world." By contrast, Kafka noted, "Miss Paddleford, whose book takes a folksier view of the American kitchen . . . has collected a great number of regional recipes from all over the country. The recipes are authentic, and, if you are either a devotee of or not fazed by the indomitable prose style, you should find lots of dishes you would enjoy making and much local history and information."

The general public, faced with competing titles published a year apart containing recipes from home cooks, might not have made the distinction so easily as Kafka. Despite its success, *How America Eats* was out of print by 1969. Claiborne's cookbook, however, went on to achieve legendary status, and is in print today (with the name of Claiborne, now dead, carried forward on the revised edition).

It was the first time the *Times* put its famous logotype on the subject of food in hard covers; as Claiborne himself pointed out in his autobiography *A Feast Made for Laughter*, the cookbook was successful enough to launch a series of *Times* books, including such successful and money-making titles as *The New York Times Natural Foods Cookbook*. This book, published in 1971, was ahead of the curve on natural foods. It was created by Jean Hewitt, a British home economist working at the paper who, according to Betsy Wade, was "smart, genteel, careful . . . and bought herself a huge, beautiful house near Watch Hill, R.I., with the proceeds." Paddleford's book launched no subsequent editions; Kafka put it succinctly: "Craig Claiborne stole her thunder."

The steamroller of the *Times* overwhelmed Paddleford's newspaper as well as her cookbook. In an article about rediscovering Paddleford's legacy carried in *The New York Times* in 2005, R. W. Apple Jr., then close to the end of his life, cited the charm of *How America Eats*. Nonetheless, he wrote: "*The New York Times Cookbook* by Craig Claiborne, published in 1961, eventually eclipsed *How America Eats*, helped by the fact that his newspaper stayed in business while hers folded in 1966." And that is it in a nutshell: In the early 1960s, Claiborne's paper was waxing prosperous while Paddleford's was fading.

The *Tribune* battled the *Times*, particularly its fat, glossy Sunday insert, *The New York Times Magazine*, to get and keep big advertisers. Although the magazine had been in existence since 1896, it achieved its prominence as a home for serious reporting about politics and "soft" subjects such as furniture and food, under the helm of the intimidating editor Lester Markel. Markel directed the magazine, and indeed all the material in the Sunday paper other than the news sections, from 1923 to 1964.

A "dominating and terrifying" presence at the paper, Markel was consumed with hard news, according to Betsy Wade, but he had the wit to realize that such subjects as fashion were important in at least one key way: They made money. As a result there were big fashion supplements in the magazine at least twice a year. The bra and clothing co-op advertisements, often humorously described as soft-core pornography, were what made the magazine. The bulky publication enriched the entire paper, paying bills for its costly international reporting. This was not only one reason Markel was held in such awe, but also one reason the *Tribune* went down. As Kluger notes in *The Paper*, there was the strong possibility that the New York department stores, the garment district and all its connected parts, were eager to reduce the number of papers they had to advertise in. So they settled on the *Times* and starved the *Trib* out. There were only so many New York–based papers that advertisers like Maidenform were going to pay to be in, and the *Times Magazine* became their choice.

The *Tribune* didn't take the increasing dominance of the *Times Magazine* passively. To fight it, in 1963 the publisher founded its own in-house Sunday supplement, glossy *New York* magazine. Edited by the now-legendary magazine editor Clay Felker, it was smart, modern, and cutting-edge—showcasing the work of many popular Tribune writers, including Tom Wolfe, Jimmy Breslin, and Judith Crist. With this innovation, the *Tribune* dropped *This Week* magazine out of its Sunday combo.

Felker is today credited with having invented the "city magazine"—a glossy insiders' guide devoted to news and service material (where to find the best locksmith, the top Italian restaurants, etc.). The early days of *New York* magazine definitely helped keep the *Tribune* afloat. However, there was no place in it for a writer like Paddleford, cozy with her readers, country-raised and friendly. *New York*'s name became wedded to food writers like Gael Greene, Mimi Sheraton, and, later, Molly O'Neill—critics with an insiders'-only voice who play to a more aspirational crowd, assuming every reader knows an Eastern Shore oyster from a Long Island one.

But she may not have wanted to move, either: Paddleford's Sunday byline was part of the fabric of *This Week*, which paid her handsomely and rewarded her with plenty of plaques for her mantelpiece. Any time she had ever threatened to leave, *This Week*—and the *Tribune*, too—had immediately increased her pay. However, despite all, both publications were becoming irrelevant.

The displacement of *This Week* in the Sunday *Tribune* by *New York* magazine and the increasing muscularity of the *Times Magazine* had a devastating impact on *This Week*. "When Clay Felker started *New York* magazine as a supplement in the *Tribune* in 1963, that washed out *This Week*," said James Boylan, an editor at *This Week* from 1951 to 1956, who later founded the *Columbia Journalism Review*. "The *Tribune* was looking around for something new to make it competitive with the *Times*, and this was one of several things they did to make themselves livelier.

"The new supplement got a lot of attention; Felker had Tom Wolfe writing for it," Boylan continued. "*New York* magazine was one key weakness for *This Week* thereafter; the magazine was not being seen by consumers in the New York market."

This Week was able to survive for a while, though the *Tribune* was not. The sixties were hard for New York newspapers, and along with the decline in advertising, the *Trib* just couldn't withstand such losses as the famous strike led by the printers union, which began on December 8, 1962, and lasted for 114 days. Paddleford crossed no picket lines—she had *This Week* business to keep her alive, so she was better off financially than most other reporters. (She was also, conveniently, in the hospital with pneunomia from December 31 to January 17.) The long strike, and others that followed, plus a decision by the *Tribune* owner to join in a merger with two afternoon papers, were death blows. The final edition of the *New York Herald Tribune* was published April 24, 1966. Paddleford's last column for the paper, titled "A Five-Gazpacho Day," had run fourteen days earlier.

Everyone except the publisher of *The New York Times* mourned the passing of the *Tribune*. The folding of the paper, for which she was unequivocally a major star, must have been particularly hard for Paddleford.

But as before, when the going got tough she worked. Only now the options were a bit curtailed. If she was tempted at this time, or earlier, to leave for greener shores, she left behind no evidence. *New York* magazine turned out to be a powerful launching pad for food journalism everywhere but Paddleford at her age would most assuredly not have stepped on to a wobbly raft, leaving the loyalty and guaranteed check of *This Week* behind. As for joining the victor in the newspaper war, it is also assuredly true that the *Times* seldom made a practice of seeking out talent. Instead, it was much more what Boylan and others refer to as "the *Times* way," which is to hire writers and editors only after the talent had approached the paper. "The style of the *Times* in the fifties and sixties was such that you had to be humble and petition them," Boylan said. Paddleford—who had spent her early career petitioning just about every major news organization in America except the *Times*—probably considered going hat in hand to the *Times* significantly beneath her.

Hence the resentment toward Claiborne, who had chosen the luckier horse, and also the curious choices she made after the end of the *Tribune*.

In the twilight of her career and in possession of clear evidence that both of her major outlets were on the decline, she pressed on. John Hay Whitney, who had bought control of the *Tribune* from the Reid family in 1958, was in control at the time and joined the *Hearst*-owned *New York Journal American* and the Scripps-Howard owned *New York World-Telegram & Sun* to form the *World Journal Tribune*, whose nickname, The Widget, was another cold wind.

For the eight months the hybrid survived, Paddleford wrote occasional columns under the rubric "Clementine Paddleford: Food in the News." These rarely contained recipes and were about such things as the new design of the Betty Crocker corporate kitchen ("New Kitchens Take in a Whole World").

But *This Week* was still going, and it was to this magazine that Paddleford dedicated the most time in her later years. Harking back to her coming of age as a reporter in the early 1930s writing about church ladies' suppers and offering those readers stipends for winning recipe contests, in 1965 she even began a new recipe challenge—this time for younger people. "Looking for 'cook young' ideas for my 'How America Eats' series in *This Week Magazine*, I introduced a nationwide recipe swap of time-saving dishes," she wrote when a collection was published. "These came from children under twelve, teenagers, career girls, young brides, mothers, grandmothers." The collection, 153 of these recipes, appeared in 1966 as *Clementine Paddleford's Cook Young Cookbook*, published by Pocket Books.

The point of this series wasn't merely age; it was also an attempt to embrace modernity. Paddleford was apparently making a big effort to show that she was changing with the times, and that she understood the altered needs of her home-cooking readers: The other focus of the series was time management. "Now there is a young revolt in the ways of cooking, as in the manner of clothing," she wrote. "Cooking is done the easy way, with convenience foods as the timesaving ingredients." Gone were the days, Paddleford asserted, when "it was considered hush-hush to own a can opener" because now "women put together three meals a day in about 90 minutes" whereas "two decades ago it took five hours." Paddleford married these two burgeoning trends—younger kids in the kitchen, and the vast array of time-saving products hitting grocery shelves—in the "Cook Young" series with an extremely popular result. She spoke of the responses she got to her request for submissions. "In all, there were over 50,000 recipes," she wrote, "every one using short-cut ingredients—meaning those convenience foods that account for more than 15 percent of today's food sales. Whatever science has developed to make cooking easier 'is for us,' the letters said."

Paddleford's focus was the same: reporting regional recipes. Only now, she found that these had changed, too. "Today even the regional dishes are being updated to a faster time tempo," she wrote. She still traveled, but this series, in which readers wrote to her rather than her seeking them out, meant she had to visit only the most interesting of her respondents: the breakneck pace slowed.

She also had to contend with people's anxiety over weight, something never dealt with in columns focused on food as celebration. "Now that the world has gone calorie mad," she wrote, "the fresh vegetable tray of crunch items appears with increasing frequency by the dip bowl." She even deigned to include a "low-cal cheese dip," which consisted of one pint of cottage cheese beaten with two teaspoons of garlic salt and served with celery sticks. Other recipes were less monastic, like Syrian beet salad, a jellied beet mold that is a kitschy example of the melding of convenience and aspiration—aspic, in this case—that typified the home cooking of the early 1960s. This from Mrs. Karl Cole of Osawatomie, Kansas, a small prairie town in the rolling hills of the eastern part of Paddleford's state. Some of her respondents for the "Cook Young" series, Paddleford noted to readers, were not so much technically young as they were "young at heart," and therefore felt free to send in their recipes, too—Mrs. Cole must have been among them.

Putting this series together not only consumed her in a project that fitted her general mission of recipe-sharing across the country, but introduced her byline to a whole new set of readers—a shrewd move. It gave her the chance to agitate and inspire, to send curious minds into the kitchen, if only in hopes of seeing their own names published in a magazine.

Throughout this period of hard work, Paddleford was suffering. Perhaps because of her earlier ill health and throat ailments, she was not a "young sixty." Photos from this period show that Paddleford had aged dramatically. As early as 1958, a shot of her in the test kitchen, pencil in hand, shows her hair more salt than pepper, and her waistline significantly rounded. Of course, some things never changed: A voluminous scarf is wrapped around her neck, her voice device still in a black velvet choker, and a full skirt flaring. The image suggests that old age came fast, and infirmities with it.

Syrian Beet Salad

4 cups water

½ teaspoon salt

2 large beets (about 1¼ pounds)

1 envelope (½ tablespoon) gelatin

2 tablespoons sugar

2 tablespoons prepared horseradish

1 tablespoon fresh lemon juice

2 tablespoons white vinegar

In a medium saucepan, bring water to a boil and add salt. Scrub beets and add them whole to the pot. Slowly simmer for 30 to 40 minutes or until tender but still firm. Reserve 2 cups cooking liquid, drain the beets, and discard the remaining liquid.

In a small bowl, cool ½ cup of liquid over ice and use it to soften gelatin. Cool, peel, and julienne beets, yielding 4 cups. Add softened gelatin to hot beet liquid and then add the remaining ingredients. Add the beets and adjust the seasoning if necessary.

Pour the mixture into a medium (2-quart) bowl or mold, chill at least 6 hours or overnight before unmolding by

continued on next page

dipping the bowl in very hot water for a few seconds at a time until it loosens.

Serve as a side dish alongside braised beef or as an appetizer with smoked fish, such as trout, and a garnish of crème fraiche.

Yield: 6 to 8 appetizer or side dish servings

Paddleford was not going to slow down unless she had to, of course. In the summer of 1962, she fulfilled yet another dream: traveling to Russia. Her files show that she had long been fascinated with Russia, and had been saving clippings since 1941. At the *Tribune*, Isabel McGovern filled in for some of Paddleford's columns for the couple of weeks she was abroad. But Paddleford also filed nine columns for the newspaper about subjects both expected, such as "Vodka: Russian Versus American," in which she visited the largest Moscow vodka distillery, which produced 600,000 bottles of 80-proof a day, and unusual, like the story "Red Farms Cultivate Thousands of Acres," in which she finagled a trip to a state-owned farm. "A visit to a collective farm and a state-owned farm was a 'must' on my schedule for Russia. I was put off and put off until the day my visa expired. Then came the word—GO! Fly to Kharkov, and by car to the farms. I had the visa extended," she began. For *This Week* was a long feature, "Inside a Russian Kitchen." The work was much the same as her usual: Visiting homes and reporting on what was cooking, being taken around by Charlotte Staples, wife of a U.S. Consul in Russia, as she went to collective markets and state-owned stores. Helping her arrange visits was a press agent named Irene Urin, who was employed by Intourist, the Moscow-based official Soviet government travel agency. An Intourist contact was essential then for any private person traveling in the Soviet Union. Paddleford sent a thank-you note to her in October 1962, with a postscript reading: "Wish I could order caviar for breakfast today."

Paddleford's trip to the Cold War enemy was covered by *Newsweek*. "Better Bread Than Dead" ran the headline in an August 1962 issue. The story opens by quoting Paddleford on the conditions of the women she met: "Almost no one wears a girdle! And almost everyone is 30 pounds overweight by our standards. Fat soups, fat meats, and sausages aren't helpful to svelte figures."

"So much for Russian women, as observed by *New York Herald Tribune* Food Editor Clementine Paddleford on a two-week tour of the Soviet," the newsmagazine continued. She was also quoted this way: "Russians eat like trenchermen with great gusto. They bite off a piece of buttered bread as if it might be the last bite of the last supper."

That trip would be one of several last hurrahs of Paddleford's career, as her health began to fail. One dramatic crisis occurred later in 1962, when Paddleford was sidelined for more than a month with pneumonia in New York Hospital. Eloise Davison had re-entered the picture, and was there with her. Jorgensen, however, was tied down in Maine with her three young children. "I am so sorry I wasn't in when Eloise was trying to reach me from your room yesterday," she wrote. "I play with the idea of coming down. . . .I know Eloise said you didn't want me to come and I am not flapping around making plans to come. If it works out easily I will." The rest of the letter is a report on life on the farm, probably meant to cheer. Mostly the news was about animals, especially the cats. "Pussy sits on the back of Mark's chair and of course Henry sleeps on the table," Jorgensen wrote. "I tell the children this just isn't done, and they mustn't tell anyone. But the animals are good and really want attention more than food."

Paddleford's prognosis was serious enough that it prompted a heartfelt letter from Nichols at *This Week*. He wrote that Ed McCarthy, editor of the *New York Herald Tribune* edition of *This Week*, "has just told me your news, and it upsets me, as does anything which touches anyone I love."

"Ed and I agreed that people live and get well who have the will to live and get well, and no one we know has a greater will than you," he continued.

Nichols goes on to make what he called a "proposal" to Paddleford, in order to proceed with their business arrangement "as though everything were completely normal" as they entered 1963. "In other words, by this letter," he wrote, "I am renewing for another year, your guarantee of $15,750.00, and this will be paid, however long it takes you to get completely well, on the understanding that if necessary during this period Mary Lyons will work with you and prepare materials to appear, subject to your approval and under your name, in the magazine."

After assuring Paddleford of her paycheck—and letting her know that Lyons, a former copyeditor of Paddleford's *This Week* column, was on standby for ghostwriting, Nichols goes on to suggest what looks like a step to protect a valuable property.

"This matter of name is important," he wrote, "because it is the basis of continuity, and it can be a basis of security, too. For, looking a long way into the future, I would like to suggest that we think now of some way that your name can be protected and used, in effect, as the trademark for all our food material for the magazine. This could be the basis of some kind of continuing payment to you or to your estate, and it is something I hope you and Ed will think about and discuss together."

In proposing to obtain the rights to "By Clementine Paddleford," he envisioned having her column carried on by others well into the future. The idea of a house byline was not without precedent. The most famous example was "Dorothy Dix," the nom de plume of a lovelorn columnist, Elizabeth Meriwether Gilmer. The column continued long after Gilmer's death, with various writers at the helm. Today the most famous examples are "Dear Abby" and "Ann Landers," both of which have had writers other than their creators.

Nichols's suggestion might be what routed Paddleford from her sickbed. According to Jorgensen, Paddleford was not about to let another writer carry on with her own life's work, no matter how lucrative the arrangement. Whatever Nichols's intentions, both well-meaning and self-serving, he was turned down flat.

Paddleford managed to get herself better and back on the job, but the days of breakneck work were done. "It will be impossible to attend the National Peach Council meeting because I am taking it very easy until at least April," Paddleford wrote to Lora Stone in a letter to the organization in January 1963. "But I am interested in a fresh peach story for *This Week Magazine* some time next summer."

By May of that year she was well enough to plan an ambitious trip to Hawaii and on to China, where she had promised to attend the opening of a couple of Hilton Hotels. A China press representative, Ellen J. Swan, whose office was in Hong Kong, had invited Paddleford to appear on several radio programs, but this was out of the question. "I can be of no help to you regarding radio panel discussions," Paddleford wrote to Swan. "I have but half or less of my vocal chords and speak in a 'whiskey tenor.' Interviewing, telephoning, etc, is fine, but no public speaking." The trip to China yielded at least two feature articles for *This Week* and eight for the *Herald Tribune*, including one about Hong Kong street food in which the author discovers tofu. "Eat dangerously (fool you may be) sampling strange tidbits at street market stalls. Have you ever had snake soup? We tried tou-fui, a soya bean curd, like a thick custard cut into cubes."

At the end of summer 1963, Paddleford traveled to Mexico. Her beloved cat Pussy Willow was left with the Jorgensens, who were spending the month at Paddleford's place in Redding. Continuing proof that animals were a bond between Paddleford and Jorgensen shows in a letter Jorgensen sent her adoptive mother on August 21, 1963. The letter imitates a girls' camp report, only the "camper" was a cat.

Jorgensen divided the letter into categories including "Aptitude Tests" ("She spends many hours each day in pure contemplation, either under the great pine trees, on our back stairs where she sits quietly and observes things known only to her, or on a favorite rock outcropping"), "Crafts" ("She neither embroiders, nor does she spin or sew"), and "Eating Habits" ("Her tastes are finicky; she does not like the same food served twice in succession and insists on Saturday and Sunday ingesting only a delicacy called fresh chicken livers. She also tries to convince her Counsellor that every weekday is Saturday and Sunday").

By this time in her career, Paddleford was a kind of éminence grise of journalism—her fame came from writing about food, but she had transcended the women's pages to become one of the country's top reporters. As she traveled the country—in her later years and even on a reduced schedule—she still made good copy. A profile of her in the *Charlotte Observer* in North Carolina in October 1964 was carried with a photo of a worn-looking Paddleford who, despite gray hair and wrinkles, still managed a twinkly smile at her overladen home desk flanked with Pussy Willow. The quotes recorded by Eudora Garrison, the homemaking editor, are equally sassy. "Looking back over her remarkable career, Clementine admits she wanted to write novels and short stories at the beginning. 'I also wanted to be sure of a living,' she says with artless candor. 'In Kansas we always believed in paying our debts.'"

The folks in Charlotte weren't the only ones who got to know Paddleford as a freestanding celebrity. The September 26, 1964, issue of *The New Yorker* contains a cartoon by the eminent Peter Arno. It depicts a couple perusing their Sunday paper under a shaded umbrella in their backyard with their dog nearby. The caption reads: "I'm getting pretty fed up with teeth marks on Clementine Paddleford."

To be paid a visit by Paddleford at this point was to be in the presence of a bona fide celebrity, according to Marianne—Mimi—Strong, the New York City–based literary agent to whom Paddleford devoted a column in the autumn of 1964. At that time, Strong had her own publicity agency and was a social figure of some standing, married to Stephen Van Rensselaer Strong, whose family were New York State pioneers and lawmakers and the founders of Rensselaer Polytechnic Institute. Strong was one of a long line of Harvard men, and every other year he and Marianne held tremendous buffet parties in honor of the

Harvard-Princeton game at their country home in Piscataway Township, New Jersey, thirteen miles from Princeton. (Upon her husband's death, Strong sold the home, called Ivy Hall, to the state of New Jersey; today it's an historic museum.) Paddleford somehow got wind of these tony buffet parties and called and asked Strong if she could attend one.

"I was really excited when Clementine called me," Strong says. "You can talk about *The New York Times* from here to hell and back but the *Herald Tribune* was a more respected paper . . . and she was highly respected, and very well liked." Paddleford arranged to come down to New Jersey a day before the party and to bring a photographer. "It was a little bit nerve-wracking," Strong says, "but she was not at all intimidating—anything but." Paddleford came over and took a tour of the house, and the following day Strong had set up the dishes in tureens for Paddleford to sample before the guests arrived. "She had a great time coming over," Strong reports, and was full of fun, and Strong's guests thoroughly enjoyed mingling with her, although she did not stay for the entirety of the event. "Her personality was glowing . . . she was magnetic."

What Strong says she most appreciated about Paddleford's visit to her party was how easygoing the reporter was. "She did not talk down to me," Strong says. The only negative words Paddleford had for anyone were reserved for Craig Claiborne, whose name apparently came up in conversation. "She sort of made fun of him," Strong says, "he could be very snotty to people and Clementine was not about that."

"Touchdown Supper for 80" came out in the November 15, 1964, *Herald Tribune*, detailing the Strong's party in which "50 were invited, 80 came"—to cheer on their team. Paddleford reserved special praise for Strong's party-planning strategies: "To serve 80 people in a 10-room house requires ingenuity. Mimi solves the problem by removing the bed in one guest room and adding two tables, each seating eight. Another room had been cleared of furniture and a long party hanger installed to take care of the coats. We expected to a see a raccoon coat revival: not one appeared." A recipe for Strong's father's beef stew was included.

"People always call you when a story comes out," Strong says, but a story by Paddleford yielded more attention than any—and Strong was flattered and buoyed by the descriptions of herself as a hostess extraordinaire. What she remembers most about Paddleford was her energy. "I think you have to say that she was not Marilyn Monroe, but she was a charismatic woman. Sometimes charisma is more important than looks, that's important to know about her."

Indeed, sources found that Paddleford, even with the graying bob and expanding waistline of a sixty-six-year-old, glowed from the inside. "Something sparkles about Clem. Part of it is her blue eyes, but more is her wit, her sense of fun," wrote Dorothee Polson, the food editor of *The Arizona Republic* in the issue of May 2, 1965. The occasion for Polson's profile was Paddleford's trip to Honolulu to serve as one of the twenty-three judges for the Kaiser Foil For Men Only Cookout Championship. This turned out to be the last big public relations shindig of her career. Polson's story gives a neat outline of Paddleford's accomplishments: "For 24 years she has been food editor of *This Week*, the magazine supplement which appears with Sunday's *Arizona Republic*. And for 27 years she has been food editor of the *New York Herald Tribune* . . . wherever she goes she is recognized by her readers, who number millions. Many spoke to her, greeted her by name, even snapped her picture as we strolled together today beneath the banana trees."

Polson also noted that Paddleford had collected more than five thousand cookbooks, and that she had "two secretaries, two writing assistants, two maids and two test kitchens." She also got Paddleford to spell out her secret: "She credits her success to 'our tremendous circulation and the fact that I write about people, not just recipes.'"

A great deal of correspondence from Kaiser and its advertising agency, Young & Rubicam, was created by this cook-off. If the heavy underlining of her notes is any indication, Paddleford was attracted to the subject because "over four billion dollars were spent on outdoor living last year"—reason to jump on the trend if ever there was one. After a five-hour cook-off, Dr. Gail S. Erbeck, a thirty-one-year-old dentist from Cincinnati, took the $10,000 prize for his "Luau Pork Ambrosia" and won a mention in Paddleford's column; Joan Crawford presented station wagons to runners-up.

Ever resourceful, Paddleford, "hearing it said that Joan Crawford, when at her home in New York City, does the family cooking," made it her business to follow up on the rumor. The result was a feature on the great—and fearsome—actress for *This Week* called "Joan Stars in the Kitchen," which ran with a picture of Mommy Dearest herself showing her teenage twins Cindy and Cathy a box grater. Crawford may have been an imposing figure to some celebrities, but Paddleford took her on with ease. The accompanying article begins quite humorously, with Paddleford detailing the way in which Crawford began their interview by applying her makeup. "Can you really cook?' I bluntly asked. Miss Crawford propped the make-up kit for a better view. Her enormous eyes fastened on the job at hand. 'I can certainly cook,' she said in her forthright way. 'I started to cook when I was nine years old to pay my tuition at the St. Agnes Academy in Kansas City.'"

The two women warmed to each other, and the rest of the short story makes the point that Crawford, "in her present status as actress, widowed mother and business woman," gives "home parties" in her apartment in New York "where she lives between acting chores." Her "pet buffet" recipe was for meatloaf, which she supplied Paddleford. "What about a fancier dish?" we asked. 'Simplicity is a lovely thing,' she said."

After the Crawford column ran, Paddleford heard from the actress several times—once when she was invited to a Pepsi-Cola reception by Crawford, whose late husband Al Steele had been the president of the board (Paddleford respectfully declined, citing "appointments that couldn't be broken"), and again after the column ran. "You just don't know the amount of mail I am getting on the article you did for *This Week*," Crawford, no stranger to vast amounts of publicity, wrote. Crawford told Paddleford that she advised all of her culinary admirers to go out and buy copies of *How America Eats*, a book that she felt "cannot be equaled."

When it came to her official duties as a cook-off judge, Kaiser now hoped to have Paddleford make the trip to Hawaii as an annual event. The next one, the 1966 edition, was to be part of something new that Paddleford had dreamed up and Nichols had agreed to: a series for *This Week* called "How the World Eats." This would widen the scope of her previous work, and give her a chance to carry on with her favorite sort of work. For copy like that, the avenues were narrowing: With the *Tribune* having met its expected demise, and no chance of begging for a job at the *Times*, Paddleford had to channel all of her energy into *This Week*.

First, Paddleford let Nichols know that she was planning to remain loyal. The previous December, she had written to Nichols: "In business 'inside notes' there have been (as of course you know) rumors of consolidation of papers. If this comes about I will leave the *Tribune*, which would give me enough time to do a bang-up job for *This Week* . . . I like to interview people, kneecap to kneecap." Nichols must have been thrilled at the news that he'd finally have the name reporter all to himself. The 1966 plans, however, did not unfold as Paddleford hoped

In a letter to an Eastern Airlines representative, Sandra Hart, dated May 23, 1966, Paddleford laid it out. "I am still interested in the Mexico City restaurant and Eastern, as we discussed earlier," she wrote. "But I had promised to be a judge at the Kaiser Cookout in Honolulu, and was going from there to Australia and New Zealand. Not a vacation, but to get material for *This Week*'s 'How the World Eats' stories. None of this came off. I was half packed, had ticket in hand, money in pocket, when I came down with pneumonia and 'emergencied' to New York Hospital. Was there for six weeks and am just home."

Two serious attacks of pneumonia at her age meant that Paddleford barely survived another year. Jorgensen says that by the beginning of 1967 doctors discovered Paddleford had cancer "everywhere." By the fall of that year, she had become a permanent resident of New York Hospital. Jorgensen also said that when Paddleford was dying, Bill Nichols came to pay his respects—and to ask once more if she'd consider selling her name. And once more, Paddleford refused.

On November 13, 1967, Clementine Paddleford died. Her obituary was carried in all of the country's major newspapers. The unsigned obituary in *The New York Times* was reported by Joan Cook and Betsy Wade, two of Paddleford's earlier colleagues at the *Tribune*.

"Clementine Paddleford is Dead; Food Editor of the *Herald Tribune*," was the headline; the copy was four columns long, and consisted of the kind of detailed character observations that would have impressed even the subject. Her accomplishments came first and were succinctly enumerated: "As food editor of the *New York Herald Tribune* from 1936 to until its demise in 1966 and of *This Week Magazine*, the Sunday supplement, from 1940 to her death, Miss Paddleford wrote for a weekly readership estimated at 12 million."

Her writing style was analyzed: "Although a brisk, matter-of-fact woman, she had a knack of embellishing even the lowliest foods so that they seemed like taste delights. An ordinary radish was not just a radish but 'a tiny radish of passionate scarlet, tipped modestly in white.' Mushrooms were the 'elf of plants' or 'pixie umbrellas.'"

Her most important rival was given a chance to pay his respects: "Clem was a dear woman with rare courage, a strong lust for life and a rollicking sense of humor. She was also indefatigable. Wherever I go in this old globe, someone is certain to say, 'Clem was here,'" was the quotation from Claiborne.

Perhaps the most fitting tribute of all, though, ran in the November 19 issue of *This Week*. It was Paddleford's last column, published posthumously. It was part of the "Cook Young" series and dedicated to one of Paddleford's favorite subjects: holiday desserts.

"It's time to reorganize the recipe files for the big stretch of holiday entertaining that looms ahead. We discovered an extravaganza dessert last month that rates star billing for ease and elegance. A Pancake Apple Torte, towering 12 layers high, crowned with soft swirls of whipped cream and giant walnut halves, was the grand finale at a buffet party we attended," she began. Paddleford encouraged readers to use a mix for the pancakes and to compose the tower a day ahead of time. "But," she cautioned in the last line, "be prepared for second requests!"

A Bundle of Longing

by KELLY ALEXANDER

No surprises are in Clementine Paddleford's last will and testament; even the care of her surviving cats is addressed. Paddleford left some token gifts to Lois Leak, her dutiful housekeeper; Bush Barnum, a bona fide *Esquire* magazine-declared dandy and her last lover; Addie Burrell, who had been Paddleford's caretaker when she had throat cancer and who had been Claire's minder when she first came to live with Paddleford; Anna Marie Doherty, Paddleford's personal secretary; Harriet Arnold, a food photographer who first shot Paddleford for *Time* magazine and was a friend; Alice Nichols, a fellow Kansan and longtime intimate, and a couple of other acquaintances. She left an apartment building that her father had owned in downtown Manhattan, Kansas, to her brother's children, Donald Paddleford and Pauline Paddleford Lantz.

The bulk of the estate, including the cats and her home in Redding, Connecticut, was left to Claire Duffé Jorgensen. An exception was all of Paddleford's work material, including nineteen hundred cookbooks, seven hundred restaurant menus, award plaques and other memorabilia, and notes for every article she ever wrote including the 845 pieces that made up *How America Eats*. All 274 of these standard-size file boxes were given to Paddleford's beloved alma mater, Kansas State University.

In February 1968, Kansas State sent two librarians to Paddleford's apartment to pack the bequest and take it to their creator's home state. According to an article in the Kansas State *Collegian* for February 15, 1968, these items arrived safely. "A trip into the library stacks and Miss Paddleford's world of food seems endless," the story suggested. And then, for thirty-four years, the material sat virtually undisturbed. The school devoted no resources to unpacking the "world of food," and, aside from a couple of distant relatives of Paddleford's, no one came to look.

That's probably because the majority of potentially interested parties had never heard of her. By 1967 the *Tribune* had folded, leaving the New York morning full-sheet newspaper field to the *Times*. Many of the journalists who had observed Paddleford in her prime as she kept up an impossible travel schedule, bustled around the office in her swirly clothing, tasting test kitchen recipes and interviewing creators of coffee-making devices, faded away themselves. By the year 2000, if you searched for someone who had known a thing about Clementine Paddleford while she was alive you'd likely have turned up empty-handed. The main source left on earth for Paddleford's life, Claire Jorgensen, had, not unlike Paddleford, cloaked herself in mystery.

Maybe because she had been virtually orphaned, and maybe

because she had been taken in by a celebrity, Jorgensen was not one to reach out and tell the world how Paddleford changed her life. Like the cats she loved so well, Jorgensen had to be coaxed out of her hiding place; she was someone who would reveal a secret only when she decided to. No amount of persuading, subtle or overt, would draw out a personality like this if she was not ready. Successive administrators at Kansas State learned this the hard way when they were rebuffed each time they reached out to Jorgensen, who assumed they were after a donation.

Of course, growing old can make a person feel like talking. And finally, that's what happened with Jorgensen. In April 2006, Jorgensen was in a posh nursing home in Maine just a few miles from the glorious saltwater farm that Paddleford bought her for a wedding present, where she raised her family and where her son still lives. She had already been diagnosed with Parkinson's, but she had not progressed to dementia. For unexplained reasons, she decided to emerge from her hiding place and clear some of the air about Paddleford.

Jorgensen was not a young seventy-five; her thick straight hair, always a source of pride, had faded pleasingly to salt-and-pepper, and it hung straight as photos had always showed it. Now it was more salt than pepper. Wrinkles acquired from years of farming goats and chasing children and riding horses in the sun had settled around her bright blue eyes. Deep in those eyes, though, was a steely glimmer, a look of plucky determination that said "don't mess with me" in a nice but firm way. Although Jorgensen spoke slowly and paused often, the spunk of the child Clem had found irresistible was obvious.

Even though Jorgensen had called a meeting of her own with us, the two women who would be Paddleford's biographers—

Cynthia Harris, an archivist at Kansas State University, and me, a food writer—she was not about to be an open book. Some questions, such as "Did Clementine ever talk about her husband, Lloyd Zimmerman?" were met with stony silence, as if she had not heard them. When the subject of what ailment, exactly, Paddleford died of, "cancer" was the terse reply. But what kind? "It was everywhere," was all she'd say. Other times, she fairly tripped over her words to tell an amusing story, such as details about how Paddleford and her boss and ostensible friend Eloise Davison "fought like cats and dogs." Asked why, she said "Eloise, who never married or had children, always wanted a family like we had, and she couldn't stand that she couldn't boss us around." Paddleford, she said, almost never cooked at home except to prepare a steak on the maid's night off. Another affirmation, Paddleford had many lovers, "Oh yes, many," Jorgensen laughed, adding that Paddleford even kept a log of which meal was served to which man.

One of the biggest uncertainties of Paddleford's life, which was how she came to be the guardian of Jorgensen, hung in the air. Many have speculated that perhaps Jorgensen was Paddleford's biological child—Paddleford herself had been so cagey about how she acquired her ward that it evoked many questions: Had she really been the child of Paddleford and Zimmerman? Uncharacteristically, Jorgensen was happy to clear this up. She showed a scrapbook containing her own birth certificate listing Marcelle Duval as her mother, plus persuasive photographs of her with Marcelle, and, further in the book, pictures of the young teenager with Paddleford. The most sensitive subject of all turned out to be Paddleford's bout with throat cancer and the rumors that swirled around the *Herald Tribune* that instead of being sick the writer had attempted suicide by drinking acid. Jorgensen was infuriated at this question, balling her arthritic hands into fists and severely, emphatically, stating: "That is not true, and you are not to write that."

Mercifully for all involved, the tense moment passed and the day ended on a happier note: Jorgensen and her son took the two biographers, Cynthia and me, on a tour of the Maine farm. It was a gray, chilly day—news of early spring had not yet reached the place—but the spread had a wonderful energy. Situated at least three quarters of a mile off a state highway, the simple white farmhouse had a cheerful cornflower blue door. "I chose that color," Jorgensen said when it was praised. She insisted on walking part of the two miles from the main house to the water, through fields and over knobby tree roots and unmarked forest paths. By the water she sat on a stone bench, absorbing the view of the Kennebec, at peace. "This is me," she said quietly.

For my part, I could not have been happier to be there; sitting at Paddleford's property represented a kind of ending to a quest that I had unexpectedly embarked upon six years before when my husband, returning from a business trip, had brought me as a present a used copy of *How America Eats*. I was not thrilled—*another* cookbook—and it was weeks before I opened the dusty peach-colored jacket. When I did, what I found changed my life.

"I have ranged from the lobster pots of Maine to the vineyards of California, from the sugar shanties of Vermont to the salmon canneries of Alaska," I read. Who was this woman, I wondered, gobbling up the words. Paddleford explained that her book was based on personal interviews with more than two thousand of the country's best home cooks and that its recipes were "word of mouth hand-downs from mother to daughter." She proceeded to introduce me to people from across the country who cooked foods with origins from all over the world. For someone who had grown up in a Southern Jewish family, where dishes like kasha varnishkes were served alongside barbecued chicken for holiday dinners, the knowledge that American food is tied to many traditions was daily grist. It was also the reason I went into writing about food in the first place, and it was the thing to which Paddleford had devoted her professional life. I grew hungrier to know more about the woman with the impossibly curious name who was behind this book.

Interested, I began cooking from the book, starting with a cake from Philadelphia because it sounded wildly delicious. Aunt Sabella's Black Chocolate Cake (page 265) turned out as promised: easy to prepare, moist, rich. Paddleford's clipped, efficient prose was equally rewarding: "Chocolate cake, now that's my meat," she wrote, after discussing her foray into Pennsylvania Dutch country for "chocolate cakes, so famous people drive one hundred miles and more to eat a slice fresh cut."

Earlier that year I had taken a job as an editor at *Saveur*, a cutting-edge food magazine born in 1990 of the idea of "savoring a world of authentic cuisine." The magazine was known for its daring—and often mouthwatering—photography that avoided the usual precision work in favor of in-your-face shots of blueberry juices spilling over the lattice of a pie, plates of nachos oozing cheese and sour cream, pans of lasagna framed in burnt rims. The articles were different, too: Not one of them was about how to wrangle dinner in a certain number of minutes; instead, stories like "Where Pizza Was Born" traced the history of what was likely the world's first pie to the hands of the baker

Aunt Sabella's Black Chocolate Cake with Fudge Frosting

For the cake:

2 ounces unsweetened chocolate, chopped

5 tablespoons plus 1 teaspoon butter,
at room temperature

1¼ cups sifted all-purpose flour

1 teaspoon salt

1 teaspoon baking soda

1 cup buttermilk

1 cup sugar

2 egg yolks

For the frosting:

2¼ cups confectioners' sugar, sifted

5 tablespoons unsweetened cocoa powder

6 tablespoons unsalted butter, melted

5 tablespoons hot freshly brewed coffee

1½ teaspoons vanilla extract

Preheat oven to 350 degrees.

continued on next page

For the cake: Melt chocolate in a small heatproof bowl set over a small pot of gently simmering water over medium-low heat, stirring occasionally with a wooden spoon. Remove bowl from heat and set aside until chocolate is cool.

Meanwhile, grease an 8-inch square cake pan with the 1 teaspoon butter and set aside. Sift flour and salt together in a small bowl and set aside. Stir baking soda into buttermilk in another small bowl and set aside. Beat sugar and the remaining 5 tablespoons butter together in a large mixing bowl with an electric mixer on medium speed until light and fluffy, about 2 minutes. Beat in the egg yolks, then add melted chocolate and beat until thoroughly combined. Add one-third of the flour mixture, then one-third of the buttermilk mixture, beating well after each addition.

Repeat process to use all of both mixtures, then pour batter into prepared pan and bake 40 to 50 minutes, until a toothpick inserted in center of cake comes out clean. Transfer cake to a rack to cool in pan, then invert onto a cake plate.

For the frosting: Sift confectioners' sugar and cocoa together in a medium bowl. Stir in butter, then coffee, then vanilla, mixing well with a wooden spoon after each addition, until frosting is smooth. Ice top and sides of cake with frosting.

Yield: 18-inch-square cake

Publius Paquius Proculus of Pompeii before Vesuvius blew in the year 79. In other words, nothing was too arcane, not even the life and times of a long-dead food writer.

Online searches for Clementine Paddleford turned up one false trail: In 1943, a book called *Clementine in the Kitchen* was published. This successful book about cooking, by Samuel Chamberlain writing under the pseudonym Phineas Beck, was about another Clementine entirely, one with an accent on her name, a cook who fled wartime France to immigrate to the United States with her employing family. Once that notion was discarded, I was quickly directed to Kansas State University's Web site. There I learned that Paddleford had bequeathed a goldmine in the prairies for someone interested in twentieth-century American food. Suddenly, I developed a burning desire to visit Manhattan, Kansas. Since most of my colleagues had those warm feelings toward places like Paris and Venice, it was not difficult to persuade my boss, *Saveur*'s editor-in-chief, Colman Andrews, to send me.

Andrews, then fifty-six years old, six foot one inches in height, girth of overadequate proportion, is one of the most important food writers in the world. With *Saveur*, he and his co-founders shaped much of the way American chefs and restaurateurs—and some home cooks, too—have come to think about food. His colleagues in this venture were the editor Dorothy Kalins and the food photographer Christopher Hirsheimer. And this formidable figure, ruling the roost in his office in New York, was my gateway to restoring immortality to Clementine Paddleford.

When Andrews was working behind his desk, it was customary for him to ignore any traffic into his office. I walked in, and he went right on doing whatever he was doing. I cleared my throat. Without turning from his computer, Andrews asked over his shoulder, "Yes?"

"I want to write a Lives column about, uh, a dead person, I think," I began. (At the time, the magazine occasionally published short columns devoted to the lives of surprising people in the food world, such as a couple of Eastern Airlines employees who gave it all up to farm exotic bananas. To my knowledge, these columns were never about the deceased.)

"What the hell are you talking about?" Andrews sighed, finally swiveling to attention.

"Have you ever heard of Clementine Paddleford?" I asked, holding out *How America Eats*. Unlike anyone else on the magazine's masthead, Andrews said yes to this question. Although he knew that Paddleford had been on the *Herald Tribune* years ago, he didn't know much more—and he was dubious about her claim to have traveled "over 800,000 miles" in pursuit of regional American recipes. "That's more than twice the distance from the earth to the moon," he said. He heard me out, though, and relented on the Kansas trip, with the words: "You won't have much in the way of expenses."

He was right. Manhattan, Kansas, has a Applebee's and a Holiday Inn across the street from campus. No Katy railroad dining car with kornettes these days. What it does have is the Hale Library, at five stories one of the tallest buildings on the Kansas State campus. And on the top floor of that building it has Cynthia Harris, the archivist who day-in-day-out for three years had nearly single-handedly organized Paddleford's papers.

Harris's most obvious connection to Paddleford is geographical, but it became so much more than that—something I learned when, about three months into the work, I contacted

Harris and let her know I'd be coming to Manhattan for research. We spent hours together, backs hunched over Paddleford's college yearbooks, her memos to her secretaries, the letters from her readers, the menus for each meal from a month-long hospital stay. ("Who saves this kind of stuff?" I asked Harris when we discovered the hospital menus. "I told you she was a Kansas pack rat!" Harris responded.)

For her part, Harris fell in love with Paddleford slowly; as she worked, she began to enjoy learning about her and to feel more and more attached to her. Such continuous work on the life of one person forges a deep connection, and Harris was not immune. Just as Paddleford's inventive food reporting had been the lure for me, the reporter's way of making each person feel special had a unique appeal for Harris. As September 27, 2002, Paddleford's 104th birthday, approached, Harris could not get the woman born and raised near her home off her mind.

That an outsize "endearingly loopy" character, as David Kamp described Paddleford in *The United States of Arugula*, could have been so easily forgotten, left out of the pantheon, was shocking. The problem was that the food landscape changed radically in the years since Paddleford died. James Beard had been able to continue his legendary cooking classes and to endow a foundation: he also wrote ten times as many books as Paddleford because he wasn't writing several newspaper columns a week. Craig Claiborne had the muscle of *The New York Times* behind him, and the newly-chic mission of restaurant reviewing with which to make his name. Julia Child had the most powerful organ of all: television. Introducing Americans to the pleasures of French cuisine proved a fruitful endeavor: Her 206 episodes of *The French Chef* are among the most watched in public television's entire history. Today we have Rachael Ray's triple-threat empire, which includes cookbooks, a magazine, and television shows, all devoted to the world that has grown up around the American stove. We have hundreds if not thousands of "regular" cooks putting up their favorite recipes on their own personal blogs, sharing their own dishes with each other the way they had been "word-of-mouth hand-downs from mother to daughter" in Paddleford's era.

Another issue at play here is the quality of the subject itself: Food is a topic that is endless in its scope. To report on it is to find that almost nothing is really new—from home to home, culture to culture, the dishes may change and grow up with different advances and innovations in the tools and ingredients we may choose, but essentially chicken soup is chicken soup. That said, the world of food is constantly being reinvented. "The concept of regional American food is totally evolving," Ruth Reichl, *Gourmet*'s editor and herself a longtime food writer, said. "The weird thing is that it is evolving so much faster now, changing as new immigrants come in. . . . We're going to see more and more African food coming in and regionally you see it's not an accident, like Asian flavors coming into American culture. The Hmong community in Minnesota is an example. One of the things that's different about America than the rest of the world is that we make room for these things."

Paddleford was a pioneer in "making room" for the innovations and in codifying our already existing traditions, which happened themselves to have come from other countries. In a food culture that has always imported its recipes, how could the people who have written about them expect to have longevity? "Isn't it amazing the way that Craig Claiborne has been forgotten?" William Rice, the legendary food and wine columnist for the *Chicago Tribune*, said when I interviewed him about Paddleford, whom he'd read but not known. (Rice had no idea that he invoked the one colleague whom Paddleford had sparred with during her life.) Rice pointed out that authentic recipes—and the traditions behind them—seem to outlive their reporters. "It's the ephemeral nature of our business, maybe," he offered.

With the aid of Harris, I finished my article. It took nineteen drafts—editing out examples of Paddleford's fanciful food descriptions proved difficult. "Hometown Appetites" was published in *Saveur* in November 2002, with a cover line. The title was based on a favorite Paddleford quotation taken from the *Saturday Evening Post* article of 1949 by Josef Israels II: "We all have hometown appetites. Every other person is a bundle of longing for the simplicities of good taste once enjoyed on the farm or in the hometown he or she left behind." The story was a sketch of Paddleford's life and a brief description of her significance to me; I called myself Paddleford's "groupie."

In the spring of 2003, the article won the James Beard Award for food journalism. The most lasting effect of this was to put its subject's name back on the lips of food professionals after thirty years. In my acceptance, I said that Beard and Paddleford must have been looking down from their foodie heaven, toasting with vintage champagne.

Almost as soon as the article was published, my phone and Harris's were rung by people who had known or worked with or had been profiled by Paddleford and who had long wanted to share their recollections. Maybe there would be a spot on the culinary Olympus for Paddleford after all. She had certainly worked hard enough—and saved and protected enough material—to ensure her arrival. It was clear to all involved parties that it was about time for the world to take notice again.

Would Paddleford have been disappointed that it took an entire generation to restore her name? Not necessarily; she was a shrewd reporter and a tough cookie, too. As she once wrote to her mother, Jennie, during her lonely first winter in New York City when she was cooped up in her Morningside Heights apartment with no job and not a friend in sight: "Isn't it queer how little people are missed. Someone else always steps in and fills the place left vacant and does it quite as well."

Our Story and Acknowledgments

$\mathcal{A}$s is clear from its title page, this narrative is the work of two people—one the archivist who saved the papers of Clementine Paddleford from encroaching neglect and rot, and the other the food writer who discovered Paddleford as role model and pioneer in her chosen field. One had never been to New York City, and the other could barely pick out Kansas on a map, which means that before this project, we were in parallel universes. To tell the adventure of how we found each other, we will separate our voices.

Cynthia Harris's story:

In Manhattan, Kansas, if you stand at the end of the Stockdale Park Road and look across Tuttle Creek Lake you can hear children's laughter on the wind; this was the place where, in the early part of the twentieth century, Clementine Paddleford grew up on a 260-acre farm. That vast acreage was part of the land flooded in 1962 by the Corps of Engineers when it built the Tuttle Creek Dam. After the flooding, the housing development where I live was established for Kansas State University people. My family moved to our home in 1985 and I drove past Paddleford's grave daily for thirteen years before I ever heard her name.

In high school in Kentucky, I had set three goals: to be the best secretary I could be; to get a college degree in history; and to write a book. In 1988 when I was promoted to administrative assistant to the two ministers at the First Presbyterian Church in Manhattan, I was on the top rung of the secretarial ladder. Goal number one.

In January 1996, when I realized that our son would be leaving home the following year and we would have an empty next, I took my husband's suggestion and enrolled in college courses. I also continued working at the church part-time until January 1998, when I resigned. A month later, with too much free time, I sought a part-time job. I started work in the Department of Special Collections at Kansas State University as a student assistant, if a bit older than most students. As an insider, I learned that Paddleford's cousin, Alice Paddleford Wood, made regular pilgrimages to Kansas State University, also her alma mater, to check on the processing of her cousin Clementine's papers. Each time Wood found no progress and more deterioration.

This project had become rather a bitter joke. When student assistants finished with one processing job, the archivist would tease them that the Paddleford collection would be their next. But the task would surely take far longer than any student assistant was going to spend in Special Collections, and as the department did not have a full-time collections processor, the papers remained in storage, for all practical purposes untouched since the day they left New York.

Graduation day—marking goal two—was in May 2000. I left Special Collections and in September, I began working at Kansas State Extension Agronomy as an administrative assistant. I soon found this job could also be done part-time, so to fill the hours, I asked about compiling a history of the Department of Agronomy. This got an enthusiastic response and for nearly a year, I concentrated on the department heads, the farm, and the experiment fields. Paddleford did not enter my thoughts.

In the summer of 2001, staff changes were on the horizon and my position was up on the chopping block, although I was allowed to stay until I had another job. One day in Hale Library, the archivist told me that my old place, Special Collections, had been authorized to hire a Manuscripts/Collections Processor. I applied, and started work that November. My first assignment: the Paddleford papers. I groaned, because there were many boxes stuffed with fragile documents. Yet I also knew that the collection was important and would complement the library's Rare Books Cookery Collection. I did not know the task would last three and a half years.

Three months in, Kelly Alexander came to research Paddleford for a magazine article. We worked through boxes and boxes, mostly still in chaos, yet she wrote an article that won an important prize.

As September 27, 2002, Paddleford's 104th birthday, approached I kept thinking about the woman born and raised so near my home. On her birthday, I took flowers to her grave and a photographer from *The Riley Countian* weekly newspaper took my photograph. The following week I was on the front page and my telephone started ringing. The callers were people either related to Paddleford or those who knew the family and were surprised to learn her papers were at Kansas State.

As I worked, I enjoyed learning about the woman. As all biographers find, the subject becomes part of you. If I pulled up an interesting article, my co-workers and I would laugh and have a "Clem" discussion. Other days, it was a heavy burden, and I sometimes thought of Churchill, in a graver context, promising blood, toil, tears, and sweat. The pins—often rusty—that Paddleford typically used to attach paragraphs from one article to another often stuck my fingers and made them bleed when I reached in for a batch of clippings. Getting boxes down from the shelves was likewise a hazard since they often weighed seventy-five pounds or more. Many days I felt like crying because I had worked so hard to get one section done then found myself dragged backward. Was this toil ever going to finish?

Along the way I figured out something important to me: Paddleford once wrote, "Ingredients mean little to me." It was the people and their stories that enraptured her and she made each person she wrote about feel special. For they all got their fifteen minutes of fame. Once the article was in print, telephone calls and letters brightened their days: they were famous and Paddleford made them so.

One day my telephone rang and it was Betsy Wade in New York City. She had worked with Paddleford at the *Tribune*. Our conversation led Wade to track down Paddleford's foster daughter, Claire Duffé Jorgensen, for me. After that, it took me two years to build a relationship of trust with Claire.

Then one day, out of the blue, I received an envelope from

Claire. Inside there was a photograph of Paddleford's convertible, a Studebaker Lark, shiny black with lush red interior, and the words "Life's a lark. Call me any time" scrawled on the back. Just as I was winding up processing the papers and the Special Collections department was planning a symposium to mark their opening in 2005, Claire fell ill; her health has continued to decline. We will lose Claire Jorgensen, the living person who was closest to Clementine Paddleford, who showered love and care upon her. We have lost Paddleford's bosses and many co-workers. We may lose her contemporary fans, as we have lost R.W. Apple Jr. But Paddleford took a bold step for her own immortality, leaving her papers to a place that could store them and, however long it took, sort and archive them. They are here in Kansas, a slice of history. They speak about journalism, about women in journalism in the first half of the twentieth century, as well as speaking volumes about food and the people who prepared and ate it. Kelly and I hope that this book introduces her to a new generation of admirers who may themselves want to research through all those pages of tireless, vigorous writing. It is worth it.

Kelly Alexander's story:

After close to ten years of slogging it out in the lower echelons of food reporting, dreaming about writing a story that actually meant something to me while I was researching articles like "50 hot wine trends" (such as "wine served in blue glass bottles"), I knew I had hit pay dirt when I happened on to Clementine Paddleford. This was confirmed by my trip to Kansas.

The small story I'd set out to get felt like it should be much, much bigger, and luckily I was able to persuade the magazine's

staff of that. But the assignment was also trickier than I'd anticipated. Reconstructing the life of a "pack rat" like Paddleford
was easy, but attempting to answer how a person like her could
have so easily slipped out of memory was another thing entirely.

The editor on the project, Kathleen Brennan, worked dili-
gently to get me to show what Paddleford the human must have
been like. "More than anything," Brennan advised, "you've got
to make us know her, not just her impressive resumé." This was
hard. Paddleford systematically culled personal material from
her vast files.

I could scarcely find a living soul who had known Paddleford. Tracing the names I encountered in her papers lead nowhere—all the people I saw as major players, like William I.
Nichols, Eugenia Sheppard, Craig Claiborne, Eloise Davison,
were dead. I had decided against contacting Claire Duffé Jorgensen; Kansas State had had bad luck with her, and it appeared
she wanted to make no public comment on Paddleford's life.

When "Hometown Appetites" was published in *Saveur* in
November 2002, the sources I hadn't been able to find emerged.
Cindy Harris had made contact with Betsy Wade in New York.
Wade did some local work for Cindy, going to the surrogate's
court to copy Paddleford's will, photographing the building
Paddleford and Davison owned. One night I had a dream that
Clem was floating over my bed, cape swirling. "You should listen to Betsy Wade," she warned me sternly as she pressed her
voice box. This wasn't the first time I'd dreamed of Clem, but it
certainly left an impression. I wrote Wade to see what was on her
mind. Not an opportunistic intruder, Wade had a desire to repay
Paddleford's long-ago helping hand. She became the link to the
living people who contributed to this book, most valuably Joyce

Jones Crosby, who had tested recipes for Paddleford at the *Herald Tribune*, and Joan Rattner Heilman, who had been one of Paddleford's editors at *This Week*. She also saw to it that Cindy Harris and I were invited to a party in 2006 marking the fortieth anniversary of the end of the *Herald Tribune*. It was held in the old *Trib* building, where Wade was able to walk us to the spot where Paddleford had her desk, "in" box stuffed with manuscripts and cats as it was.

I also got a letter from Edward Weiss, whose family had owned Paprikas Weiss, the Hungarian import store that Paddleford put on a wider map. Weiss, an amateur food historian, took Cindy and me to lunch in New York to share his recollections. He was nearly moved to tears when describing how Paddleford had helped his business grow for three generations.

After this, I began writing other food stories for *Saveur*, traveling to report the pieces. It wasn't exactly "How America Eats," but I was finally doing the work I had longed to do. When in the field, I found my thoughts turning to my role model. Once in Stockholm, I was assigned to visit the kitchen of a graphic designer. Unfortunately, my cab driver confused one suburb with another, and left me, six months pregnant, in the middle of February, on the wrong doorstep. "What would Clementine do?" I thought. Cautiously I rang the doorbell, and the family, not panicked by a pregnant American, arranged to get me where I was supposed to go. I should have stayed longer, though, because there were smells of a fabulous stew on the stove; Clem would have.

It also seemed that Clementine wasn't ready to let me go either: A literary agent who specialized in food writing, Michael Psaltis, took me for a frank conversation. He had liked "Hometown Appetites" and thought it should be a book. I said I was not interested in turning out "350 Recipes for Classic American Food" based on Clem's work, an idea that had already been broached to me. I told Psaltis that what did interest me was a serious telling of Paddleford's life, illustrated by recipes she sought and saved. And by the way, I said, there is a librarian in Kansas who's essential.

Enter the great R. W. Apple Jr. of *The New York Times*, a longtime colleague and friend of Wade's. She alerted him when Cindy finished cataloguing the archive and pressed him to go take a look. He did, and "A Life in the Culinary Front Lines" appeared in the *Times* on November 30, 2005. In it, Apple introduced readers to his gustatory forebear. The piece announced that Kansas State was making Paddleford's papers available to scholars. A day later, the agent sold the book.

Soon after I was able to interview Apple. I'd brought several pounds of Eastern Carolina barbecue from home in Chapel Hill, and he was delighted. His enthusiasm for the project was obvious, and he urged me on.

As Cindy and I continued research, I kept being surprised at how hard Paddleford fought to cloak her personality. Every last detail about her professional life was documented, down to notes about her favorite kind of stapler. But so many personal questions led to dead ends. What was it like to go out to dinner with Clementine Paddleford? Was she funny? Was she serious? What made her angry?

Only one way to learn: her foster daughter. Claire wrote that she had enjoyed the article in *Saveur*. Fortunately for our relationship, I'm sure, she noted a few errors. For instance, in a caption we identified the cat Prince Peter as Pussy Willow. Claire, who, like Clem, is deeply private, let out some details. Despite her usual attempts to steer conversation away from Clem—a trait I attributed to Celebrity Child Syndrome—Claire was keen for us to come to Maine. Ultimately, Cindy and I met Claire at her nursing home near Bath in April 2006.

Most of the conversation was genial. But after about thirty minutes, Claire seized a scrapbook and said, "That's enough of that." Still no answer to how such an outsize character could have been so easily forgotten. I have been asked this question more than any other. I finally have concluded it was luckless timing. Clem's death followed closely the closing of the *Herald Tribune*. Then the advent of food television did her entire legacy in. No amount of column-saving would have secured her reputation in the face of those odds. Her paper died, and her voice was not right for television, and that was that.

Yet, without Clementine Paddleford's early columns describing the concept of "regional American food," would we have the Food Network, the countless cookbooks devoted to this subject, and Rachael Ray and her empire? Today in America with food and cooking major hobbies, what would Paddleford make of it?

She might be horrified by the commercialization, but she might be overjoyed at the outsize role cooking plays in general social conversation. She knew that food connects us to each other, and she wrote about it in unerringly sassy, smart prose. I feel about her life story the same way that she felt about *How America Eats*: "My files are bulging with America's best eating. I had a hard time to choose this small sampling, which I sincerely hope you will enjoy to the last mouthful."

Acknowledgments

We come together again to offer our deepest thanks to the members of Clementine Paddleford's family, who without reservation supported a project that probed into the private and public life of its subject. Paddleford's foster daughter, Claire Duffé Jorgensen, invited us to her home; Claire's son, Mark, was patient with our many questions and showed us around, allowing us to roam freely on the farm. Claire's daughter, Jenny Jorgensen, a professional pilot who was named for Paddleford's mother, described her own passion for flying, which sounded like something her grandmother would have written.

Paddleford's cousin, the late Alice Paddleford Wood, greatly admired her noted relative and sought to follow in her steps. In addition, she reared her own children to respect the cousin who left Kansas to become a great food editor. These children, Meredith McCaughey, Lauralee Maas, and Barry Wood, have seen to it that their mother's pilgrimages to Kansas State University were not for nothing. Other cousins and friends, Jane Hendrickson and Nancy Paddleford, and their mother, Laurie Paddleford; Mary Jo Hageman, Bonnie, John, and Casey DeVore, Peggy Hubbell, Grace Goff, and Curtis and Gladys Goff Phillips, did not let us down when we needed them.

Andrea Reusing took time away from running Lantern, a thriving restaurant based in Chapel Hill, North Carolina, and rearing her family to perfect recipes that were forty to eighty years old; she did this to honor the memory of the earlier cooks who trusted Paddleford with their best dishes. Her diligence, good humor, and perfect palate were indispensable. Silvia Pahola and Vera Fabian, Lantern restaurant staff, tested, too, researching and preparing historic recipes so we could get them right.

Dr. Mark Weissler, professor of surgery in otolaryngology, head and neck surgery at the University of North Carolina at Chapel Hill, patiently explained what throat cancer would have looked and felt like in the 1930s, and how it would have been treated.

Several of Paddleford's colleagues and friends took us under their wing. Besides her colleague Betsy Wade, whose role is noted above, Joyce Jones Crosby, who was the home economist in the kitchen where Paddleford's recipes were tested, not only shared her subtle, close-in memories, but fed the authors, a spouse, and Wade on their voyage to Maine.

Others of Paddleford's surviving colleagues, especially Joan Rattner Heilman, Judith Crist, Richard Wald, Jill Krementz, Morris Warman, Jim Boylan, Stanley Alpern, Frances Fitzgerald, Denise McCluggage, and Ray Price talked about their old co-worker in ways that helped us to color in the outlines of Paddleford's life.

Edward Weiss, owner of the now defunct Paprika Weiss and a dear friend of Paddleford's, often expressed his devotion; his telephone calls and reminiscences were priceless.

Colman Andrews recognized that Paddleford's memory needed to be revived, and his foreword is a testament to his willingness to believe. Other key former members of the staff of *Saveur* magazine were also there early: Kathleen Brennan, who edited the original *Saveur* article; Melissa Hamilton, who tested the recipes, and Margo True and Ann McCarthy.

Paddleford talked to numberless people for her thousands of articles. We were lucky enough to track down a few who could tell us what it was like to be under Paddleford scrutiny. Rocky Aoki, Mary Call Collins, Emma Contrearas, Edna Eby Heller, and Sigrid Howell described their fifteen minutes of fame created by Paddleford. Occasionally we were able to track down children of Paddleford's subjects. Richard Coffin told of his father, the poet and professor Dr. Robert P. Tristram Coffin, making lobster stew. Jackie Kronenberg and Barbara Sims spoke lovingly of the hamantaschen prepared by their mother, Regina Less. Margaret Norris discussed her mother's tricky lime chiffon pie. While Barbara Sargent was not interviewed by Paddleford, her wedding cake decorator was. Sargent never forgot the description of her cake "as dark as sin." Sandi Burr, never interviewed by Paddleford, was a faithful follower of "How America Eats." She said she enjoyed impressing her guests by preparing recipes from Paddleford's column. Like so many others, she felt a kinship to the writer and, in cooking her discoveries, felt herself part of a wider circle.

The newspaper women Kathleen Kelly and Marianne Strong and the cookbook writer Barbara Kafka showed us the side of Paddleford that other journalists saw: competitive and gung-ho.

A huge thank you goes out to these friends who helped fill gaping holes: Cindy Von Elling, who pored through articles and correspondence for us; Lindsey Bird, Nelda R. Brown, and Darla Hanks, who cheerfully went through historical records; Charley Couch of the Redding, Connecticut, Historical Society, who examined land records; Lisa Holley of Arrowsic, Maine, who did the same, as did Linda Glasgow and Brian Sutton of the Riley County Historical Society in Kansas. Pat Patton, Tamara DeRossi, and Mallory Peterson made photocopies. Tammy Doboney of the Beardstown Houston Memorial Library in Beardstown, Illinois, found out that Paddleford's ex-husband, Lloyd Zimmerman, remarried and had a daughter named Martha. Zimmerman died in 1969.

Anne Hecker supplied information about the Chicago Theta Sigma houses and the women who were Paddleford's roommates there. Sam Hamlin described his grandmother, Hilda Hamlin, who never gave up corresponding with Paddleford and continued to be a friend until the very end. Meredith Litchfield and James Hathaway, Kansas State University librarians, made the trip to New York City in February 1968 to pack up and deliver Paddleford's papers.

Others who provided support were Kevin Arnovitz, Brooke Balick, Julie Bender Cevallos, Jerry Bennett, Dr. Laura Bennett, Robert Bennett, Tim Blacker, Catherine Bigwood, Jeb Brody, Elaine Byrd, Andrew Cadel, Ashley Cassell Carson, Kevin Christian, Patrick and Susan Clinton, Salvatore Conti, Edwina Davis, Susan Davis, Maggie Dietz, Stephen Curry, Paul Duffé Jr., Maryellen Dugan, Elizabeth Dunham, Betsey Elbogen, Eric Etheridge, Andrea Eisen, Marcie Ferris, Beth Galloway, Dr. Patricia Gammon, Shoshana Goldberg, Margo Harkradder, Chris Henry, Larry Huber, Shelly Larkins, David Mathias, Alex May, Mac McCaughan, Reggie Miller, Leslie Moye, Dr. Chris Munoz, Donald J. Mrozek, Kate O'Malley McCulloch, Anna Lee Pauls, Adam Platt, Beth Posner, Steve Prockish, Steven Shaw, Nikki Sixx, Judith Sonntag, Dr. Charles Thompson, Paul Thomsen, Tina Ujlaki, Peter Van Pelt, Bonnie Vaughan, Suzanna Yorgey, and Michael Zeiss.

Definitely not least are our agent Michael Psaltis and our editor Erin Moore. Spouses and children, Andrew Davidson and young Louis and Dylan, and Joe Harris and Barry, cheered us on even as they had to listen to still more stories of Clementine Paddleford. And finally, we must thank the late R. W. Apple Jr. Johnny believed we had the power to bring Paddleford back from the brink of obscurity; we hope we have.

A Note on the Recipes

by ANDREA REUSING

The fifty-five recipes in this book were collected by Clementine Paddleford and originally published between 1920 and 1967 in the *Christian Herald, The New York Herald Tribune,* or *This Week* magazine. They represent traditional regional specialties prepared by what seems to be a dying breed, Americans who cooked at home, mostly for their families.

When I agreed to test these recipes to determine how today's cooks might best replicate them, my main concern was to respect the original intentions of each cook. While cooking, I rooted for each recipe to "work" and my goal was no substantive changes at all. Sometimes this was easy, as with the Philadelphia Pepperpot (page 104). Other times, it was difficult; the "soft" molasses cookies, for example, were inedibly hard until we abandoned the instruction to add flour "until the mixture is stiff enough to hold a spoon upright." As it became clear that a "no changes" mandate would help no one, my job became to recommend to the authors what ought to change and what be left alone. In making these choices, I was influenced by my grand-mother Marie, whose own recipe for braised pork and sauer-kraut would have been at home in one of Paddleford's columns.

Every Thanksgiving while I was growing up, Marie served her version of Oysters Rockefeller. In the original dish, created in 1899 at Antoine's restaurant in New Orleans, oysters are topped with bracing green herbs, butter, and breadcrumbs and then lightly broiled until just tender, with a delicate crust (see page 143). Strangely delicious, Marie's recipe had been inspired by a version she'd eaten in a New York City seafood restaurant in the early seventies. White wine and bacon were the key ingre-dients in the tiny, boozy casseroles baked in enormous scallop shells nested in rock salt, served crusty and still bubbling, with cocktails. Marie took a small lump of freshly grated horseradish with hers. In the years after she died, we debated the authentic "Marie" version—the now-forgotten restaurant had used grated parmesan cheese, had she? But when I decided to surprise my family by bringing her oysters back to Thanksgiving, my dad and I were secretly glad that we couldn't find the old scallop shells, since it gave us an excuse to buy a peck of fresh Blue-points. We upgraded the other ingredients, too—fresh spinach didn't seem to violate the spirit of the dish, although we knew Marie had used frozen. We enjoyed the new oysters with our cocktails that year, but it would never occur to us to prepare them again. They had nothing to do with Marie.

With that vision in mind, I tackled Paddleford's recipes. There is great value in the "improved," adapted, or tinkered-with recipe. You test a recipe in enough permutations to come up with an "ultimate" version of it—"the best" macaroni and cheese—that anyone can reliably prepare. But these meta-recipes loose their individual point of view as they are molded to suit broad tastes and purposes—they are as disconnected from the people who helped originate them as my oysters Rockefeller were from Marie.

In choosing which recipes to include from Paddleford's forty-plus years of newspaper and magazine columns—more than one thousand in all—we tried to pick dishes that sounded curious and delicious. Does the world need another Caesar salad? Well, yes (page 155). In 1953, Paddleford returned from a trip to Cincinnati, recipe in hand, turned it over to a test kitchen whose employees had probably never heard of it before. Making a Caesar from the vantage of someone getting a first taste of that salty romaine-egg-anchovy combination can erase a thousand awful ones by taking us back to the beginning.

That said, some minor and a few major changes have been made. For instance, long cook times were a frequent issue. In Dr. Coffin's lobster stew (page 180), carefully written instructions suggested gentle, repeated simmering to maximize the essence of lobster in the milky broth, yet this process toughens the meat without intensifying the flavor. Often, we met dishes that included a lot more flour or cornstarch than current tastes expect. The rich crab imperial casserole (page 198), called for ¼ cup of flour, which is overkill when combined with bread crumbs; we reduced it to 2 tablespoons.

Another concern was cuts of beef. We were puzzled over the frequency of the suggestion for top round, the ultra lean and often dry cut from the cow's hindquarters, when the more succulent chuck from the animal's breast and shoulder seemed a better call. But tenderness and juiciness are evolving ideas. The meat-purchasing chart in the back of *America's Cook Book*, prepared by the *Herald Tribune* Home Institute in 1941, put steaks from the eye under the "very tender, juicy; excellent flavor, choice cuts" column and chuck, now thought of as a braising cut, in the "less tender" steak category

Not everything is better nowadays. The industrialization of the modern dairy industry has given us less flavorful, less thick cream that is more often served sweetened and whipped rather than simply poured over desserts, as in the strawberry shortcake (page 17). People cook at home less and in some key ways, have forgotten how to do it. A cook in 1950 would not have had to be reminded to preheat the oven, bring a large cut of meat or eggs to room temperature before cooking, or be told to season food with salt and pepper. Some Paddleford sources gave vague instructions on cooking temperatures (many recipes instruct the cook to bake a dish in a "hot oven"). Cooks today want precision and so we suggest specific cuts of meat and correct pan sizes. We sometimes eliminated lard and shortening when butter can readily be substituted, and we reconsidered some such as the Syrian beet salad (page 245), which originally called for lemon Jell-O. We updated the dish with fresh lemon juice and by adding a little more horseradish; these additions made it taste so much better we knew Paddleford would agree.

Food has grown since the days of these recipes—literally. Our modern portion sizes are larger. The original recipes for both the marble layer cake (page 5) and the coconut-marshmallow cake (page 69) yielded only enough batter for ½-inch layers; these were not only difficult to handle but created puny cakes. Both recipes were doubled to yield the amount of batter a home cook of today might expect. Occasionally, we ran into the opposite problem, as with the weird but excellent Swiss pear bread that had so vexed the *Herald Tribune* home economist, Joyce Jones Crosby, in 1952 (page 157). The original recipe made three fat foot-long loaves, each weighing a couple of pounds; one loaf alone was enough to provide breakfast to a family of four for a week.

A few recipes contained actual problems no matter when or where they were first cooked. The temperature of oil for frying the cod fritters (page 174) needed amending if the reader was ever to actually cook them. The original amount of potatoes in the New England boiled dinner (page 127) could have fed the entire crew on the USS *Skipjack*. A recipe for "Iowa barbecue" does not appear. It called for tenderloin, a slim, lean cut that would never be used for the long-cooked, pulled pork dish. If only we could have asked Paddleford why it was there.

But occasional glitches in fifty-year-old recipes are not surprising. What amazed me was that the recipes, quaint as they sometimes seem, are full of interesting lessons and fresh ideas. I loved the method of moistening roast pork with a little water (page 30), and the flavor of fresh grated nutmeg in biscuits for shortcake (page 17). Ouida Hill's frozen bananas (page xxviii), quickly coated with fresh cream and crunchy sugar, struck me as very modern. Imagining eating kornettes (page xxii) on a train, I found that the thing that I had been missing all my life was small, hot buttered corn cakes. The Kansas fried chicken (page 20) calls for a combination of butter and lard, which at first seemed superfluous. But it's a fact: we should all fry chicken exactly this way.

Finally, there was one recipe that we couldn't resist thoroughly adapting. We found a recipe for mitzutaki from Paddleford's 1963 trip to Tokyo and couldn't pass up the chance to add it to ingredients not available in American supermarkets in 1963. To make it taste more as it did in Japan, we have included ingredients like kombu and bonito flakes. The "hot pot" here is much more likely to resemble the one Paddleford enjoyed than what she offered in print for her readers.

The dishes in this book were often created to put dinner on the table, but also as an expression of creativity and love. My hope is that in cooking these recipes, you will revive the spirit of these women who worked hard to feed their families—that in your kitchen, you will continue Clementine Paddleford's mission of sharing recipes across geography and generations.

Andrea Reusing is the chef and owner of Lantern restaurant in Chapel Hill, North Carolina.

Mitzutaki

8 cups water

8 dried Chinese mushrooms

1 6-inch piece dried kombu

½ cup sake

¼ cup soy sauce

1 teaspoon salt plus, to taste, on chicken

4 whole chicken legs, thighs and drumsticks separated,
skin removed

6 green and white scallions

1 small head Napa cabbage, cored and cut into 2-inch chunks

In a large casserole bring water, mushrooms, and kombu to a boil. Remove from heat and let steep for one hour. Add sake, soy sauce, and salt.

Salt the chicken to taste.

Strain broth, discarding kombu and reserving mushrooms. Return broth to casserole.

Add chicken and two of the scallions and simmer over low heat, partly covered, for 25 minutes or until chicken is very tender. Trim tough ends off mushrooms and return them to the pot with the chicken. Add the cabbage.

continued on next page

After five minutes, or when the cabbage is just tender, re-move chicken pieces, cabbage, and mushrooms and arrange in separate piles on a heated platter. Thinly slice remaining four scallions on the bias and use as garnish. Serve family style with ponzu sauce for dipping. If you wish to finish the meal in the traditional style, serve each guest a small bowl of hot rice topped with a ladleful of the cooking broth.

Ponzu

4 cups water

1 packet bonito flakes (about 2 tablespoons)

½ cup soy sauce

¼ cup mirin

1 tablespoon plus 1 teaspoon lemon juice

2 tablespoons very finely grated daikon,
preferably grated on a microplaner

2 teaspoons very finely grated ginger,
preferably grated on a microplaner

In a small saucepan, heat water to a boil. Remove from heat and add bonito flakes. Strain through fine mesh strainer. Add remaining ingredients. Serve alongside mitzutaki.

continued on next page

Sushi Rice

2 cups uncooked sushi rice

2½ cups water

small pinch salt

Wash rice in several changes of cold water until the water runs clear. Combine rice, water, and salt in a medium saucepan and bring to a boil uncovered over medium-high heat (6 to 8 minutes). Cover and adjust heat to low and cook for about 7 minutes. Check to make sure that all water has been absorbed and that the rice is done before removing from heat. Replace lid and allow pot to sit for 10 minutes before fluffing with a fork and serving.

Notes

PROLOGUE

xvii   42 . . . 13 million: William I. Nichols, *New Patterns in Publishing The Story of* This Week *Magazine* (New York: The Necomen Society in North America, 1960), p. 2.

xxiv   fifty thousand miles a year: "Clementine Paddleford," *K-Stater* Magazine, March 1961, p. 32.

CHAPTER 1

1   six o'clock: "Union Pacific Train Schedule," *The Daily Mercury* (Manhattan, KS), March 6, 1913.

2   seven thousand: Note-1910 Census Record for Manhattan, Kansas, shows the population at 6,855 and the 1915 Census record for Manhattan, Kansas, shows the population at 8,037. The authors estimated this amount for the year 1913.

3 800,000 miles in twelve years: Clementine Paddleford, *How America Eats* (New York: Charles Scribner's Sons, 1960), Foreword.

7 population of one hundred: Mary Duroche, "Progress Fells a Town," *Topeka Daily Capitol,* October 14, 1953.

19 By eight o'clock: Clementine Paddleford, *A Flower for My Mother* (New York: Henry Holt and Company, 1958), p. 28.

25 the student body of 2,406: "K-State Enrollment Statistics Yearly Totals," accessed online September 17, 2006, http://www.lib.k-state .edu/depts/spec/flyers/enrollment.html.

29 seven hundred: Cynthia Harris, "An Introduction to the Life and Papers of Clementine Haskin Paddleford" (presented at *Celebrating the Legacy of Clementine Paddleford* Symposium, Hale Library, Kansas State University, Manhattan, KS, September 26, 2005).

29 three-thousand cirulation: Clementine Paddleford, "1933 Resume," Paddleford Papers.

33 *The Collegian* with 234 inches of type; . . . had 112; *The Industrialist* . . . placed first with 90 inches, . . . with 21: "First Place in Two Contests," *The Kansas State Collegian,* January 7, 1919, p. 1.

CHAPTER 2

40 $8: Josef Israels II, "Her Passion Is Food," *The Saturday Evening Post*, April 30, 1949, p. 56.

44 $35: "Personal Fact You Will Want to Know," 1928–1937 Portfolio Material, Paddleford Papers.

45 July 10, 1923: Clementine Paddleford and Lloyd D. Zimmerman marriage certificate, in private holdings.

46 one hundred papers: Clementine Paddleford, "Boys' and Girls Clubs to Help Fill Uncle Sam's Seed Bin," *Streator* (Illinois) *Times,* March 6, 1924, 1920–1923 Porfolio Scrapbook, Paddleford Papers.

47 listenership more than doubled . . . : Clementine Paddleford, "Lullaby Tots Have Big Station Party," *Chicago Evening Post,* July 17, 1924, 1920–1923 Portfolio Scrapbook, Paddleford Papers.

48 September 8, 1924: Clementine Paddleford to Jennie Paddleford, September 8, 1924, in private holdings.

53 twelve to twenty; "Hundreds of mothers . . ."; 62,000 requests: Clementine Paddleford to Andrew Wing, March 27, 1925, Paddleford Papers.

54 thirteen-day exploratory trip; forty: Clementine Paddleford to George Martin and Andrew Wing, July 16, 1925, Paddleford Papers.

55 one hundred years; five foot five inches tall in blue overalls: Clementine Paddleford, "Two Jolly Red-Headed Girls Who Love to Farm," *Farm & Fireside Farm Journal,* 1925.

55 December 18, 1925; eighteen people: Clementine Paddleford to George Martin and Andrew Wing, February 23, 1926, Paddleford Papers.

56 fifty-acre spread: Clementine Paddleford, "Two Women Who Farm Like Men," *Farm & Fireside Farm Journal,* 1926, Paddleford Papers.

57 October 1926; Seventy; eight: Clementine Paddleford to George Martin and Andrew Wing, October 20, 1926, Paddleford Papers.

57 three-month temporary position; $35 a week: Fulton Oursler to Clementine Paddleford, December 20, 1926, Paddleford Papers.

58   On Monday, January 31, 1927, Jennie died: "Mrs. Paddleford Died Mon. Night," *The Manhattan Mercury,* February 1, 1927.

59   June 20, 1927, in Asheville, North Carolina . . . ; eleven hundred; five: Clementine Paddleford to George Martin and Andrew Wing, July 7, 1927, Paddleford Papers.

60   December 1927: Clementine Paddleford to George Martin and Andrew Wing, April 8, 1928, Paddleford Papers.

60   three days in Manhattan: Clementine Paddleford to George Martin and Andrew Wing, December 16, 1927, Paddleford Papers.

61   summoned her to New York in 1928; "reading the slush": Helen P. Hostetter, "A New Angle on Bleeding Kansas," *K-Stater* Magazine, March 1954, pp. 10–11.

CHAPTER 3

66   "From 1924 to 1930": Edward P. Seymour, "Personal Facts You Will Want to Know," Paddleford Papers, 1928–1937 Portfolio Material.

67   200,000 copies: Porter Caruthers, "Personal Facts You Will Want to Know," Paddleford Papers, 1928–1937 Portfolio Material.

68   June to October 1930; forty-three: Note-A typewritten note attached to: Clementine Paddleford, "Church Suppers Go Modern," *Christian Herald,* October 11, 1930.

68 $25: Clementine Paddleford: "$25.00 for Your Best March Menu," *Christian Herald,* November 1, 1930.

77   "Congratulations on a 35 percent increase . . .": Godfrey Hammond to Clementine Paddleford, January 5, 1932, Paddleford Papers.

78 "Hundreds of thousands . . .": Clementine Paddleford to H. L. Mencken, April 20, 1932, Paddleford Papers.

80 45 to 50 percent . . . : Interview with Dr. Mark C. Wiessler, University North Carolina, Chapel Hill, G0412 Neurosciences Hospital, June 2, 2006.

81 choice of treatments: Catherine Royer, "A Country Girl Whom Misfortune Stirred to Great Achievement" within radio broadcast of "Women in the Free World, Voice of America," December 23, 1954, p. 2.

84 divorced in 1932: Israels II, "Her Passion is Food," p. 57.

91 March 1936; six days a week; $40 a week: Clementine Paddleford Portfolio Material 1928–1937, Paddleford Papers.

91 6,077; 7,429; 78,337 compared with 28,489 in 1935: "Food Markets Editor of the Herald Tribune," Clementine Paddleford's 1928–1937 Portfolio Scrapbook, Paddleford Papers.

92 1938, Paddleford bought; 17 acres: Register of Deeds, Redding, Fairfield County, Connecticut, Warrantee vol. 40, p. 199.

CHAPTER 4

100 about 52 percent: Clementine Paddleford, "America Makes the Cheese," *This Week* Magazine, September 8, 1940.

102 "the average production is 25,000 pounds": Clementine Paddleford, "Philadelphia Scrapple Welcomes the Delegates," *New York Herald Tribune,* June 24, 1940.

108 "Give a Dime"; $355: Clementine Paddleford, "Give-a-Dime Menus Net $355 for War Relief," *New York Herald Tribune,* July 12, 1940.

110 sixty-two dehydrated food products: Clementine Paddleford, "Dinner Dehydrated," *This Week* Magazine, December 7, 1941.

111 "Last year 100,000,000 gallons": Clementine Paddleford, "Our American Wines," *This Week* Magazine, April 19, 1942, p. 18.

113 $25,000 a year; hundreds of letters and 1,000; 28 receptions; 11 a.m.: Israels II, "Her Passion Is Food," pp. 43, 57, 58, 11.

120 "60,000 Miles of Eating; "three books with over a million sales every year"; "12 all-time favorite"; 10 cents:" Clementine Paddleford, *This Week* Magazine, January 12, 1947, p. 24.

128 "Found: the world's best potato salad, 20 cents . . .": Clementine Paddleford, "Secret Salad," *This Week* Magazine, January 2, 1949.

129 $15,250: Mortgage Records, Register of Deeds, New York County, New York, MTG 5563, p. 611, August 15, 1955.

137 "300% increase in pie sales": Frank Orrin Carpenter to Clementine Paddleford, ca. July 20, 1949, Paddleford Papers.

144 "*This Week* has over 10,000,000 circulation . . .": Clementine Paddleford to Joan Rattray, September 12, 1949, Paddleford Papers.

148 "For fifteen years . . .": Israels II, "Her Passion Is Food," p. 43.

CHAPTER 5

159 $28,000: "Women in Journalism," *K-Stater* Magazine, October 1952, p. 11.

166 "own 10½s fit . . .": Clementine Paddleford, "Fire Island Clams in Jars Win Praise of Amateur Clam Digger," *New York Herald Tribune,* January 23, 1950.

168   planning a weekly luncheon for four hundred: Clementine Paddleford, "She Cooks to Please," *This Week* Magazine, March 4, 1951, p. 50.

170   "the eight best-loved . . .": Clementine Paddleford, "Clementine Paddleford Picks America's Favorite Recipes." *This Week* Magazine, December 23, 1951.

170   "with the 14 sharp pencils ...": Barbara Clendinen, "Clementine Paddleford, Gourmet, Visits Tampa," *Tampa Morning Tribune,* March 7, 1952.

181   "ten American food editors ...": Clementine Paddleford, "Denmark, Home of Bleu Cheese, Welcomes Food Editors of U.S.," *New York Herald Tribune,* March 7, 1951.

181   178 varieties of "smørrebrød": "The House of Davidsen," retrieved on January 17, 2008, from http://www.idadavidsen.dk/index .php?page=9

182   eight hundred invited guests; one hundred dishes: Clementine Paddleford, "Banquet For Elizabeth," *This Week* Magazine, June 7, 1953, p. 47.

188   1956; thirty-five pages ...: Clementine Paddleford, "Westward Ho!" in letter Clementine Paddleford to William I. Nichols, Stewart Beach, Dick Dodson, Advertising Staff, Anyone Interested, August 29, 1956, Paddleford Papers.

189   air navigation classes in 1953: Clementine Paddleford to Mrs. Robert Swanson, January 12, 1954, Paddleford Papers.

190   150-acre farm: Register of Deeds, Warranty Deed, pp. 274–275, Arrowsic Sugadahoc County, Maine, November 8, 1952; Mark Jorgensen to Cynthia Harris, October 3, 2007, in private holdings.

192 "twenty-four hours": Clementine Paddleford to William I. Nichols, December 12, 1957, p. 1, Paddleford Papers.

192 "furnished with antiques . . .": David L. Cohn, "Chippendale and Gumbo Creole" (s.l., s.n., n.d.), Paddleford Papers.

192 $68: George Beveridge to William I. Nichols, December 20, 1957, Paddleford Papers.

CHAPTER 6

209 "I had asked for it . . ."; 75 to 100; brownies to feed 80 and hamburger pie for 100: Clementine Paddleford, "How to Cook for a Whole Crew," *This Week* Magazine, July 10, 1960.

211 "endearlingly loopy": David Kamp, *The United States of Arugula: How We Became a Gourmet Nation* (New York: Broadway Books, 2006), p. 4.

211 "Clementine was down here . . .": James Beard, *Love and Kisses and a Halo of Truffles: Letters to Helen Evans Brown* (New York: Arcade Publication, 1994), p. 251.

212 "Today there must be 20 big firms . . .": Clementine Paddleford, Summer Salads All Dressed Up," *New York Herald Tribune,* August 11, 1960.

213 twelve years of Paddleford's career: Paddleford, *How America Eats,* Foreword.

219 $1,500: Burroughs Mitchell to Clementine Paddleford, July 18, 1957, Paddleford Papers; Clementine Paddleford's Checkbook, Paddleford Papers.

219   Christmas 1960 at $10 a copy: Grace Warlow Barr,"A Pleasant Safety Belt Is Hot Soup For The Road," *Orlando Evening Star,* ca. January 9, 1961.

228   "the eminence in the ...": Joe Nagelschmidt, "Twelve Years in the Writing: A Lifetime in the Eating: How America Eats," *Chapel Hill Weekly,* Chapel Hill, North Carolina, May 1, 1961.

228   "Residents of Central Pennsylvania ...": Edna Nash, "Milady's Bookshelf," *Sunday Patriot News,* Harrisburg, Pennsylvania, December 18, 1960.

232   "well worth the ten bucks it sells for ...": Grace Warlow Barr, "A Pleasant Safety Belt Is Hot Soup for the Road," *Orlando Evening Star.*

233   one thousand copies; thirty-two hundred; five thousand more: AnnaLee Pauls (Rare Books and Special Collections, Princeton University Library) to Cynthia Harris, September 26, 2007. In private holdings.

233   The Cookbook Guild . . . by 1962: Elinor Parker to Clementine Paddleford, May 29, 1962, Paddleford Papers.

234   1861; ". . . two hours of sight-seeing . . .": Clementine Paddleford, "Happy Cooks of Napa Valley," *This Week* Magazine, February 14, 1960.

235   "viewed as eccentric, if not downright . . ."; dollar a quart; $8 million; 2000: Margalit Fox, "Obituary: Paul K. Keene, 94, Organic Farming Pioneer," *New York Times,* May 18, 2005.

243   "In all, there were over 50,000 recipes . . .": Clementine Paddleford, *Clementine Paddleford's Cook Young Cookbook* (New York: Pocket Books), 1966, p. 1.

246 600,000 bottles of 80-proof a day: Clementine Paddleford, "Vodka: Russian Versus American," *New York Herald Tribune,* September 13, 1962.

253 "For 24 years she has been food editor . . ."; five thousand cookbooks; "two secretaries, two writing assistants, two maids . . .": Dorothee Polson, *Arizona Republic,* May 2, 1965, Paddleford Papers.

254 "over four billion dollars were spent on outdoor ...": Joanne Schreiber to Clementine Paddleford, January 20, 1964, Paddleford Papers.

254 After a five-hour cook-off . . . : Young & Rubicam Publicity, Honolulu, Hawaii, news release, April 21, 1964, Paddleford Papers.

EPILOGUE

260 February 1968: Nancy Scheetz, "K-State Acquires Paddleford's Personal Library," *Kansas State Collegian,* February 15, 1968; Meredith C. Litchfield, interview, May 3, 2006.

263 more than two thousand of the country's best . . . : Paddleford, *How America Eats,* Foreword.

269 206 episodes: "Celebrated Chef Julia Child Dies at Age 91," *Associated Press,* August 13, 2004.

271 "We all have hometown appetites . . .": Israels II, "Her Passion Is Food," p. 43.

Index

Christmas, 10–11, 74–77, 107, 114
Churchill, Winston, 119–20
"Churchill Enjoys Home-Cooked
    Missouri Meal" (Paddleford),
    119–20
Cider punch, spiced, 76
Cioppino, Tarantino's, 134–36
Claiborne, Craig, 203–7, 236–38, 242,
    252, 257, 269–71, 278
Clementine in the Kitchen
    (Chamberlain), 267
*Clementine Paddleford's Cook Young
    Cookbook*, 242
Cloudy, Helen, 152, 162, 166
Coconut marshmallow layer cake,
    69–71, 290
Cod fritters, 174–75, 291
Coffin, Robert P. Tristam, 179, 180,
    190, 289
Cole, Mrs. Karl, 244
Collegian, The, 29, 260
    "Doomsday Edition," 32–33
Colson's College Inn Café, 28, 29
Cook, Joan, 150, 152, 162, 257
Cookbook Guild, 233
Cookies:
    hamantaschen, 193–96
    molasses, soft, 144–46, 287
    schokoladeplatzchen (little chocolate
        drops), 222, 223
"Cook Young" series (Paddleford),
    242–44, 258
Copenhagen, Denmark, 181–82
Corn cakes, 94
Corned beef dinner, boiled, 126–28,
    291
Cornmeal rolls (kornettes), xxi, xxii, 291
Country Gentleman, The, 44
"Country Girl Whom Misfortune
    Stirred to Great Achievement, A"
    (radio segment), 168
Country Home, 66
Covington, Euclid M., 98
Crab, baked, imperial, casserole of,
    198–99, 289

Crackers, souffléd, 11, 13
Crawford, Joan, 254
Creole cookery, 137, 140–44
Crist, Judith, 16, 239
Crosby, Joyce Jones, 278–79, 291
Crowell Publishing, 57–58
Crullers, 164–66
Currey, Margery, 43

Daily Chronicle, 2
Davison, Edith, 168, 170
Davison, Eloise, 87–88, 91–92, 129,
    131, 247, 262, 278
Delmarva Chicken Festival, 160–61
Desserts:
apple dumplings, 222, 226–27
    black bottom pie, 121–23
    black chocolate cake, 264–66
    cheesecake, Lindy's, 134, 137–39
    coconut marshmallow layer cake,
        69–71, 290
    frozen bananas, xxvii–xxix, 291
    Maids of Honor, 183–85
    marble layer cake, 5–6, 290
    orange maries, 68, 72–73
    strawberry shortcake, 14, 16–18,
        290, 291
Dickens, Charles, 75
Dobson, Dick, 56
Dr. Coffin's lobster stew, 179, 180, 289
Doherty, Anna Marie, 185, 259
Dole Corporation, 233–34
Doyle, Pat, 151, 162
Drop biscuits, 106
Duchess potatoes, 23–24
Duffé, Claire (*See* Jorgensen, Claire)
Duffé, Paul, 113

"Easy Does It!" (Paddleford), 110–11
Edwards, Arthur, 182–83
Eggs sardou, 141–42
Elizabeth II, Queen of England, 107,
    182
El Mundo, 170, 175
Engels, Joe, 161